The Atonement
in the
Light of Nature
and
Revelation

by J. H. Waggoner

TEACH Services, Inc.
New York

2006   07   08   09   10   11   12   · 5   4   3   2   1

Copyright © 2006 TEACH Services, Inc.
ISBN-13: 978-1-57258-078-7
ISBN-10: 1-57258-078-X
Library of Congress Control Number: 96-61844

Published by
TEACH Services, Inc.
www.TEACHServices.com

PREFACE.

By all who have faith in the efficacy of the blood of Christ to cleanse from sin, the Atonement is confessed to be the great central doctrine of the gospel. On this they agree, however much they may differ on other doctrines, or on the relations of this. And yet the number of books on this subject is not large, compared with the number on many others, not held to be as fundamental in the Christian system as this.

In developing the argument we have tried to follow the Scriptures in their plain, literal reading, without regard to the positions of others who have written before us. It would be a pleasure to us to agree with all who are considered evangelical, and we have differed with them only because our regard for the truths of the Bible compelled us to do so.

With those who consider it necessary to apologize for the Bible, the writer has little sympathy. It is a noticeable fact that of all the writers and speakers whose words are recorded in the Bible, no one ever undertook a defense of the sacred word. "The Scriptures" were appealed to as final authority by both Christ and his apostles; and if any denied their authority, they were considered beyond the reach of proof—they would not believe though one should rise from the dead. Luke 16 : 31. And when men of a certain class denied a Scripture truth, the Son of God did not meet them with philosophy or science, but settled the question by an appeal to the word itself, answering: "Ye do err, not knowing the Scriptures nor the power of God." Matt. 22 : 29.

The reader may then question why we have departed from the beaten track in laying the foundation of an atonement by an appeal to principles of reason and of law. It was because we believe that something is due to those who have received erroneous ideas of the doctrine from those who stood as religious teachers. Many have assailed the Atonement

because of the unwise teachings of its professed advocates.
They affirm that it is a doctrine which leads to license and
immorality; and they are confirmed in their opinion by the
positions of learned theologians who deny that justice un-
derlies the Atonement, virtually, and often openly, declar-
ing that the gospel does not establish and vindicate the law
of God. We do not believe that outside of "theology" a
soul could be found who would insist that pardon of a crime
absolved the criminal from obligation to the law which condemned him for the commission of the crime! The power to
pardon should be used with prudence, and is always committed to those who are sworn to maintain the authority of
the law.

In the Government of God, as in all Governments, *law* is
the basis upon which everything is made to rest. The very
idea of *probation* enforces the Bible declaration that to fear
God and keep his commandments is the whole duty of man.
The "golden rule" is the embodiment of "the law and
the prophets," Matt. 7 : 12, and the love of God, the very
object and essence of the gospel, is the keeping of his commandments. 1 John 5 : 3. Our positions in "Part First"
have been examined by eminent jurists and declared to be
well and safely taken; and we appeal to every reader that if
the doctrine of the Atonement *did* conflict with these principles, then the skeptic would have solid reasons for rejecting
it. This part of our argument was the result of long-contin-
ued and careful examination of the ground, and it has been
a delightful task to trace the harmony between these principles and the word of revelation.

The more we examine it the stronger are our impressions
that no language can do justice to the subject of the Atonement of Christ. The mind of man, in this present state, cannot realize its greatness and its glory. It is the prayer of
the author that the reading of this book may arouse in others
the desire which the writing has strengthened in his own
heart, to enter that immortal state where we may, through
ceaseless ages and with enlarged powers, contemplate and
admire "the unsearchable riches of Christ."   J. H. W.

Oakland, Cal., August, 1884.

"Sincere respect for the men of early times may be joined with a clear perception of their weaknesses and errors; and it becomes us to remember, that errors, which in them were innocent, because inevitable, may deserve a harsher appellation if perpetuated in their posterity. — William Ellery Channing.

CONTENTS.

PART FIRST.

AN ATONEMENT CONSISTENT WITH REASON.

PART SECOND.

THE ATONEMENT AS REVEALED IN THE BIBLE.

THE ATONEMENT.

CHAPTER I.

COMPARISON OF NATURE AND MORALITY.

THE psalmist well says: "The heavens declare the glory of God; and the firmament showeth his handiwork." Ps. 19:7. The works of the material creation are wonderful. When we look at the countless globes in the heavens, and consider the inconceivable distances which separate them, and consider that they move in exact and harmonious order, compared with which the working of the most perfect machinery that man ever made is rough and jarring, we may somewhat appreciate the words of the psalmist; and we cannot wonder that Dr. Young said: "The undevout astronomer is mad." Every well-executed work of design speaks the praise of the designer. And wherever we see arrangement, order, harmony, especially in mechanism, in movements, we know that there is a designer. We cannot be persuaded that any successful piece of machinery is an accident; we cannot by any effort bring our minds to believe that the works of a watch, or anything similar to them, came by chance, or *happened so*. They need no voice to speak to us to assure us that they had their origin in power and intelligence, or in mind. So said David of the material heavens: "There is no speech nor language; without these their voice is heard." Or as Addison beautifully expressed it:—

> "What though no real voice nor sound,
> Amid their radiant orbs be found;
> In reason's ear they all rejoice,
> And utter forth a glorious voice,
> Forever singing as they shine—
> The hand that made us is divine!"

But, while the works of nature may arouse us to devotional feelings, they cannot guide our devotions. They but give evidence of the existence of an almighty Designer, but they cannot reveal him to us. Man himself is "fearfully and wonderfully made;" and he may stand in awe at the thought of his Maker; he may feel a sense of responsibility and of accountability to his Creator; but if left to the voice of nature alone, the highest shrine at which he will bow will be that of "The Unknown God." He may even recognize the voice of conscience within him reproving him of the wrongs which he is conscious that he commits; but nature does not reveal to him the manner of service which would be pleasing to his Creator and Preserver, nor the means of freeing him from the guilt and consequences of his wrongs.

The psalmist, no doubt, had this train of thought passing through his mind, for, after ascribing to the creation all that it can do to incite us to devotion, he abruptly turned his subject, saying:

Ps 19:7,8

"The law of the Lord is perfect, converting the soul; the testimony of the Lord is sure, making wise the simple. The statutes of the Lord are right, rejoicing the heart; the commandments of the Lord are pure, enlightening the eyes." Man is highly exalted as to his *capacities;* there are wonderful possibilities in his being. Yet left altogether to himself he is helpless, especially in the understanding of morals. And this is not at all surprising; for no one is expected to understand the will of a governor, or the laws of the Government under which he lives, unless they are revealed to him. The psalmist, as quoted in this paragraph, ascribes to the law of the Lord an office which it is not possible for creation or nature to fill. The commandments of the Lord impart instruction, important and necessary instruction, which we cannot learn by observation, nor by the study of the material universe. No proof ought to be required on this point. The most powerful telescope or microscope can never reveal a single moral duty, or point out a remedy for a single moral wrong.

Now we attach no blame to nature because it does not perform the office of a written revelation. No such purpose was embraced in its design. We do not learn the laws of our Government by walking through the fields, by studying her dimensions and natural advantages, nor by noting her public improvements. When we have learned all that we can possibly learn from nature, we find beyond that an absolute necessity for direct revelation.

Opposers of the Bible are often met who declare that the doctrines of Christianity are contrary to reason; contrary to the conclusions legitimately drawn from our study of nature, of the deepest researches of science. Especially has the doctrine of the Atonement been made the subject of strong opposition, some affirming that it is immoral in its tendency, and is based on principles which are not in conformity with justice. But we think the whole objection is founded on misapprehension; and the object of this present argument is to show that reason is not opposed to the idea of atonement, but rather leads to it; that a coincidence of strict justice and mercy demands it; and that it vindicates the majesty of law, and therefore honors the Government. It is also our object to show that a written revelation is but the supply of an acknowledged want; that the gift of such a revelation is but a conformity to the plainest, simplest principles of government, principles which are universally recognized. And, therefore, consistency requires that such a revelation, when given, should be universally received and accepted.

The present is a mixed state, of good and evil. It is not our purpose now to inquire *why* it is so; we are viewing it as we find it—as it is; not as we might wish it were. And confined in our views to the present state, and to observation alone, or merely to reason without a written revelation, it is impossible to vindicate the justice of the *controlling power*, whether that power be called God or nature. Virtue is often trampled in the dust, and ignominiously perishes in its representatives. Vice is exalted on high, triumphs over justice and right, and its very grave is decorated with flowers, and honored with a monument. In the operations of nature, there is *no discrimination* manifested, and without discrimination there can be no conformity to justice. True, we see many exhibitions of benevolence, but we see also many things which cannot be reconciled with it. The righteous and the wicked, the just and the unjust, the innocent and the guilty, the aged and the little child, alike share the bounties of Providence, and together fall by the pestilence, or sink beneath some sweeping destruction. These facts have troubled the minds of philosophers, and caused the short-sighted philanthropist to be faint of heart. Many, reflecting on these things, and judging in the light of their own unassisted reason, have doubted that the world was ruled in wisdom and justice, and even denied the existence of a supreme, intelligent Being.

It seems singular that they who discard the idea of an intelligent Cause, of a personal supreme Being, generally invest nature with the attributes of such a Being, and ascribe to it all the wisdom of design and the merit of virtue. They talk of the laws of nature, of their beauty, their harmony, their excellency, as if nature were the sole guide of correct action, and the proper arbiter of destinies. They lavish encomiums on her operations as if she never tortured an innocent person nor permitted the guilty to escape.

*encomium -n- a formal expression of praise / accolade / commendation

As before remarked, we find no fault with nature; but we do find fault with the unreasonable position assumed by her devotees. The laws of nature answer well their purposes. But this class of philosophers endeavors to make them answer a purpose for which they never were designed, and which they cannot fulfill. And we think that by correct reasoning it will be easy to show that their ideas are mere fallacies.

We would raise the inquiry, When they who deny the work of a supreme, personal Creator, speak of "the laws of nature," what do they mean by the expression? It cannot mean the laws made by nature, as we speak of the laws of man, or of the laws of God; for nature never made any laws. Nature never knew enough to make a law. She could not deliberate; she could not plan; she did not have a knowledge of the future, whereby she could judge what was suitable, and devise means adapted to the end. Or, if she made the laws, she must have existed before she made them. How, then, were her operations regulated before laws existed? Is there a man living who will claim this for nature? Not one.

We have been thus particular in our queries on this point because we wish to notice another phase of this subject. It has been said by some that they do not deny the existence of the God of the Bible—of a personal, supreme Being; but yet they believe in *the eternity of matter;* that there never was done such a work as that of *creating,* in the sense of causing things to exist.

And that matter, or nature itself, being eternal, the laws of nature must be eternal also, because they inhere in matter. Thus, they say, you can-not imagine that matter could exist and gravitation not exist. And so of all the laws of matter. But, we reply, this leads to the same result which we have been examining. If the laws inhere in matter, they are essential to the very existence of matter; and it follows that, to suspend or reverse these laws would be to suspend the existence of matter, that is, to destroy it. In this view *a miracle is an impossibility.* Thus: Matter is not dependent on any power in the universe for its existence. But its existing laws are necessary to its existence. Therefore the laws of matter, or of nature, are beyond and independent of any power in the universe.

Against this theory we have objections to bring. It is not a part of our present purpose to argue against it from the Bible, as we shall try first to establish *principles*, natural and legal, outside of Bible proof. It is possible to present an argument which must be conclusive to believers of the Bible, besides the direct declarations of that book in favor of the existence of miracles, such as causing iron to swim upon the water, raising the dead, etc. But we waive this, and affirm that, in admitting the existence of God, these have not changed the issue before examined. This theory is open to all the difficulties which we find in the hypothetical theory of *nature making her own laws.* We have, then, harmony of movement without intelligence; mechanism without a mechanic; a design without a designer; a result in marvelous wisdom without plan or deliberation. To avoid the unscientific fact of a miracle, they have presented before us the greatest miracle which could be imagined! And David was mistaken when he said "the heavens declare the glory of God;" for if nature, and its laws, and its harmonies, and its almost infinitely varied operations attendant upon them, existed from eternity, and not by the creative power and act of God, then we ask, with an earnest desire for information, What did God ever do? What can He do? Why does He exist? And would not nature and its laws "move and have their being," as they did from eternity, if God did not exist? Other theories are projected to prove that God does not exist. This is complaisant—it is accommodating; it does not deny His existence; its object is only to prove that he is not needed! that everything existed by chance; it acts by chance; and the interference of an all-wise, supreme, personal God, could only destroy the harmony of the work! Great is the philosophy of the nineteenth century, and modest and reverent as it is great!

We think there is but one reasonable and allowable construction that can be put upon the phrase, namely: They are the laws which the Supreme Being made for the government of nature. The Infinite Creator, He who *made nature*, subjected her to the operations of those laws, under which she is held in control. And, of course, those laws are within the power and under the direction of their Maker. That which we term a miracle is but a temporary suspension of, or change in, the operations of those laws. And this can require no greater exercise of power on the part of the Almighty than to set, and to keep, these laws in operation.

It is truly strange that men, of ability and intelligence in other respects, will deny that there are any but *natural laws*, or laws of nature. They ignore the distinction between natural and moral laws. But when judged in such a light the laws of nature are found to be imperfect and incomplete. In what respect? In this, that *they present no standard of right*, and are therefore no sufficient guides for human action. We cannot shape our conduct after such a model with reference to the rights of our fellow-men. As lovers of the most expansive benevolence, we may strive to imitate nature when she spreads abroad her bounties: her precious fruits and golden grain. But again she withholds these, and famine is the dire result. Shall we imitate nature in the desolations of the whirlwind, the earthquake, and the pestilence? Shall we indiscriminately spread ruin and destruction around us, involving alike the innocent and the guilty, the gray-headed and the prattling child? All answer, No. But each hand that is raised to check such a mad career practically acknowledges that nature, which is so blindly worshiped by many, presents to us no example worthy of our imitation.

Thus in fact the laws of nature do not and cannot satisfy the aspirations of man; no one can accept them as a standard of action, no matter what his theory may be, because *they are destitute of the element of morality.* We cannot trace a single moral element in their frame-work or their execution. He who studies them intelligently must be convinced that they are designed solely for a natural system,—not at all for a moral system. And this being so, it follows that *they have no penalties, but only consequences.* On this point many well-meaning men err, who recognize the distinction of moral and natural law; they speak of the penalties of the laws of nature, when no such penalties exist. The violations of natural laws are attended with consequences, uniform in operation, so that in nature we see an unbroken series of causes and effects, the results being the same whether issuing upon a responsible or an irresponsible object, regarding no distinctions of moral good or evil.

That the laws of nature have no penalties must be apparent to all if we consider the fact that they are never accepted as, or considered, *a judicial system.* In executing penalties there must be a consideration of the just desert of the crimes committed. But there is no such consideration, there is no discrimination whatever in the case of a consequence of the violation of natural law. In this respect the operations of natural law are as blind and unreasoning as nature itself. There is implanted in man *a sense of justice*, or convictions of right, to which he finds no counterpart in the operations of nature. These convictions are entirely on a moral basis. This sense of justice is erected in the human mind as a tribunal, a judgment seat, whereat we determine the nature and desert of actions. And mark this truth: before this tribunal we always arraign the actions of intelligent agents, *but never the operations of natural law*. And in this, what is true of one is true of all; and it shows that all, whatever their theories may be, do in fact and in practice make a proper distinction between moral and natural laws. This should be well and carefully considered.

The prime distinction between moral and natural laws is this: the first has respect to intention —the other has not. Fire will burn us, and water will drown us, whether we fall into them accidentally or rush into them madly. The little child, who is yet unconscious of any intention of good or ill, suffers as certainly and as keenly on putting its hand into the fire, as the man of mature mind who presumptuously does the same thing. And should the man willfully and maliciously set fire to his neighbor's house, and the child, playfully and without intention of wrong, do the same thing, all would blame the one and not the other. And were a judge, in the administration of law, to visit the same penalty upon the man and the child, because the actions and results were the same, all would detest such a perversion of justice. Thus we not only find men acting upon the difference between moral and natural laws, but we find them also with great unanimity judging of the actions of moral agents according to their intentions.

But the operations of natural law cannot thus

be judged, and its consequences, often miscalled penalties, have no regard whatever for the claims of justice. As before said, the child is burned in the fire as certainly as the man; the good suffer under a violation of nature's laws as severely as the most hardened and brutal. The idea cannot be too strongly impressed upon the mind that, confined in our reasoning to the present state, to observation without a written revelation, justice cannot be attained unto nor vindicated. A moral system is necessary, and the idea of probation must be accepted, in order to meet the requirements of justice.

Another point should be noticed. When the demands of a moral law and a natural law conflict, as they often do in this mixed state of good and evil, men always give preference to the former, unless their sensibilities are blunted. And they are often false to the theories which they have adopted to be true to this fact. We sometimes meet with men who deny these distinctions; who assert that there are no laws aside from the laws of nature; yet they *act* in harmony with the propositions herein set forth. Should one refuse to attempt to rescue his fellow-man from impending destruction by fire, and plead in extenuation that it would have involved the violation of law, as he must have been somewhat burned in the effort, they would, as readily as others, abhor his selfishness. Here they recognize the distinction claimed, and place the moral duty of assisting our neighbor above conformity to natural law.

CHAPTER II.

THE MORAL SYSTEM.

HAVING sufficiently shown that there is a distinction between moral and natural law, and that all men recognize it and act upon the fact, even if they do not admit it in theory, we have a question of great importance to propose. None but the reckless and unthinking can pass it by without giving it attention. The candid must admit that it is one of great interest. It is this: Will these aspirations for the right, this innate sense of justice, to which we have referred, ever be gratified? That they are not, that they cannot be gratified in the present state, scarcely needs further notice. Is my moral nature, my sense of right and justice, satisfied to see virtue trodden under foot? to see the libertine mocking over the grave of blighted hopes and a broken heart? to see the priceless treasure of virtuous purity, around which cluster the fondest hopes of earth, sported with as a mere toy of little worth? to see honest toil sink unrequited, and hide itself in squalid poverty and a pauper's grave? to see the vain rolling in wealth accumulated by fraud and oppression? to see vice exalted to the pinnacle of fame? to hear the praises of him whose very presence is loathsome by reason of the filthiness of his iniquities? And when words fail to express the horrors of such and kindred evils, must I smile complacently and say, This is right? in this my soul delights? But this is but a mere

glance at the facts as they exist, as they have
existed, and are likely to exist in this present
state. Is it possible that these aspirations, these
discriminations of right and wrong, were placed
within our breasts to be mocked—to look and
long in vain? Is it possible that the Supreme
One, who has so nicely arranged the material
world, and subjected it to certain laws, has placed
moral balances in our hands to no purpose? that
we are to long for, but never see, a vindication
of the great principles of justice? Is it not
rather *reasonable* to conclude that he has a moral
Government, and that our moral sense is evidence
that we are within the limits of a moral system?
Are not our convictions of wrong proof to ourselves of our amenability to such a system?

The very fact that we discriminate between
moral and natural laws, as we have seen that all
men do, and that all pronounce upon the *right* or
wrong of the actions of mankind, is proof of the
general recognition of the existence of *a moral
Government.* And so to look above nature, to acknowledge God as *a moral Governor*, is necessary,
to be true to our own natures, to the convictions
planted in every breast. In this great truth our
aspirations find rest. Here our sense of justice
takes refuge; for a Government is *a system of laws
maintained*, and the very idea of a moral *Government* leads us to look forward to a vindication of
the right principles or laws now trampled upon.
Why should we pronounce upon the merit or
demerit of human actions, if there is no accountability for those actions? Our feelings of respon-

*assize - a judicial inquest; the time or place of holding such a court, the court itself, or a session of it.

THE MORAL SYSTEM. 23

sibility (the movings of conscience) are but the expectation of a great assize, in or by which injustice, fraud, and every wrong, will be requited, and down-trodden virtue and injured innocence be exalted and vindicated. This is, indeed, but a legitimate deduction from the propositions established, and in this we find a sure vindication of the divine Government in regard to the anomalies of the present state.

anomaly - something different, abnormal, peculiar

It must, however, be admitted that there are some who deny the existence of moral wrong, and, of course, of accountability for our actions. But their denial or our admission does not weaken our argument, for the denial is only in profession, not in practice. The denial is based on the alleged inability of man to act except in a given line. Man (say they) is a creature of circumstances; the motives which impel him to action are outside of his own will; he is led of necessity to do just as he does, and he cannot do otherwise. Therefore he is not responsible for his actions. But we affirm that this is only their professed belief; not their actual belief. For in practice we find them uniformly false to their theory. They will, as readily as others, sit in judgment upon, and condemn the actions of their fellow-men. They will blame any for encroaching on their rights. But it were surely the height of folly, the grossest injustice, to blame one for doing that which he cannot avoid. And how unreasonable to think that God bestows a moral sense, and plants within us the monitor of conscience, to lead us to do right, and yet *compels* us to do wrong. We count

the man immoral and degraded who disregards
the distinctions of right and wrong; what contempt, then, is thrown upon the originator of the
present system by the theory which admits that
these distinctions exist; that of right they should
be preserved, yet affirms that they cannot be
preserved to any extent whatever. Admitting
the existence of a God (and we now speak to the
consciences of some), what shall we, what must
we, think of a God who would frame a system
wherein these distinctions could not be preserved?
And yet such is the case, if man has no freedom
to act. We all acknowledge the difference between right and wrong, as principles; that it is
right to regard our neighbor's life and property;
and hence, he that disregards them does wrong.
And all are conscious that the wrong we do is of
ourselves; and no one ever seeks to throw it
back to any other cause until his moral sense is
perverted by selfishness and false reasoning.

Akin to the above position—at least in its un-
reasonableness—is the theory which admits the
existence of God the moral Governor (though
this admission is not essential to the theory), and
admits that man is responsible for his actions, and
admits that all violations of law are certainly
punished, and yet denies a future judgment.
This is intimately connected with, or is the outgrowth of the error that there are penalties to
natural laws; and that all penalties are inflicted
immediately upon the violation. Thus (they say),
if a man puts his hand in the fire he violates a
law of his being; and he does not wait to an

indefinite future time for judgment and punishment; he suffers immediately and certainly; and for the violation there is no atonement or forgiveness. This, to some, appears to be truth, for they advance it; to us it seems like a puerility. We repeat, the suffering from contact with fire is not a judicial infliction to serve the ends of justice, as penalty is; it is but a consequence of the violation of natural law; and that it falls as certainly and as severely on the innocent as the guilty. The innocent and unconscious babe suffers by the fire as readily, as certainly, as the willful man. And we can go further in the illustration: the man in cruel malice may hold the hand of the child in the fire; the child does not offend against law, for it did not put its hand in the fire, and it vigorously tries to withdraw it. Here the man does all the wrong, and the child suffers all the penalty! Such is the wisdom, such the justice of this theory. The truth is, that the child suffers as a consequence of the man's wrong-doing. He deserves punishment (the infliction of a penalty) for the action; and if justice is ever vindicated, he will be punished, according to his intention and his commission of a great moral wrong. The admission that all sin will be punished makes necessary the admission of a future judgment; for without that, justice will never be vindicated, and our aspirations for the right will never be satisfied.

But one more fallacy of this character we will notice. It is found in the oft-repeated idea that God is so loving, so kind, that he will not mark to condemn our aberrations from duty. It is not necessary to say that this is a denial of the Scriptures in regard to the character of God. But, laying the Bible aside, where is the *evidence* that God so loves his creatures that he will not mark their faults or maintain the justice of his government? Surely it is not learned from nature that love is the sole attribute of Deity. How came any by the idea that the Deity must possess that degree of love supposed in the statement? Whence do they derive their conceptions of such love, and of its necessity in the divine character? Can any tell?

They may reply that these conceptions are intuitive; that they are evolved from their own consciousness; that they have an innate knowledge of the moral fitness of things, and according to this, they clothe Deity with such attributes as their moral sense determines to be fitting to such a Being. Our reply to this is twofold. 1. We deny that such ideas are developed by intuition. The intelligent skeptics of this land and in this age do not derive their knowledge of right, and of the abundance of love in the character of Deity, from the light of nature. They derive this from their surroundings; from the prevalence of Christian influences and Christian literature. To show just what man can learn from nature and by mere intuition, we must take him entirely separated from the influence of the Bible and Christianity. And we hazard nothing in saying that, where Christian example and the teachings of the Bible were entirely unknown, man never developed an exalted idea of Deity. To the contrary, where men have trusted to the light of nature and to the power of human reason, their conceptions of Deity were low and base, generally vile; and this was the case even where there was considerable proficiency in philosophy and the arts. Many deny the Scriptures who are indebted to them and to their influence for very much of the knowledge of which they are proud. 2. In thus exalting love in the divine character at the expense of other attributes, they are only partially true to their higher nature; partially just to their own consciousness. Our consciousness, our self-judgment of the moral fitness of things, gives us as definite and clear conceptions of *justice* as of *love*. All the propositions established in this argument tend to this point. We are apt to lose sight of justice, and to exalt love. This is quite natural with all who have any sense of wrong (and who has not?), for we feel the need of love or mercy, and are ever willing or anxious to screen ourselves from justice. But in this, as before remarked, we do violence to our moral sense, to gratify our selfish feelings. Can any one dispassionately reason and reflect on this subject, and accept the idea of a God of even partial justice? The idea is alike repugnant to reason and to reverence. God must be strictly, infinitely just. Who would not choose to be annihilated rather than to possess immortal existence in a universe governed or controlled by a being of almighty power, but lacking justice?

Many professed believers in the Bible manifest

the same tendency, to exalt the love of God **above** his justice. It is a great perversion of the gospel. God is *infinite* in *every* perfection. His love cannot be *more* than infinite. If his justice were *less* than infinite he would be an imperfect or finite being. The gospel plan was not devised, and Christ did not die, to exalt his love above his justice, but to make it possible to manifest his infinite love toward the penitent sinner, without disparagement to his infinite justice; "that he might be just, and the justifier of him who believeth in Jesus." Rom. 3 : 23–26. But this will be examined when we come to the Biblical argument.

Perhaps there never was a time when the idea expressed by Pope, " Whatever is, is right," was so distorted and carried to an absurd extreme, as it is at the present.] Some say that every action, whatever its nature, is acceptable to God, because it is performed under his overruling hand. One well-known "reformer" says that such a thing as "sin, in the common acceptation of the term, does not exist." It is affirmed that sin cannot exist; that "there is no room in the universe for wrong to exist." We heard a somewhat popular speaker declare that "what men call crimes are most valuable experiences in the march of human progress." And these state ments are not made by wild fanatics alone; they are argued in their most plausible forms by men, and women, also, who pass in their communities for staid and sober people. But on examination we find that the propagators of these theories get them up to relieve the mind of a sense of responsibility. This class of moral philosophers always frame their theories to throw the blame of wrong, if any wrong exists, upon God, the Creator, and never to leave it upon themselves!

We trust the reader will pardon the relation of "a true story" which contains an argument in itself worthy of consideration. Two men, machinists, working in a railroad shop, were conversing on this subject. One contended that if he did wrong he was not responsible for the wrong, for, said he, "I act out the disposition that was given me. If I make a locomotive and it will not work, you do not blame the locomotive, you blame me for my faulty workmanship. Even so, if I do not answer the end of my being, it is not my fault. The blame attaches to my Maker, who made me what I am." His friend replied: "Your illustration is just and forcible, provided you insist that your Maker gave you no more brains than you put into a locomotive!"

The truth is that the possession of brains and will-power brings responsibility; and this responsibility necessarily attaches to creatures on our plane of being. If they who deny the existence of moral wrong would reflect a moment, they could not fail to perceive that their theory is really degrading to themselves. They are irresponsible if they are mere machines or unreasoning animals. But if they have the power to reason, to will, to choose, and have moral consciousness, a sense of right and wrong, responsibility must necessarily attend the use of these powers. And every one *feels* this responsibility; his conscience will not permit him to deny it, until he has seared his conscience, and blunted his moral sensibilities; that is to say, he has, in a greater or less degree, brutalized himself, and degraded his manhood, either by pernicious and false reasoning, or by an immoral life.

And now, looking over the whole field of argument on this subject, we ask: Is it not a humiliating thought that a word is necessary to prove to any one that moral wrong exists? Must I stop to reason with a man, a human being, with all his faculties in exercise, to prove to him that it is wrong to steal, to murder, or to commit adultery? To argue the subject, nay, to admit that it is a debatable question, is an insult to the sense of mankind. The real question at issue is, How shall we dispose of the evil which exists? or, How shall criminals be rescued from the awful consequences of their violations of the law of Him who is infinitely just? We do not ask the reader, or our doubting friend, to consider the question as to whether the guilty might not be suffered to escape by overruling or suspending justice, or how they might stand before a finite being, or a judge who is comparatively just. The real question is, How shall they stand before the judgment seat where justice is maintained and vindicated on the scale of infinity? where every evil thought and intention is counted as an overt act of iniquity and rebellion against a righteous Government? This, and nothing less, is involved in the very idea of a Supreme Being, an Infinite One who is a moral Governor, whose perfections demand that He shall take cognizance of every offense against His authority; every invasion of the rights of His subjects.

These are solemn questions, and demand our candid consideration. If God *is* infinitely just—and can he be otherwise?—if he *will* bring every work into judgment, and we shall have to meet our life records there, how shall we stand in His presence? It certainly becomes us to deal candidly with ourselves, and to understand, if possible, those principles of justice which must prevail in a wise and righteous government. Sin is everywhere, and in our own hearts. What shall be done in regard to it?

We may indeed flatter ourselves that our sins have not been very great; we may persuade ourselves to believe that, compared to those of others, our lives have been quite creditable. But we must remember that *wrong never appears odious to the habitual wrong-doer;* therefore no one is competent to judge in his own case. The decision will not be made upon our actions as they look to us, but as they look to the Infinite Lawgiver and Judge. We will not be compared with our neighbor, in the Judgment, but with the law which is holy, and just, and good. The spirituality of that law we cannot comprehend, even as we cannot fathom the mind of its Author. We must stand in the light of Heaven's purity and glory.

CHAPTER III.

THE administration of government is a simple, easy, yes, a pleasant matter, where all the subjects are perfectly obedient. No such Government now exists on this earth; but every one can picture to himself how happy the State would be where there was no sin; no violation of the law; no invasion of rights; no denial or disregard of authority; no discord, but each seeking the peace and happiness of the other. Who would not pray, "Thy kingdom come," if its coming will introduce such a state of things?

But when sin enters, everything is changed. New and strange relations are introduced. New interests spring up. New duties devolve upon both the Government and the criminal. The governor must then take steps to maintain the integrity of the law, the honor of the State, and thereby to protect the subjects from the consequences of wrong-doing. For every violation of the law is an invasion upon the rights and liberties of the citizens. As we shall notice more particularly hereafter, two parties then arise; one, pitying the criminal, pleading for mercy; the other, fearing for the safety of the State and the welfare of its subjects, pleading for justice. And such are the realities now before us. With such an unfortunate state of things we have to deal. Such difficulties and diverse interests are found everywhere upon the face of the earth.

While we consider the requirements of a moral system in such a state of things, we must bear in mind that *there is no moral Government on earth.* That is to say, there is no Government on earth entirely of moral principles, or administered solely upon a moral basis. And, from the very nature of things, it is impossible that there shall be in the present state. No human Government is administered with regard to the *intentions* of the subjects aside from their *actions.* No governor, no judge, no jury, has been able to "discern the thoughts and intents of the heart." Secret things are not, and cannot here, be brought into judgment. A moral system, or a moral Government, can be administered by God alone. All that we have said or shall say respecting a moral system, we say in reference to the rule and authority of God, who only can defend moral principles, and bring into judgment the violators of the spirit of law as well as the violators of its letter.

But *the principles* of justice and of government we may understand, and are able to discern in regard to their requirements under various circumstances. According to the measure of our ability, we are under obligation to maintain these principles; and though we cannot discern the intents of the hearts of others, *we are required to guard our own hearts,* and to respect these principles *in our lives.* And however much we might shrink from the strict enforcement of these principles, we must bear in mind that law not only *binds* us, but it *protects* us; and we would have every reason to dread the results of a failure to uphold and enforce law. We deprecate tyranny, but it is seldom as blindly cruel as anarchy.

We will now proceed, as briefly as possible, to examine some of the well-known and well-accepted claims and requirements of government.

§ I.   SIN OUGHT TO BE PUNISHED.

Penalty gives force to the law, and without it, law is a nullity. And no matter what consequences may result from the violation of law, the criminal is not punished till the penalty is inflicted. We might find many cases in our courts where the accused has suffered consequences more severe than the punishment which the law inflicts; but the judge cannot regard these—his office is to see that the penalty prescribed by the law be inflicted. He who violates the law risks the penalty and the intermediate consequences. In behalf of the affirmation that the transgression of the law ought to be punished, the following reasons are offered:—

1. *It injures the subjects of the Government.* One great object of government is the good of its subjects. The imprisonment of the thief, the robber, and the murderer, answers a double purpose, punishing the crimes, and preventing their further preying upon our property and our lives. The same law that restrains the evil-doer, secures the rights of the well-doer. Hence, every violation of the law of a Government is an invasion of the rights of the subjects thereof. Its tendency will be more clearly seen if we imagine for a moment that the law be disregarded by not one

only, but by many, or by all. Then all rights, all safeguards, would be trampled down, and the objects of government entirely defeated. This, of course, is the tendency of every transgression.

2. *It brings contempt upon the Government.* In case of war we have seen thousands offer their lives as a sacrifice to uphold the Government and maintain its honor. If it cannot secure respect, it cannot maintain its authority. And if authority be despised, no rights and privileges are safe. All the evils noticed in the preceding paragraph are involved in this.

3. *It insults and abuses the Creator and Governor.* So blinding is the influence of sin that men despise the authority of God, and insult him daily, without any apparent compunction. All violations of law are insults to, and abuse of, authority. Every individual has *rights* in his own sphere, and there is no right more sacred than that of the Supreme authority to claim the respect and reverence of the subjects. And if the Governor be not respected, his Government cannot be; and if that be not respected, of course the rights of the subjects under it will not be. Consider again, if this example were followed by all—by all the intelligences of the universe; if all the men on earth and all the angels in Heaven should unite in abusing and insulting the God of Heaven, his Government would be turned into one vast field of anarchy, and individual rights would no longer be recognized. No one could consent that God should suffer such a state of things to continue without making an effort to

reclaim the Government, and to maintain and vindicate right laws. Of course all must agree that sin ought to be punished.

§ II.   CAN THE SINNER BE CLEARED?

This question is of the greatest importance, and no one should pass it lightly. All would say at once that the sinner *can be cleared;* but of necessity something must be involved in securing his acquittal. It must appear to all that he *cannot possibly* be cleared *unless* one of the following things takes place:—

1. *The law be suffered to be trampled upon with impunity.* This, of course, *should not* be permitted, for reasons given above; and we may say, *will not* be permitted, if the executive has a proper sense of right and justice to himself and to his subjects, and requisite power to enforce his authority. But the divine attributes must be a sufficient guarantee to guard this point.

2. *The law be abolished.* But this would be an acknowledgment of weakness or error on the part of the Government rather than evidence of wrong on the part of the transgressor. Or if the law were not acknowledged to be wrong, nor the Government in error, the case would be equally bad, presenting the pitiable spectacle of a Government abolishing a good law to accommodate a bad subject—one of rebellious tendencies. This would not be restraining sin; it would be rather favoring or licensing sin, and justifying the sinner in his evil course. And it would have a tendency to bring in all the evils of anarchy and ruin that

we have considered as the unavoidable results of destroying governmental authority. To suppose that God would act thus is a libel on the wisdom and justice of the King of Heaven which we would not dare to utter. These suppositions are inadmissible.

3. *The Governor pardon.* This is a prerogative that may, under proper restrictions and conditions, be safely exercised. Therefore we must accept this as the only alternative; as the only means whereby the sinner may escape from the punishment of his crimes.

By examining the foregoing points, it will be perceived that the acts of *abolishing the law*, and *pardoning the transgressor*, cannot in any case be united. One would be a nullity if both were attempted. This will be better appreciated when we consider the conditions under which pardon may be granted, and how the Government (which must ever be the first and chief concern) will be affected thereby.

§ III. PARDON SUPPOSES OR RECOGNIZES,

1. *The guilt of the condemned.* This is evident. To pardon an innocent man would be preposterous. Human Governments sometimes professedly do this, as when it is ascertained that a man, who is in prison for a term of years, is innocent of the crime of which he was convicted, the Governor issues a pardon as a means of his release. But it is a misnomer, and really an insult to the innocent man. The law should make provision for release from unjust confinement

without subjecting a man to the disgrace of receiving a pardon when he had committed no crime.

2. *The power of government.* This is equally evident. To pardon is to remit a penalty which might be inflicted. It would be a mere farce to offer a pardon to those whom the Government had no power to punish.

3. *The justice of the law transgressed.* This is nearly parallel with the first proposition, and like it, evident; for to pronounce a man *guilty* is to say that he has *done wrong.* And if a violation of law be wrong, the law violated must be right. An unjust law is, in a moral view, a nullity. When a law is found to be unconstitutional, or a nullity, the prisoner under it is not really pardoned; he should be released from false imprisonment; and such release is of justice, not of mercy. But pardon is of favor. Thus it is clear that the justice of the law is acknowledged in the article of pardon. Now as pardon supposes the guilt of the prisoner, the power of the Government, and the justice of the law, in all these it may be made to honor the Government and vindicate its integrity.

But there are other principles involved. The act of pardon recognizes the *claims* of law, by recognizing its *justice.* Thus far it honors the Government. But the question still remains, Are those claims *satisfied* as well as acknowledged? According to a plain truth before noticed, the sinner ought to be punished; justice imperatively demands it. How then can pardon be granted, and *strict justice* be administered? In this case there will arise two conflicting interests; one of sympathy for the accused, leaning toward mercy; the other, strenuous for the integrity ef the Government, leaning toward justice. How can these principles be reconciled? Can both parties be satisfied? Here is a difficulty; and this will lead us to notice the conditions or restrictions under which pardon may be granted with safety. For an indiscriminate, unconditional pardon is dangerous to the Government. Closely examining this subject we find

§ IV. WHAT THE GOVERNOR MUST DO IN GRANTING PARDON.

He must do one of the following things:—

1. *Disregard the strict claims of law and justice.* But this, of course, is evil in its tendency, giving license to crime, and favoring lawlessness, rather than restraining it, which latter must remain the true object of government. This, indeed, is the very thing we have all the time been guarding against. We cannot admit this, it being dangerous to the Government. Because if the claims of the law may be disregarded in one case, they may be in many—they may be in all; and then government is at an end. And if the executive sets the example of disregarding the claims of the law, others may thereby be led to follow his example, or all may; and the result is the same —lawlessness and anarchy. And all this from following the example of him who occupies the throne of justice! The very thought is, in the highest degree, abhorrent. Only one way re-

mains possible by which pardon may be granted without trampling on justice, and endangering the Government; that is

2. *Make satisfaction to the law by voluntary substitution.* If the substitution be voluntary, so that the substitute be satisfied, and the full penalty of the law be inflicted, so that the law and justice be satisfied, all must be satisfied—all conflicting interests and feelings must be reconciled. Let no one say, to oppose this, that such is not the case when pardon is granted in human Governments; for these are imperfect, and instead of conforming strictly to justice they can only hope to approximate it. The interests above referred to are *never* harmonized in human Governments. In these, if the prisoner is punished less than the penalty indicated by the law, then the law is deprived just so much of its due. In such case, justice is not reconciled or vindicated; it is suspended. All must see at a glance that the means herein proposed alone obviates all difficulties. Let us further examine its effects.

§ V.   VOLUNTARY SUBSTITUTION,

1. *Recognizes the claims of law.* We have supposed substitution wherein all parties are satisfied —all conflicts reconciled. But if the law were unjust, if the accused were not really guilty of a wrong, the act of condemning would be tyrannical. There could then be no satisfaction, either to justice, or to the condemned, or to his substitute. Hence, to obtain the desired result, there must be acquiescence in the justness of the pro-

ceeding, which is a recognition of the justice of the law which condemned.

2. *It honors and maintains the Government.* It must be admitted that every infringement on the claims of law, every departure from strict justice, is a violation of common rights, and endangers the Government. Whatever honors and vindicates the claims of law and justice, tends to maintain the Government; and of course to vindicate personal rights under it. This voluntary substitution does, as has been shown.

3. *It dispenses mercy*, which could not otherwise be offered consistently with the great principles of right and justice. Hence, all the objects of government—justice and mercy, truth and love, —meet in this arrangement. This is precisely the idea of an Atonement—not a thing to be deprecated, as some have vainly imagined, but to be loved and esteemed, as a certain vindication of right and justice, and a beneficent dispensation of love and mercy.

In the examination of principles thus far we have found that the Atonement affects our relation to the Government in two respects, looking to the past and to the future. To the past, in that it frees from condemnation for past offenses; and to the future, in that it recognizes the claims of the law, thus binding us to future obedience to the law.

But some affect to discover no harmony between these objects, though it is plain that a proposed Atonement which should lose sight of either of these would fail to unite justice and mercy; it would leave the sinner condemned, or dishonor the Government. It may, however, be noticed further,

§ VI.   WHY AN ATONEMENT IS NECESSARY.

1. *Future obedience will not justify the guilty.* To argue this seems hardly necessary, as it has been shown that justice and mercy meet in no way but by an Atonement. But some deny the *use*, by which it is presumed they mean the necessity, or justness, of obeying a law which will not justify the guilty. But the deficiency lies only in their own oversight. They make no distinction between justifying the *innocent* and the *guilty*. The innocent are justified by law; the guilty cannot be. But the innocent are justified by law only if they *remain* innocent; that is, if they continue to obey. While the transgressor, already condemned, is not freed from condemnation of past offense by future obedience. In this, no more is claimed than is settled as a principle of action in legal and even in commercial transactions. He who killed, last year, cannot offer in justification that he has not killed, this year. The judge has no right to listen to the plea of the thief, that he has not recently stolen, while the evidence of his past guilt is clear. It does not release a man from a past debt to pay for what he buys to-day. Present justice and present morality simply answer a present demand, leaving the past unsettled. But we have a question to ask to those who think it is not required to keep a law because it will not justify

the transgressor. If the law condemns a thief, and he can only be cleared by pardon, does the granting of a pardon release him from obligation to keep the law, and leave him free to steal thereafter?

2. *We have no ransom to bring.* The demand of the Government is *obedience;* and the duty is *perpetual.* Any cessation or suspension is a break in the chain that we cannot restore. We cannot on one day perform the duties of another, in such a manner as to suspend obligations on that other day. Presenting this idea on a moral basis purely, we will be better able to appreciate it. The obligation to love God with all our heart binds us every day of our life. Suppose we fail on one day, it would be absurd to say we could make amends by another day's obedience; for that would be to love God that other day *with more than all the heart*, so as to apply some of our superabundance of love to the past! Hence the transgressor could not save himself, even though he retained all his original strength to obey; but the following truth is well known:—

3. *We are incapacitated by immoral practices.* In this, appeal is made to the consciousness of every candid, reflecting mind. We all acknowledge ourselves to be subjects of temptation, and often find in ourselves a proneness to do that which our convictions forbid. If we allow ourselves to do wrong, these feelings become still stronger, and we are less able to resist the temptation. Wrong-doing becomes a habit, hard to resist or overcome. Thus, he who has a mod-

erate desire to drink ardent spirits will find that desire greatly strengthened by indulgence and it will finally, if indulged too far, bring him completely under its control. This is the tendency of all wrong-doing. Now we all feel conscious of having done more or less wrong; and it is but reasonable to say we have done more than we are conscious of, inasmuch as we have not been sufficiently tenacious of the right, nor very watchful to observe our own wrongs. And, according to the plain truth herein stated, we have become weak according to the wrong we have done, and so much the more need the assistance of a third party to set us right with the power we have offended.

An Atonement must not only unite justice and mercy, and reconcile the transgressor to the law, but the perpetuity and stability of the Government should be the *first* consideration, as they are first in importance in our relations and duties, because on them the perpetuity of all private relations and rights depends. We all assent to this, that public good should be held paramount to private interest. But these only come in conflict when we place ourselves in opposition to the Government. Hence, if our interest conflicts with the Government, which is the conservator of general rights, it is proved to be a *selfish interest.* For, had we honored and sustained the Government in our lives or actions, it would justify or sustain us; but if our rights are forfeited by disobedience, wherein is the Government to blame? Because the transgressor has sacrificed his own rights, it is not therefore reasonable to ask that justice be dishonored, and the rights of others be sacrificed for his benefit. As *right* should be the *first* consideration in all transactions, the interest of the Government, which is right, should certainly be held paramount to the good of the transgressor, who is wrong. Therefore, in making an Atonement, the upholding of law—the maintaining of governmental authority—should be held as of the first importance. This is the only manner in which an Atonement can honor the Government in behalf of which it is made.

By a single violation of law, we forfeit our rights and privileges; but by persisting in such violation, or inducing others so to do, and thus disregarding the authority of law, we take the rank of rebels or traitors against the Government. Our relation to the Government while we are in that position, and our relation to the means of our restoration, should be considered with great carefulness and candor.

VII. THE SINNER MUST ACCEPT, NOT MAKE, CONDITIONS.

1 This proposition must be evident to all, for

1. *Treason is the highest crime.* He who commits murder takes a life, but he who seeks to subvert the law, seeks the destruction of life's safeguard, of that which is to protect life by preventing and punishing crime. Hence, it is the aggregation of all crimes.

2. *The Government has the sole right to free therefrom.* By this is meant that the Government has

the sole right to dictate the terms or conditions by which rebels may be restored to citizenship. This is true, also, in regard to all crimes for which pardon is desired. And this right, Government ought to exercise. No criminal has any right to dictate the terms of his own pardon, or the means by which he may be restored to the favor of the Government. And no one who has any regard for violated rights, for down-trodden justice, for the sacred principles of law and order, could be willing to see the traitor unconditionally restored to place and favor. No Government would be safe pursuing such a course; neither could it command respect.

3. *He who will not accept the conditions is a traitor still.* If the Government has the sole right to dictate terms to rebels, which all must allow, then the transgressor can only change his relation to the Government by accepting those terms; and if he refuses to accept them, he, of course, persists in maintaining his position in rebellion. Or to substitute terms of his own would be no better, but rather an insult to the Government, a denial of its right and authority. If a criminal were to dictate how crimes should be treated, government would be a farce and become the contempt of honest men. Therefore two things must be required of a transgressor or rebel, which only can be accepted, to wit:—

1. UNQUALIFIED SUBMISSION TO THE LAWS WHICH HAVE BEEN TRANSGRESSED, and,

2. A HEARTY ACCEPTANCE OF THE PLAN OR CONDITIONS OFFERED FOR HIS RESTORATION.

An objection is often urged against this view, viz., that if a substitute be accepted and the penalty of the law be laid upon him, then there is no pardon—no mercy, but justice only in the transaction. For, says the objector, if the debt be paid by another person, it cannot justly be held against the principal; payment cannot be twice demanded. The fatal fault of this objection is this: It regards *crime* as a *debt*, which it is not.

A man may owe a debt without any guilt attaching to him; but not so of sin. In the very first step there is mercy toward the sinner in the acceptance of a substitute in his behalf; and after the substitute has suffered the penalty, the sinner is as deserving of punishment in his own person as He was before. *He* has done nothing to relieve himself of the odium of his crime. All must see, at a glance, that what has been said about the *acceptance of conditions* is a necessary part of this system of pardon, as the Government not only needs satisfaction for the past, but a safeguard for the future. This the mere payment of a past debt would not furnish. Therefore the acceptance of a substitute who volunteers to bear the penalty of crime *opens the way for pardon* to be granted consistently with justice. Now if the criminal accepts that substitute so as to make the offering *his own*, and fulfills the required conditions, so that he unites his efforts with those of the substitute in honoring the law, then the Government has its safeguard against future rebellion. But without this, all the evils of *unconditional pardon* may accrue from the action of the sinner, even though a substitute have suffered in his behalf. But if the law be honored by the suffering of the substitute, and the sinner cease to sin, and accept the conditions, as herein proposed, there remains no difficulty. The Government is honored in the justice of the transaction, and the sinner is justified and saved by its provision of mercy. But if any of these particulars be lacking, the system will then be defective. Pardon granted on any other terms tends to iniquity, violating the principles of right and justice, and subverting government.*

It is unnecessary to argue, but well to mention, that a substitute, to render satisfaction to justice, must be free from condemnation in his own life; he must be innocent in the sight of the law, or free from its transgression. For one criminal to offer his life for another would not be any satisfaction to justice, seeing his own was already forfeited.

RIGHTS OF SUBJECTS.

While advocating the claims of the Government, we must not lose sight of the truth that the subjects have claims on justice also. As very much is due from the subjects to the Government, so

---

*This is a necessary deduction from the very plain facts set forth in this argument. There are two theological systems extant which stand opposed to these principles; one, claiming that man may and will be saved without accepting and complying with conditions, or without substitution. This is Universalism, which really denies the Atonement. The other is Antinomianism, which claims that the law is abolished when the Atonement is made, instead of being honored and vindicated by it. Both these systems are denials of justice, and tend to subvert the principles of government as established by reason and the Scriptures. But as these principles lie at the very foundation of the divine Government, the above systems are, though *professedly Christian, practically infidel.*

something is due from the Government to the subjects. It is expected of a Government to establish its laws, and of the subjects to obey them; but it should be able to present tangible and substantial claims to obedience. We notice, then,

1. *The Government must plainly reveal its laws.* It is recorded of a certain tyrant that he caused his laws to be posted at such a height that they could not be read, and then punished those who did not keep them. This was injustice—it was indeed tyranny. It is *law* that defines our duty; and in order that obedience may be justly enforced, such declaration of duty should be clear and distinct: not left to supposition, or to doubtful inference. We have before considered that a moral government, a system above nature, is acknowledged; but what is due to that government our consciousness, or moral sense, does not inform us. On this point, our opinions, if not guided by revelation, will be as various as our impulses, our interests, or the difference of our circumstances and education. But if our duties be left to our own judgments, with our conflicting feelings and interests, our determinations will be so various that confusion and anarchy must unavoidably be the result. It would in truth be no law—no government. Was ever a government known that proclaimed no laws, but left all actions entirely to the choice of the subjects? No! there could be no government under such conditions. Shall we then admit that God, the Creator of heaven and earth, is a moral Governor, and this we do by admitting a moral system, and yet deny his justice,

4

his wisdom, and, in fact, his very government, by denying the revelation of his will, or law, to man? Such a denial is too unreasonable to be tolerated; it involves conclusions too absurd and derogatory to the divine character. It is really sinking Deity below our ideas of a wise human governor.

But again: As it is the prerogative of the Government to ordain its laws, so it is its sole prerogative, as we have seen, to determine the means whereby a rebel may be restored to citizenship, and as the law must be plainly revealed to serve the purposes of justice, so,

2. *The Government must plainly reveal the conditions of pardon.* The right to ordain conditions being exclusively in the Government, the subjects or offenders can have no means of ascertaining them, except by direct revelation. If left without this, they can never be restored; for it would be absurd to leave the offenders to devise their own means. That would be to place the dearest rights of the Government into the hands of criminals, a thought unworthy of consideration. In all this we plainly see that one demand of justice is a written revelation. And so reasonable is this, so consistent with the plainest principles of justice, that, instead of objecting to a written revelation, every one that is capable of reasoning correctly should expect such a revelation, as strictly necessary to the moral Government of God.

CONCLUDING REMARKS AND QUESTIONS.

1. If God has instituted morals, he is a moral Governor, and has a moral law; for there can be

no government without a law. If there is a moral law, it must be the only standard of morality; and it follows that we can only determine a man's character in a moral point of view, by comparing his life with the law of God—the moral rule. For, as we have before noticed, there is no earthly Government which is administered on purely moral principles. God alone can govern on such a basis. Therefore, whoever has violated God's law has lost his moral character by such violation as surely as morality consists in obedience to moral law. But we are all conscious of having violated the principles of right and justice—most of our race in a most glaring manner. All around us are evidences that man has ruined himself by sin. *How may he be acquitted and restored?* Can you devise a plan which will honor the Government, vindicate justice, maintain the authority of the law, and yet save the sinner? Have you ever considered this matter?

2. We have considered that the Government has the sole right to dictate the terms whereby man may be restored to favor. We trace a plain distinction between the systems of nature and morality; but in neither, unassisted by direct revelation, can we discover the measure of obedience due to the divine Government, or the method or means whereby we may be reconciled to our Creator. *How shall we obtain this information?*

3. We have also seen the utter inability of man to save himself from the penalty of his transgressions, and the imperative necessity of a mediator to atone for us, and to vindicate justice in our

pardon. And our fellow-men are all in the same condition, as helpless and unworthy as ourselves. *Who shall act as our mediator?*

Friendly reader! if you have trusted in reason and nature; if you have been skeptical as to divine revelation, we entreat you to turn not hastily away from these thoughts; pause and reflect. Have you made your boast of reason? "Come, now, let us reason together." Can you invalidate, or with reason deny, the positions taken in the preceding pages? Can you answer the three questions proposed above? Can you tell with certainty what duty you owe to your Creator, the moral Governor? or on what principle you expect to be justified before God? Do you know how you may be restored after you have offended? Can you show where we may learn all this? In a word, Do you not need a written revelation?

Again, would it not serve the cause of justice, and the true purposes of government, to have the laws of our lives, moral laws, published for the benefit of those amenable thereto? Surely, it would. So far from being astonished at the idea of a written revelation—a publication of the divine laws—we should expect it; justice demands it. And, if we could not produce such a document, would you not esteem it an oversight in the Governor?

Once more: An Atonement has been supposed to lead to immorality. But, according to what has been proved, it is the *only possible method* of restoring the sinner to favor which *does not* lead to immorality. It is readily granted that any theory by which the Atonement is claimed to have abolished the law of the Most High, or relaxed its claims, leads to immorality. And we regret exceedingly that there are some systems professing to represent Christianity, which uphold such a demoralizing view; some professedly Christian ministers who preach that the gospel set aside, superseded, or abolished the law of God which he had revealed to man. Such teachings are a perversion of the gospel; subversive of justice and every right principle of Government, and highly dishonoring to the Son of God who came to establish the law and to put down rebellion against his Father. But can that lead to immorality which acknowledges the justice of law, removes rebellion, and restores the wrongdoer to obedience? You will see that this objection arises, not from any defect in the system of the Atonement, but from the ignorance of the objector as to what that system is. We readily admit that to abolish a good law because it has been disobeyed, and thereby leave men free from its obligations, is to license the crime committed and to utterly subvert all government. We claim nothing for an Atonement on such grounds, and should be obliged to reject anything purporting to be a revelation from God which led to such unjust and unreasonable conclusions. The Bible presents a pure system of morality, and, through the Atonement, a means of pardon, consistent with every requirement of justice, and every correct principle of government. It neither favors indulgence nor gives license. *Pardon* maintains law;

license upholds crime. There is as great differ-ence between pardon and license as there is be-tween liberty and licentiousness; and he who cannot discern the difference as recognized in the Atonement, may well be pitied.

Do not think that we discard reason because we plead for the Bible and its truths. And we entreat you not to abuse your reason in a vain effort to make it answer a purpose which it will not, and for which it was never designed. *Reason is not evidence;* nor can it create evidence. It can only weigh the evidence when presented. But revelation and evidence are the same. And now if it can be shown, as we claim, that the Bible is in perfect harmony with these principles, and enforces them strictly, there will remain no *reasonable objection* against it as a revelation from the great "Lawgiver." Will you join in a patient investigation of this matter? No subject can be more worthy of your attention. Let us examine the Bible itself, and discover what is the morality which it teachers, and what means it reveals for the salvation of those who have dared to disre-gard the claims of the divine Government.

THE ATONEMENT.

CHAPTER I.

PRINCIPLES OF THE DIVINE GOVERNMENT.

In our examination of the teachings of the
Bible concerning the principles of the Divine
Government, and the means therein revealed for
the pardon and salvation of the penitent sinner,
we ask the reader to keep in view the principles
already established, and to mark how perfectly
the Bible harmonizes with, and how strongly it
enforces, these fundamental principles of justice.
In this respect, we insist that the Bible stands
alone. Among the pretended revelations which
have existed or now exist in the world, it has no
worthy rival. Of all known religions that of the
Bible alone offers pardon on terms which do honor
to divine, infinite justice. It alone offers a substitutionary sacrifice worthy to meet the claims
of the violated, yet immutable law of Jehovah,
through whom it is possible for God to be just—
to maintain his infinite justice—and yet justify
or pardon the believer in that sacrifice. And if
it shall clearly appear that the Bible is the faith-

ful expositor and upholder of these principles, then we ask the reader, even though he may have been skeptical as to its merits and its claims, to accept it as the needed light from Heaven, a revelation of the Divine will. If such be the nature of its teachings; if such be its claims, then every one who is truly guided by reason and a love of right and truth, must so accept it.

There is a tendency among men, and we think it is increasing, to make the love of God the sole element in the gospel. Universalism is the true exponent of this theory, though thousands are inclining to it who would readily repudiate the charge that they are Universalists. We never could see the consistency of that system which taught that all men will be saved, while teaching that there is nothing in all the universe from which they need to be saved. We consider that view equally faulty which is now advocated by eminent men of almost all schools, namely, that the death of Christ was not a penal infliction, that it was not a vindication of justice, but merely a manifestation of the love of God, calculated and designed to move the hearts of men that they may be led to appreciate his love. In several respects this theory fails to commend itself. 1. It is not according to the teachings of the Bible, as we shall endeavor to show in these pages. 2. The result is not at all commensurate to the expenditure. If that were the sole object, the necessities of the case did not require such an immense sacrifice as was made in the sufferings and death of the Son of the living God. 3.

It is a fact that men's emotions are more easily aroused by a consideration of human woes, by a recital of the sufferings of their own kind, than by reading of the sufferings of Christ. Dr. Clarke made some striking remarks on this fact. And we might add that they who claim the *emotional* ground of the death of Jesus are seldom aroused to such exalted views of the love of God in Christ as they are who believe in the *judicial* ground. The truth proclaimed in the word of God, that "he was wounded for our transgressions, and bruised for our iniquities," is attested by the Spirit of God, who bears witness of it to the consciences of the truly convicted and converted.

But we are not now presenting an argument on this question; that is reserved for the future. We merely call attention to these points here, while the simple principles of justice which have been examined are fresh in the mind of the reader, (1) to lead him to consider that the *emotional* view of the death of Christ does not at all meet the requirements of the divine law. It ignores the claim of justice in the divine Government, and really makes sin a matter of small account; (2) that we may be prepared to appreciate the importance of those principles and rules of duty which underlie all the purposes and dispensations of God toward man; that we may understand and realize why the gospel is needed to bring man back to God, and renew his hope of everlasting life and glory.

Our first inquiry, then, relates to the principles of the Government of God, or, in other words,

to his law. This is fundamental; all else must
be based on it. It is difficult, if not impossible,
to form just ideas of secondary principles if we
have not just ideas of their primaries.

There can be no difference between the attributes of God and the principles of his Government. If God is just, justice will show forth as
a principle of his Government; it will be administered in justice. If God is love, love must per-
vade his Government. If God is immutable, the
principles of his Government must be likewise
unchangeable. We cannot conceive of his possessing an attribute which does not shine forth
in his Government. But as law is the basis of
Government, without which it cannot exist, whatever applies to the one applies to the other.
Therefore to understand the attributes of God is
to understand the nature or character of his law,
as the latter necessarily springs from the former.
This is too plainly evident to require proof, for
his law is but the expression of his will, and his
will must surely correspond to his attributes.

We do not consider it necessary to examine at
length the attributes of Deity. All will agree
that to him belong wisdom, power, holiness, truth,
justice, love, and mercy. It may be said, however, that these qualities are ascribed also to man.
Thus the Scriptures speak of men who were holy,
true, just, wise, etc. But such expressions in regard to man must be taken with the limitations
arising from man's nature. There are three attributes which belong to Deity which may be applied to all those mentioned above, but which

man cannot possess, namely, infinity, immutability, and eternity. While man is wise, just,
merciful, etc., in a certain degree, God is infinitely,
immutably, and eternally wise, just, holy, true,
etc. These three qualify all the others. They
are "perfections of perfections," essential to the
divine character, but belonging to it alone. So
let it be understood that when we speak of the
justice of God, the word is not used in any ordinary sense, or as it is used in respect to man.
The justice of God is infinite, immutable, eternal.
We are in danger of making God (in our minds)
such an one as ourselves, and of imagining that
he looks upon sin with as little abhorrence as we
do, who have always associated with it, and in
some of its forms have always been inclined to
love it instead of abhorring it. When we speak
of God and his attributes, of his will, his law, we
should do it with more than respect—with reverence.

It has been noticed that the governor must
make a plain revelation of the law to which the
subjects are amenable. This the Lord has done.
In the beginning the Creator talked with man
in person, and made known to him directly the
rules which were to govern his life. But the
book of Genesis is not a book of law; it is a very
brief history of the race, covering a period of
more than two thousand years. We have fre-
quent mention of men's violation of law, with
references to the law itself, but no code left on
record in the book. But all nations chose their
own way—"they did not like to retain God in

their knowledge"—and he separated from the nations the seed of Abraham, to be a people to his own glory. After they had been in long servitude and under deep afflictions in the land of Egypt, he "took them by the hand," as a father does his children, to bring them into the land of Canaan, and to lead them in the way of truth and righteousness. While all the families of the earth were turning away from God, going farther and farther into the darkness of hea thenism, it is not surprising that the people of Israel, oppressed in cruel bondage, should have imbibed much of the spirit of their surroundings, and retained but imperfect ideas of the sacredness of the divine law. That this was the case is proved by the readiness with which they wor- shiped the golden calf, after the manner of the Egyptians, when the circumstances would seem to forbid their yielding to the force of such super- stitions. It was a wide departure from the faith and godliness of their fathers Abraham, Isaac, and Jacob, and of Joseph.

In revealing his will to his chosen people, the Lord made known through prophets and priests, civil and ecclesiastical duties; but he taught them, and all who should come after them, to look with peculiar reverence upon *the moral code*, by pro- claiming it with his own voice, and writing it with his own finger on tables of stone. That men have always considered the ten command- ments a moral code, could only be expected from the manner in which it was given by Jehovah and placed in the ark over which the high priest made atonement for sin; from its containing a summary of duty covering all moral relations; and from the teaching of the Scriptures in regard to it.

When God brought Israel out of Egypt, he entered into an agreement or covenant with them, promising to regard them as a peculiar treasure above all nations, if they would obey his voice and keep his covenant. This they readily promised to do. Ex. 19:5–8. "Obey my voice," and "keep my covenant," are two expressions used by the Lord, referring to the same thing; for when they heard his voice, the third day after the covenant was made with them, he declared his covenant which he commanded them to perform. This was the ten commandments. Deut. 4:12, 13. The word "covenant" is of such extensive signification that we can only learn its meaning in any text by the sense of the passage or its connection. According to the lexicons, and to Scripture usage, it applies to a great variety of things, as, a promise; Gen. 9:9–11; an agreement; Gen. 21:22–32; mutual promises with conditions; Ex. 19:5–8; a law; Deut. 4:12, 13; and a covenant of law may be the condition of a covenant of promises, as in 2 Kings 23:3. And so also in Ex. 19:5–8, the expression, "Keep my covenant," refers to the covenant which he commanded unto them, and not to the covenant or agreement made with them. The agreement was based upon the condition, namely, "Obey my voice;" that is, obey that which he spoke to them when they heard his voice. They did not hear his voice when this covenant was made with them: Moses acted as mediator between the Lord and them. But the ten commandments were spoken by Jehovah directly to the people. This law in all things bears the pre-eminence above the revelations made through the prophets. It was not committed to Moses to bear to the people, as were the other laws. It bears the impress of Deity alone.

The Lord also said that if they would obey this law they would be a holy nation. Now it is an acknowledged truth that character is formed by our actions in reference to law; and *the nature of the character* is determined only by *the nature of the law*. Obedience to a bad law can never make a good character. It is hence evident that *the character of the actor is the exact counterpart of the law obeyed*. But we have the Lord's own testimony, that if they would keep the ten commandments, they would be holy; that is, they would thereby form holy characters; and as their characters would be but a copy of the law, we have herein the word of the Governor of the universe that this is a *holy law.*

As law is the basis of all government, and as the Government or law is a certain exposition of the mind, the character, or the attributes of the lawgiver, and as the character of man is according to the law which he obeys, it follows that to obey the law of God is to attain unto *the righteousness of God*, or true holiness. The conclusion is undeniable that the holiness derived from obedience to God's law of ten commandments is that growing out of the divine attributes, as pure and changeless as Heaven itself. The law being a transcript of the divine mind, perfect obedience to the law would bring us into perfect harmony with God.

Let no one object that by the law no such character is now formed, for Paul informs us in Rom. 2 and 3 that there are none who completely obey the law. And his testimony is corroborated by many other scriptures. We are a fallen, degenerate race. The law cannot make us perfect, because of the weakness of the flesh Rom. 8:3. But if we would see what the law would do in the formation of character where the weakness of the flesh was not manifested, where perfect obedience was rendered, let us look to Jesus, who said, "I have kept my Father's commandments." He did no sin; he never strayed from the law of his Father, and a pure and holy character was the result. And this is not a strange result, as all must admit who consider the force of the texts of Scripture which will presently be quoted.

As there cannot be diverse or unlike attributes of Deity, so there can be only one rule of holiness growing out of those attributes—one moral law for his Government. And upon obedience or disobedience to this law must all good and evil, life and death, be suspended. Therefore the following declarations apply to these commandments, or to this law, and to no other:—

Lev. 18:5. "Ye shall therefore keep my statutes, and my judgments; which if a man do, he shall live in them."

Deut. 30 : 15, 16. "See, I have set before thee this day life and good, and death and evil; in that I command thee this day to love the Lord thy God, to walk in his ways, and to keep his commandments and his statutes and his judgments." See verses 19, 20; chap. 11 : 26–28.

Isa. 51 : 7. "Hearken unto me, ye that know righteousness, the people in whose heart is my law."

Ps. 19 : 7. "The law of the Lord is perfect, converting the soul."

Ps. 40 : 8. "I delight to do thy will, O my God: yea, thy law is within my heart." Also Ps. 119.

Eccl. 12 : 13. "Fear God, and keep his commandments; for this is the whole duty of man."

Matt. 19 : 17. "If thou wilt enter into life, keep the commandments."

Rom. 2 : 13. "The doers of the law shall be justified."

Gal. 3 : 12. "The law is not of faith; but the man that doeth them shall live in them."

1 John 3 : 4. "Sin is the transgression of the law."

Rom. 7 : 12. "The law is holy, and the commandment holy, and just, and good."

Verse 14. "For we know that the law is spiritual."

This law is also referred to in certain scriptures wherein it is called God's holy covenant, and the covenant commanded.

Deut. 4 : 13. "He declared unto you his covenant, which he commanded you to perform, even ten commandments."

1 Chron. 16 : 15–17. "Be ye mindful always of his covenant; the word which he commanded to a thousand generations; even of the covenant which he made with Abraham, and of his oath unto Isaac; and hath confirmed the same to Jacob for a law, and to Israel for an everlasting covenant.

Gen. 26 : 3–5. "I will perform the oath which I swear unto Abraham. . . . . Because that Abraham obeyed my voice, and kept my charge, my commandments, my statutes, and my laws."

For breaking this "everlasting covenant," the inhabitants of the earth will be desolated with a curse, and burned up. Isa. 24 : 5, 6.

By indignation against the "holy covenant," was the man of sin, the abomination that maketh desolate, set up. Dan. 11 : 28, 30.

As this law has sometimes been confounded with other laws, to which the foregoing declarations of Scripture will not apply, it will be in place to notice the distinction of laws.

The *system* (not *the law*) under which the people of God lived in the past dispensation was complex; its elements were moral, civil, and ceremonial. The *moral* was the basis of all, existing prior to, and independent of, the others, and was from the beginning the standard of duty to God and to our fellow-men.* The *civil* enforced the

---

* "The decalogue having been spoken by the voice, and twice written upon the stone tables by the finger of God, may be considered as the foundation of the whole system."—*J. Q. Adams.*

Alexander Campbell, speaking of these commandments, called them "God's Ten Words, which not only in the Old Testament, but in all revelation, are most emphatically regarded as the synopsis of all religion and morality."—*Debate with Purcell, p. 214.*

moral, especially in men's relations to their fellow-men, making application of its principles to every-day life. The *ceremonial* expiated the violations of the moral, and had especial reference to their relations to God. But both the ceremonial and civil were merely typical, looking forward to the priesthood of Christ and to his kingdom; and therefore illustrated the true relation we sustain under Christ to the law of God, the moral rule, in this and the future dispensation.

This distinction of the two laws, moral and ceremonial, is shown in the following scriptures:—

Jer. 6:19, 20. " Hear, O earth; behold I will bring evil upon this people, even the fruit of their thoughts, because they have not hearkened unto my words, nor to my law. but rejected it. To what purpose cometh there to me incense from Sheba, and the sweet cane from a far country? Your burnt offerings are not acceptable, nor your sacrifices sweet unto me." Here one was kept and the other rejected; but the observance of the ceremonial was not acceptable when the moral was disregarded. That this was illus-trative of our position in this age is proved by Matt. 7:21–23, and John 7:16, 17, where the efficacy of faith in the Son, and of the knowledge of his doctrine, is dependent on obedience to the will or law of the Father.

Jer. 7:22, 23. " For I spake not unto your fathers, nor commanded them in the day that I brought them out of the land of Egypt, con-cerning burnt offerings or sacrifices. But this thing commanded I them, saying, Obey my voice."

We have seen that to obey his voice was to keep his covenant, the ten commandments; and this shows that when God gave his law, which himself declared to be the rule of holiness, the ceremonial law of burnt offerings and sacrifices was not included. He spoke only the ten commandments, and wrote only this law on the tables of stone; this alone was put into the ark over which the priest made atonement for sin. No other law had such honor bestowed upon it.

The Saviour himself explicitly declares that he came not to destroy the law; yet we know he did set aside the ceremonial law, by introducing its antitype.

The same is proved by Paul in his letters to the Ephesians and Romans. In one, he speaks of a law which Christ abolished (Gr. *katargeo*), Eph. 2:15, and in the other, he speaks of a law which is not made void (Gr. *katargeo*), by faith, but rather established. Rom. 3:31.

It has been noticed in another place that it is not consistent with justice to relax the claims of a just law, neither can the acts of abolishing the law and pardoning the transgressor be united. Hence, if the law of God had been abolished by the gospel, justice would be trampled under foot. But the Bible is not thus inconsistent with reason. God is infinitely just, and his law must be satisfied; Christ, a voluntary substitute, is set forth as our Saviour, that God might be just, and the justifier of him who believeth in Jesus. Rom. 3:26.

Though many other scriptures might be given to the same intent, those quoted are sufficient to show that the Bible truly harmonizes with the great principles of Government examined in the light of reason.

As objections are stronger with some persons than even positive proof, it will not be amiss to notice a few objections urged against the perpetuity of the law of God, by those who would make it void through faith, and pervert the gospel to a system of license.

Luke 16 : 16. "The law and the prophets *were* until John; since that time, the kingdom of God is preached, and every man presseth into it."

It is unjustly inferred that the question of *the existence* of the law is here introduced. The trans· lators saw that the passage was elliptical, but violated the laws of language by inserting the word "were," which does not make the sentence complete; the verb "is" being the antithesis of "were," the word "preached" is redundant. The following must be the correct view. The word or words understood or to be supplied must be antithetical to the words "is preached;" and therefore "were preached" would complete the sentence. The omission of these words prevents tautology, while nothing would require the omission of the word "were" if it alone belonged there. "The law and the prophets *were preached* until John; since that time, the kingdom of God *is preached*." Now no one will claim that the law and the prophets *ceased* with John; even the ceremonial law remained in force later than the time of his death. Thus it is evident that the subject of the existence or continuance of the law and the prophets is not introduced in this scripture; therefore there is no objection in it.

Rom. 3:21. "But now the righteousness of God without the law is manifested, being witnessed by the law and the prophets."

In considering this text, and any other in this argument, we must bear in mind that *the subject* is justification by faith, and *the object* is "the remission of sins that are past." And no one who understands the principles of Government will for a moment insist that a sinner can be justified by the law which he has transgressed. Justification to the transgressor comes by pardon without the law; *but it never comes at all to the person who continues in transgression.* Pardon, in the gospel system, stands closely related to conversion, for none but the converted will ever be pardoned. But none are truly converted without an amendment of life. Paul says we shall not sin that grace may abound. Grace superabounds above sin, to save from it; but grace never combines with sin to save any who continue in it. That justification for past sins is without law, by faith only, does not prove that a right character in the future may be formed without law, or by faith only. We are aware that without faith it is impossible to please God; and we are as well aware that faith without works is dead, being alone.

But there is another part to this text which objectors to the law never consider. It says that the righteousness of God is "witnessed by the law." But a law cannot witness concerning that to which it does not relate. Now Paul says that "the doers of the law shall be justified." Rom. 2:13. That does not prove that any can now be justified by the law, for alas, there are no doers of it. Rom. 3:9–19. But it does prove that the law contains the principles of justification; that it is of that nature that it would justify man if he had always kept it. In other words, it contains the true principles of righteousness; it is holy, and just, and good, and spiritual. Rom. 7:12, 14. And Solomon attests the same truth when he says the commandments contain "the whole duty of man." Eccl. 12:13, 14. For man is a moral agent, under a moral Government in which the Supreme Governor says: "Be ye holy, for I am holy." 1 Pet. 1:16; Lev. 19:2. And the law of God is *the only rule of holiness* given to man. To a sinner it is no longer *the means* of justification, but to all classes and under all circumstances it is *the rule* of justification, or of righteousness. It witnesses to the righteousness of God because it contains the principles of his righteousness; it is the expression of his will; the foundation of his moral Government; the very outgrowth of his attributes. Surely, we find in Rom. 3:19 no ground for objecting against the law of God.

Rom. 6:14. "For sin shall not have dominion over you; for ye are not under the law, but under grace."

It is not difficult to show that the objection based on this text arises from an entire misapprehension of its meaning. As sin is transgression of the law, sin surely has dominion over the transgressor of the law. It is only the obedient that are free from the dominion of sin. To set man free from sin, to turn him from violating the holy law of God, is the object of the gospel. Of Jesus it was said by an angel, "He shall save his people from their sins." Matt. 1 : 21. And Paul said "he appeared to put away sin by the sacrifice of himself." Heb. 9 : 26. That is, he saves us from breaking the law. of his Father; he puts away transgression. He had no transgression of his own to put away, for he kept his Father's commandments. John 15 : 10. Of course he came to put away our transgression; to restore sinful, fallen men to allegiance to the divine law —to loyalty to the divine Government. But this object is not accomplished in him who continues to transgress the law of God. Such are not saved from sin. Over such sin has dominion; how then can they be under grace?

If it be replied that *all* are under grace now, because the dispensation of law is past and the dispensation of grace has taken its place, we say, then, that is destructive of the sense of the text. The apostle offers the fact of our being under grace as the reason or the evidence that sin shall not have dominion over us. But if the relation is *dispensational* and not *personal*, then the distinction noted in the text is obliterated; if *all* are under grace, then also the multitudes are under grace over whom sin has dominion, and the text has no force.

This expression, "under the law," does not

mean, under the *obligation*, but under the *condemnation* of the law. Thus Paul says to the Galatians, "Christ hath redeemed us from the curse of the law." Gal. 3 : 13. But it were surely absurd to speak of redeeming from the curse of a law which is abolished. An abolished law can inflict no curse. Now if the ungodly are not under law, it is because there is no law for them to be under; if they are under grace, they are on the same plane with the godly. Indeed, if such were the case, the distinctions of godliness and ungodliness could not exist; and the scriptures which say that sin is the transgression of the law, and, by the law is the knowledge of sin, would have no place in this dispensation. Even such a text as this: "Sin is not imputed when there is no law," would be valid proof of the truthfulness of Universalism. Then to save from sin would be to save from the possibility of sinning; and to put away sin would be putting away that which proves sin to be sinful. See Rom. 3 : 20, and 7 : 13.

That "under the law" has respect to the condemnation and not to the obligation of the law, is sufficiently proved by Rom. 3 : 19. After showing that all, both Jews and Gentiles, are sinners, the apostle adds: "Now we know that what things soever the law saith, it saith to them who are under the law; that every mouth may be stopped, and all the world may become guilty before God." It is the guilty, those who are convicted by the law of sin, who are under the law. If man had never sinned, he would never have been "under the law" in the sense in which Paul uses the expression. He would never have been "subject to the judgment of God," as the margin of Rom. 3 : 19 reads. The experience of the Psalmist would then have been the happy experience of all: "I will walk at liberty; for I seek thy precepts." Ps. 119 : 45. Compare Jas. 1 : 25; 2 : 10–12.

The truth is that they only are under grace, in the sense of Rom. 6 : 14, who are in Christ; who are converted, and have received the grace of the gospel. All who are not Christ's, who are sinners, who are rejectors of this grace, are under condemnation—under the curse of the law— "under the law" in the sense of the text. But no one is naturally a Christian; all are "by nature the children of wrath." Eph. 2 : 3. Therefore all who are converted, who become Christians, in their experience pass from being under the law to being under grace. Before conversion, sin has dominion over them; after conversion, it has not.

But we must not forget that "sin is the transgression of the law." Now what is the position of a man when the transgression of the law has no dominion over him? It is that of yielding obedience to the law. We care not what may be his profession, as long as he transgresses the law, so long sin has dominion over him. This is undeniable.

The position of the *antinomian perfectionists* on this point is weak and deceptive; it is opposed to the whole scope of the gospel, and subversive of that system of grace which has its foundation in immutable justice. Thus the so-called perfectionists say: "Sin has no dominion over us; we are under the sole dominion of Christ, who frees us from the law; we are no longer bound to keep the law, but it is not sin in us who are in Christ."

The fatal defect in this statement is that it denies the plainest truths of the Scriptures, and builds up that which it calls a Christian character on a false basis. It denies the Scriptures by its utter disregard of the inspired declarations: "By the law is the knowledge of sin," and, "Sin is the transgression of the law." They use the term "sin" without any regard to Scripture definitions. According to the above-quoted texts, *a man cannot transgress the law and not be a sinner*. If we would know what is sin, we must go to the law for the knowledge, according to Rom. 3 : 20. And when a man disregards or breaks the law, he is proved a sinner, according to that text. There is no possibility of evading this truth. And if faith in Christ absolved us from obligation to keep the law, *then Christ would be the minister of sin*. But he is not; he is the minister of righteousness, which is equivalent to obedience, as will be further seen by our remarks on Rom. 10 : 4.

But we have something on this point which is conclusive without any argument. It is the declaration of the apostle in the context. Following the verse on which the objection is raised, he says: "What then? shall we sin [transgress the law], because we are not under the law, but under grace? God forbid. Know ye not, that to whom ye yield yourselves servants to obey, his servants ye are to whom ye obey; *whether of sin unto death, or of obedience unto righteousness?*" This declaration is a finality on the subject. Sin is the transgression of the law, and transgression leads to death, even though we have been under grace. Obedience leads to righteousness, through faith in Christ. The law cannot justify us without faith, because by transgression we have fallen under its condemnation. Rom. 3:19, 20. And faith does not make void the law, but establishes it, Rom. 3:31, which is in perfect harmony with the undeniable principles of justice laid down in Part One, of this work.

The grace of Christ to man is a system of favor made necessary by violation of the divine law. It is "a remedial system"—a means of pardon. The apostle's argument is highly reasonable; he says that pardon does not make void the law, and that we again fall under condemnation if we sin after we are placed under grace. *Pardon is not license.* God must be just in the justification of the believer. Rom. 3:26. *And he will be just whether man is justified or not.* This is proved in the case of every sinner lost. God could save all mankind, believing or unbelieving; obedient or disobedient. But he will not, because *he cannot do it and be just.* Oh, what a perversion of the gospel is that which tramples down the justice of God, professing to find a warrant for so doing in the gospel of Christ!

Rom. 10:4. "For Christ is the end of the law for righteousness to every one that believeth."

There are three points in this text which claim our attention.

1. Christ is not the end of the law in the sense of abolishing it; for he says himself that he came not to destroy it, and Paul says it is not made void. The word "end" is here used as it is in Jas. 5:11: "Ye have heard of the patience of Job, and have seen the end of the Lord," that is, the design or intention of the Lord. See also Rom. 14:9. Paul says the commandment was ordained unto life, which agrees with the scriptures which have been quoted in reference to the law. But we have merited death by transgression, for "the wages of sin is death." Christ now fulfills the object or design of the law, by granting the forgiveness of sin, and bestowing eternal life. In this sense, and in this only, is Christ the end of the law. This view is confirmed by the other points in the text.

2. He is the end or object of the law for righteousness. Unrighteousness is sin, and sin is the transgression of the law; this shows righteousness to be the equivalent of obedience. And Christ brings the sinner to obedience, as it is said in Rom. 5:19, "By the obedience of one shall many be made righteous," or obedient. He kept his Father's commandments, and calls upon us to follow him. He said, "Thy law is within my heart," and promises in the new covenant to write it also in the hearts of his people. Ps. 40:8: Heb 8:10.

3. This is only "to every one that believeth." He is not the end of the law in any sense to the

unbeliever. This proves that it does not mean the abolition of the law, for when a law is abolished it is abolished to everybody alike. It shows that the object of the law is not accomplished in the unbeliever.

Gal. 3 : 13, 14. "Christ hath redeemed us from the curse of the law, being made a curse for us; for it is written, Cursed is every one that hangeth on a tree; that the blessing of Abraham might come on the Gentiles through Jesus Christ."

If Christ abolished the law it would not then be true that he redeemed us from its curse, for, as we have seen, abolition of law and pardon cannot go together. And we have also seen that to abolish the law which curses the transgressor, or condemns sin, is subversive of government, and does not reform the evil-doer, or save him from sin. Again, this redemption from the curse of the law is necessary, that the blessing of Abraham might come on the Gentiles. Two important ideas are presented in this declaration. 1. The curse of the law rests on the Gentiles, which proves that the Gentiles were and are amenable to it, as is also proved by Rom. 3 : 9–19. 2. The curse of the law stands between the transgressor and the blessing of Abraham. Of course the law is the basis of the Abrahamic promises or blessings.

Some deny that the blessing of Abraham has any relation to the law; but if they were right, how could the declaration of this text be true? If they were not related the curse of the law could no more deprive us of the blessing of Abraham than the curse of the law of Russia could deprive us of American citizenship. When God gave the promises to Abraham, he connected them with his commandments. Thus he said to Isaac: "Sojourn in this land, and I will be with thee, and will bless thee; for unto thee, and unto thy seed, I will give all these countries, and I will perform the oath which I sware unto Abraham thy father; . . . because that Abraham obeyed my voice, and kept my charge, my commandments, my statutes, and my laws." Gen. 26 : 3, 5. And the same is taught in 1 Chron. 16 : 15–18: "Be ye mindful always of his covenant; the word which he commanded to a thousand generations; which he made with Abraham, and of his oath unto Isaac; and hath confirmed the same to Jacob for a law, and to Israel for an everlasting covenant, saying, Unto thee will I give the land of Canaan, the lot of your inheritance." See also Ps. 105 : 8–11.

This scripture contains two things—closely connected, but entirely distinct in their nature— namely, *a law*, and *a promise*. Both are embraced in the Abrahamic covenant, according to the words just quoted, both in Gen. 26, and 1 Chron. 16. God's promises are based on conditions. He made the promises to Abraham and his sons because of his obedience to his law. If it be asked, What law was it that he obeyed? the reply is found in the quotation above. It was that law which was confirmed to Jacob, and to Israel for an everlasting covenant. Although there are many covenants mentioned in the Scriptures, of promises, agreements, etc., there is but one covenant mentioned in the Bible which is solely a law, and that is the ten commandments. See Deut. 4: 13: "And he declared unto you his covenant, which he commanded you to perform, even ten commandments; and he wrote them upon two tables of stone."

This is that law upon which the promises to Abraham were based; it was confirmed to Jacob for a law; to Israel for an everlasting covenant; it is the word commanded to a thousand generations. And if we would inherit the blessing of Abraham we must "walk 'in the steps of that faith which Abraham had," or keep that law upon which the blessing was based. But having already broken that law (for all have broken it, both Jews and Gentiles, see Rom. 3 : 9–19), and therefore incurred its penalty, we have forfeited all right to the blessing which can only be restored through Christ, who redeems us from the curse of the law that the blessing of Abraham may come upon us, as says our text, Gal. 3 : 12–14.

The text says also that the Gentiles can receive the blessing by having the curse of the law removed from them. This is further proof of what Paul said to the Romans, that the Gentiles are amenable to that law, and by it are cursed as transgressors. But why should such an evident fact need proof? Are not the Gentiles all sinners? Is not God's law universal? Is he not the "Supreme moral Governor?" Are not all of Adam's race alike moral agents, traveling to the same Judgment? And is not "the whole duty of man" marked out in his commandments, or law? All men, of all nations, are naturally carnal, naturally opposed to the law of God (Rom.

8 : 7), and to be reconciled to God must become converted by and to the law of God.

Some will not admit that the law of God has any agency in conversion. But no one can be truly converted without conviction of sin; and no one can have thorough and intelligent conviction of sin without knowledge of the law, "for by the law is the knowledge of sin." Hence the Scriptures are strictly true (they are always true) when they say, "The law of the Lord is perfect, converting the soul." Ps. 19 : 7. In this age of superficial conversions many consider this passage obscure, and some endeavor to change its terms. We believe that President Finney was altogether correct in his expression of the opinion that the multitude of superficial conversions of late years is owing to the practice which is becoming so prevalent, of preaching a system of pardon without any heartfelt conviction, the conscience of the sinner not being aroused by a faithful presentation of the claims of the broken law. Genuine repentance is of sin; repentance for the transgression of the law. Therefore, where the claims of the law are not recognized, there can be no real conversion. True conversion is not merely emotional; not alone a matter of the feelings. It is a radical change of life; a turning from wrong to right. And how shall this be effected unless we are guided by the divine rule of right? By it alone is wrought that conviction which will lead us to Christ, who only can set us right.

Paul's relation of his own conversion, in Rom.

7, is highly instructive on this point. He says: "I had not known sin, but by the law." And in no other manner can any one know it. "For I was alive without the law once." His conscience was at ease while he was in the way of sin. So little was he aware of the true nature of his own actions that he thought he was doing God service in persecuting the church of Christ. "But when the commandment came, sin revived." In the absence of the law, or of his understanding or receiving the law, sin did not appear. "I had not known sin, but by the law." And when sin revived, or he knew sin, then, says he, "I died." It will be noticed that he speaks of the life and death of sin, and the life and death of himself, but never of the life and death of the law. The contrary has been inferred from verse 6, which says, in the text, "But now we are delivered from the law, that being dead wherein we were held." But the margin gives the correct reading: "Being dead to that wherein we were held." This is certain, for, 1. It agrees with all the context; see verse 4, and others. 2. Every other version, and all authorities, give this construction. 3. The original for "being dead" (*apothanontes*) is plural, and therefore *cannot* refer to the law, which is singular, but must refer to the brethren.

Turning back to chap. 6 : 1–8, he speaks of our being both *dead and buried*. Dead with Christ; dead to sin, or transgression; dead to the law as far as it has a claim on our lives on account of sin, for "the wages of sin is death." It was be-

6

cause Paul was a sinner that he found the law
to be death unto him. It was "ordained unto
life." This is confirmed by many scriptures.
The Lord repeatedly said of his commandments
that they who did them should live. Lev. 18:5;
Neh. 9:29; Eze. 20:11; Gal. 3:12. Life and
death were set before them in the commandments.
Deut. 30:15–20; Matt. 19:17, 18, etc.

Some have become confused over the expressions, "dead to sin," "dead to the law," thinking,
perhaps, there was identity in the two; but Paul
directly contradicts that idea, in verse 7: "Is
the law sin? God forbid." The law is against
sin and the sinner. By the commandment sin
becomes exceeding sinful. Verse 13. The conclusion to which the apostle comes is the point
of great interest to us. Did conversion to Christ
turn him away from the law, and lead him to
speak of it in terms of disrespect? By no means.
After the commandment came, convincing him
of sin, and thereby leading him to Christ, he said:
"Wherefore the law is holy, and the commandment holy, and just, and good." And again:
"For we know that the law is spiritual." And
of his own feelings—the feelings of a divinely
renewed man—toward the law, he said: "For I
delight in the law of God after the inward man."
And of the relation of mankind in general to
the law, he said: "The carnal mind is enmity
against God; for it is not subject to the law of
God, neither indeed can be." Conversion to Christ
takes away the carnal mind, and removes the
insubordination to, or rebellion against, the law
of God.

If it be yet claimed that the law of God is abolished, we would say, there can be but two reasons urged why it should be abolished. 1. Because it was faulty in itself, and not worthy of being perpetuated. But this is a grave reflection on the wisdom of the Lawgiver; for if that law were not perfect, then he gave only a faulty law, not worthy of the respect of his creatures. This is, in effect, the position which some take. But we wonder they are not shocked at their own irreverence. And this reason also contradicts all the scriptures which have been quoted which speak of the law as holy, just, good, perfect, spiritual, and containing the whole duty of man. 2. It may be urged that the circumstances of the transgressors made it necessary. On this we refer to the remarks before made on the conditions of pardon. It is certainly not consistent with good government, with justice, to abolish a perfect, holy law because rebellious men have violated it. Nor can even that necessity be urged, since a system of pardon has been instituted which is sufficient to fully meet the wants of the transgressor. But in harmony with every principle of justice and right, it avails only for those who penitently turn away from their transgressions.

As this law is holy, just, good, and perfect, it must be so in all its parts. No one part of a holy law can be impure, or, of a perfect law be imperfect. But the man of sin, the papal power, despite its professions, has sought to corrupt and pervert or change the holy covenant. Dan. 7 : 25,

To establish the worship of images, it has decided that the second commandment is ceremonial, and therefore not proper to be associated with moral laws. To introduce a festival day, the Roman Sun-day, it has decided that the fourth commandment is ceremonial, so far as it relates to the observance of a particular day, notwithstanding God blessed and sanctified the particular day on which he rested, to wit: the seventh day.*

None can deny that the Sabbath was instituted or made at creation; for then God rested on the seventh day. This day was not, therefore, a Jewish Sabbath, as it is so much claimed, but the Sabbath (rest) of the Lord, as the Bible *always* represents it to be. Space will not here admit of an argument on this point of the law, but we will notice two prominent objections urged against it, namely, that its observance was not required from the date of its institution; and that it is not moral as the other parts of the decalogue. In regard to the first, the Saviour says it " was made for man;" and we well know in what period of man's history it was made. The following remarks seem decisive on this point:—

" The Hebrew verb *kadash*, here rendered *sanctified*, and in the fourth commandment rendered *hallowed*, is defined by Gesenius, 'to pronounce holy, to sanctify; to institute an holy thing, to

---

*Alexander Campbell, in his debate with Bishop Purcell, charges upon the Catholic Church, that it has made a change in the ten commandments, which, he says, are "a synopsis of all religion and morality." This declaration, warranted by the Scriptures, places those who teach the abolition of the ten commandments, or any one of them, in a very unenviable position.

appoint.' It is repeatedly used in the Old Tes-
tament for a public appointment or proclamation.
Thus when the cities of refuge were set apart in
Israel, it is written: 'They appointed [margin,
Heb. sanctified] Kadesh in Galilee in Mount
Naphtali, and Shechem in Mount Ephraim,' &c.
This sanctification or appointment of the cities
of refuge, was by a public announcement to Israel
that these cities were set apart for that purpose.
This verb is also used for the appointment of a
public fast, and for the gathering of a solemn
assembly. Thus it is written: 'Sanctify [i. e.,
appoint] ye a fast, call a solemn assembly, gather
the elders and all the inhabitants of the land
into the house of the Lord your God.' 'Blow
ye the trumpet in Zion, sanctify [i. e., appoint]
a fast, call a solemn assembly.' 'And Jehu said,
Proclaim [margin, Heb. sanctify] a solemn assembly for Baal.' Josh. 20 : 7; Joel 1 : 14; 2 : 15;
2 Kings 10 : 20, 21; Zeph. 1 : 7, margin. This
appointment for Baal was so public that all the
worshipers of Baal in all Israel were gathered
together. These fasts and solemn assemblies
were sanctified or set apart by a public appointment or proclamation of the fact. When, therefore, God set apart the seventh day to a holy use,
it was necessary he should state that fact to those
who had the days of the week to use. Without
such announcement, the day could not be set
apart from the others.

"But the most striking illustration of the meaning of this word may be found in the record of
the sanctification of Mount Sinai. Ex. 19 : 12, 23.

When God was about to speak the ten commandments in the hearing of all Israel, he sent Moses down from the top of Mount Sinai to restrain the people from touching the mount. 'And Moses said unto the Lord, The people cannot come up to Mount Sinai; for thou chargedst us, saying, Set bounds about the mount and *sanctify it.*' Turning back to the verse where God gave this charge to Moses, we read: 'And thou shalt set bounds unto the people round about, *saying*, Take heed to yourselves that ye go not up into the mount or touch the border of it.' Hence, to sanctify the mount was to command the people not to touch even the border of it, for God was about to descend in majesty upon it. In other words, to sanctify or set apart to a holy use Mount Sinai, was to tell the people that God would have them treat the mountain as sacred to himself; and thus also to sanctify the rest-day of the Lord was to tell Adam that he should treat the day as holy to the Lord.

"The declaration, ' God blessed the seventh day and sanctified it,' is not indeed a commandment for the observance of that day; but it is the record that such a precept was given to Adam. For how could the Creator 'set apart to a holy use' the day of his rest, when those who were to use the day knew nothing of his will in the case? Let those answer who are able."—*J. N. Andrews' History of the Sabbath, pp. 16–18.*

In regard to the morality of this commandment, we may compare it with any of the others, assured that it will be sustained by any argument that will prove their morality. Take the eighth for example. No one can be proved guilty by merely proving that he took and used a certain piece of property; beyond this it must be proved that the property was another's, to which he had no right. Thus this commandment rests upon the right of property; and if this were not recognized, it would be a nullity. But surely no one can prove a clearer right, or put forth a more positive claim to any property, than has the Lord to the seventh day. Many times in his immutable word has he told us it is his; that he has hallowed it; and he warns us against desecrating it, or appropriating it to our own use. If it be an immorality to take without license what our neighbor claims as his, how much more so to take against God's positive prohibition what he claims as his own.

A little reflection or examination will be sufficient to convince every one that the position here taken in reference to the maintenance and perpetuity of the law of God is in strict harmony with the immutable principles of justice and good government. While every argument presented in favor of its abolition, is contrary to those principles, and subversive of government. No one who has regard for the honor of God and for the integrity of his Government, should hesitate for a moment to decide where the truth lies on this important subject.

CHAPTER II.

OUR present relation to the law is easily ascertained. Though we rest under a perpetual and everlasting obligation to obey the law of the Most High, we have not fulfilled our obligation. On this point the Scriptures are very explicit. Rom. 3 : 9–23 contains sufficient evidence. Jews and Gentiles are on a level—all have sinned and come short of the glory of God; there is none that doeth good, no, not one. The law stops every mouth, and proves all guilty, and subject to the judgment of God.

What is the penalty for sin? We have before said that *Government is a system of laws maintained.* This is a simple definition that all can understand; and that it is truthful is evident from this, that a Government cannot exist without law, and if the law is not maintained the result is anarchy and the subversion of Government. It is for this reason that a law without a penalty is a nullity. All the force and sanction of law is its penalty, and, whenever the law is violated, justice requires the infliction of the penalty. Therefore, if we understand the penalty of the law—the nature of the infliction to be visited upon the sinner or violator of God's law—we shall of course understand what justice demands for our redemption. It has been fully considered that justice can only be satisfied by the infliction of the penalty, either upon the offender or upon a voluntary substitute,

The idea so often advanced, that Christ did not suffer the same penalty to which the sinner was subject, cannot be reconciled either with justice or with the Scriptures. If the law itself be strictly just, the penalty of the law, neither more nor less, will answer the demands of justice. Many systems of theology have had this error incorporated into them to avoid other apparent difficulties; sometimes because the distinction between the penalty and mere consequence is overlooked, and sometimes because errors in the systems have made it necessary to resort to this, or some other expedient, as a means of relief. That a conclusion is demanded and insisted upon which is so greatly at variance with reason, with justice, and with the Scriptures, is strong evidence of defects in the systems which require it.

Dr. Barnes was an able writer, whose memory we respect. Were it not that his theology made the conclusion necessary, we should be much surprised to read the following paragraph from him:—

"It will be impossible for a substitute to endure the same sufferings which the sinner himself will endure in the future world for his sin. There are sufferings caused by sin which belong only to the consciousness of guilt, and these sufferings cannot be transferred to another. The sin itself cannot be transferred; and, as it is impossible to detach the suffering from the consciousness of guilt, it follows that a substitute cannot endure the same kind of sufferings which the sinner would himself endure. Remorse of conscience, for example—

one of the keenest sources of suffering to the guilty, and which will be a most fearful part of the penalty of the law in the future world—*cannot* be transferred."—*Atonement, p. 228*.

And again he said:—

"Remorse of conscience is manifestly a part of the penalty of the law; that is, it is a portion of what the law inflicts as expressing the sense which the lawgiver entertains of the value of the law and of the evil of its violation."—*Id., p. 235*.

We are fully convinced of the correctness of the positions taken in remarks on the reasonableness of the Atonement, though the above paragraphs from Dr. Barnes squarely conflicts with them. We unhesitatingly aver that remorse of conscience is no part of the penalty of the law. That view, which is indeed the corner-stone of Universalism, is as contrary to reason as to Scripture, and grows out of the error before noticed, of making no distinction between the penalty of the law and mere consequences. The penalty is a *judicial infliction*, prescribed by the statute, administered by authority, and its infliction must be subsequent to the Judgment. Consequences are various according to circumstances, and not according to desert, and may flow immediately out of the action without any relation to the penalty or to the Judgment. The wicked all suffer more or less remorse in this present state, but the Bible informs us that they are *reserved* "unto the day of Judgment to be punished." 2 Pet. 2 : 9.

There are two kinds of sorrow for sin: a "godly

sorrow," and a "sorrow of the world." 2 Cor. 7 : 10. The first is that of the penitent, sorrowing that he has violated a holy law and grieved a holy God. The other is that of the worldling, sorry that he is detected in crime, or in danger of punishment. No one doubts that the sorrow of the God-fearing penitent is deepest; that his remorse is the keenest. Yet the nearer he is to God, the finer his sensibilities, and the deeper his hatred of sin, the stronger will be his remorse for his sin. Therefore, if this be part of the penalty of the law, it is evident that this part is inflicted more severely on the penitent than on the impenitent and incorrigible.

Again, Paul speaks of those whose conscience is seared with a hot iron. 1 Tim. 4 : 2. That is, they run to such lengths in sin that their sensibilities are blunted, and they feel little or no remorse of conscience. Now, both reason and revelation teach us that the punishment must be proportioned to the guilt; but if remorse of conscience be a penalty, it is executed by inverse proportion; that is, the punishment decreases according to the increase of crime.

But we are led to inquire, Where did Dr. Barnes (or any other person) learn that remorse of conscience is a part of the penalty of the law? Does the Bible say so? It does not; there is nothing in the Bible which gives the least sanction to such an idea. Why, then, do men say so? Where did they get authority for such a declaration? As it is the duty and sole prerogative of the governor to reveal his law, so he alone can define the penalty.   This He has done in his word: "*The wages of sin is death.*"   Any effort to evade this plain truth, or to make it anything but a plain truth, involves difficulties and contradictions.   For it will not obviate the difficulty to *spiritualize* the term death, so as to make it embrace remorse of conscience; for if that be included in death, whatever will remove the remorse will remove so much of the penalty, or of death, and bring a proportionate degree of life.   But sin does this, as the apostle shows; therefore, according to that theory, sin removes a portion of its own penalty, which is absurd.

Dr. Barnes asserts that Christ did not suffer the penalty of the law, but something *substituted* for the penalty.   There is no cause for such a declaration, except it be found, as before said, in the necessities of a theory.

In the teachings of the Bible there is no uncertainty in this matter   They plainly inform us that "the wages of sin is death;" and that "Christ died for our sins."   Rom. 6 : 23; 1 Cor. 15 : 3.   As sin is the transgression of the law, death, the wages of sin, is its penalty; and as Christ died for our sin, the penalty was laid upon him for our sake.   Now that "Christ died" is not only plainly declared in the Scriptures, but it is a fundamental truth in the gospel system; for it is easy to show that, if Christ did not die, there can be no atonement and no redemption.   It appears evident, then, that those who assert that Christ did not suffer the penalty of the law, do not so assert because the fact is not revealed in the Bible, but, as before intimated, because of certain difficulties supposed to lie in the way of that fact. These difficulties are concerning the nature of the penalty, death.

It is assumed that death, the penalty of transgression, is three-fold in its nature, consisting of temporal, spiritual, and eternal death. If this assumption were true, we should at once give up the Atonement as a thing impossible. Yet it has been advanced by men of eminence, and incorporated into works recognized as standard. Let us examine it.

1. The death of man is temporal only by reason of a resurrection. But the resurrection belongs to the work of Christ, and as his work was not necessary or a subject of promise till after the transgression, it cannot have any place in the announcement of the penalty. When death was threatened to Adam, it was not said that he should die temporally, spiritually, and eternally; nor that he should die a first or second death; nor the death that never dies; but that he should *surely die*. It was death—simply death. Had not a promise been given afterward, of "the seed" to bruise the serpent's head, it would necessarily have been eternal death. But Christ, introducing a resurrection for Adam and his race, causes it to be temporal. But since this time, this death, temporal, has not been the penalty for personal transgression. This is evident for two reasons: (1) Infants die who never have transgressed; and (2) In the Judgment we stand to answer for our deeds, and the second death is inflicted for per-

sonal sin. But on those who are holy, "the second death hath no power;" the penalty does not reach them. So it appears the death we now die is occasioned by Adam's transgression, and is rendered temporal by the second Adam, and comes indiscriminately upon all classes and ages, thus precluding the idea that it is now a penalty, except as connected with that first transgression, in which we are involved only by representation.

2. Spiritual death cannot be a penalty at all. A penalty is *an infliction* to meet the ends of justice. But spiritual death is a state of sin, or absence of holiness; and to say that *God inflicts unholiness* upon man is not only absurd, but monstrous. That is confounding the crime with it punishment. God does not make man wicked or sinful as an infliction; but man makes himself wicked by his own actions, and God punishes him with death for his wickedness.

Again, there will be a resurrection of the dead, both of the just and the unjust; for as in Adam all die, even so in Christ shall all be made alive. Now if the penalty upon Adam included spiritual death, the resurrection through the second Adam would be to spiritual life, or holiness; and if all were restored to spiritual life through Christ, there would be none to fall under the second death, for it falls not on the "blessed and holy."

The text above quoted, 1 Cor. 15: 22, " For as in Adam all die, even so in Christ shall all be made alive," has been " spiritualized " so much that it has been fairly conceded to the Universalists by many who call themselves orthodox.

But it does not at all favor Universalism unless it is perverted, and made to conflict with other scriptures. Jesus says, all that are in the graves shall hear the voice of the Son of man, and come forth; they that have done good to the resurrection of life, and they that have done evil to the resurrection of damnation. The text in question (1 Cor. 15:22) says no more than this, that all that have died shall have a resurrection; but if some are unjust, and have a resurrection to damnation, that affords no help to Universalism. But if death here means spiritual death (as we say it does not), then the Universalists must have the truth; for to be made alive from spiritual death is to be made spiritually alive, which is none other than a state of holiness. This conflicts with the words of Christ just quoted, of a resurrection to damnation. Death is simply *the absence of life;* all die and go into the grave, and all are raised again from the grave, without respect to their character or condition. There will be a resurrection of the just and of the unjust; one class to eternal life, the other to the second death.

of Adam *became* temporal by reason of a resurrection, so we may say that the infliction for personal sins, the second death, is eternal, because no resurrection will succeed it. Thus, it appears plain that from the beginning death was the penalty of the law of God, circumstances determining the *duration* of it. This view, which is in strict harmony with the Bible, really removes all difficulty in regard to Christ having suffered the penalty due to sin.

But still another difficulty is presented to us by giving an extraordinary definition to death; it is said to mean *eternal misery*. But on examination of this, the difficulty will be entirely on the side of those who present it. If, however, the definition is correct, there is an insurmountable difficulty, involving the whole doctrine of the atonement, and making it utterly impossible for God to be just, and also the justifier of him that believeth in Jesus.

First, then, if the signification of death is "eternal misery," Christ never died at all; and then all the scriptures that say *he died* are untrue; and thus the atonement would be proved impossible, and further consideration of it would be useless. But admitting the Scripture testimony, that the wages of sin is *death,* and that Christ *died* for sin, and we have *the scriptural view of the term death;* utterly forbidding such an unnatural and forced construction of a plain declaration.

Secondly. If the correct definition of death is eternal misery. the relative terms, first and second, as applied to death before and after the resurrection, are used absurdly. For how can there be a first and second eternal misery? Sin entered into the world, and death by sin; and death passed upon all men. But the very fact that man may be resurrected, released from death, as the Scriptures teach, clearly proves that the Scripture use of the term death is entirely different from the "theological use," as given above.

And, thirdly, If death means eternal misery, then that is the penalty of the law; but Christ did not suffer it, and the redeemed will not suffer it, so it follows that justice is never vindicated by the infliction of the penalty, either upon them or a substitute; and thus justice is *suspended*, not satisfied; and Christ's death (if it could with any reason be called so) is not truly vicarious. As before considered, justice demands the infliction of the penalty of a just law; and as God is unchangeable and infinitely just, the penalty will surely be inflicted upon the transgressor or his substitute. But the above view makes it impossible. According to that, mercy does not harmonize with justice, but supersedes it, and God's justice is not manifest in justifying the believer. The sum of the matter is this: that if the penalty be eternal misery, then all that have sinned must suffer it, and be eternally miserable, or else the demands of the law are never honored. But the first would result in universal damnation, and the other would degrade the Government of God, and contradict both reason and the Scriptures.

This definition of death has been adopted of necessity to conform to the popular idea of the inherent immortality of man; yet it involves a contradiction in those who hold it. For it is claimed that the wicked are immortal and cannot cease to exist, and therefore the death threatened in the Scriptures is something besides cessation of existence, namely, misery. But immortality signifies exemption from death; and if the Scriptural meaning of death is misery, and the wicked are immortal, or exempt from death, they are, of course, exempt from misery! The advocates of this theory do not mean to be Universalists, but their position necessarily leads to that result.

It was well said by that great Christian philosopher, John Locke, that "it seems a strange way of understanding law, which requires the plainest and most direct terms, that by death should be meant eternal life in misery." Life and death are opposites; the first is promised to the justified, the second is threatened and inflicted upon the unjust. But life and misery are not opposites; misery is a condition of life. In everything but "theology" such a perversion of language would not be tolerated, as to make eternal misery and death, or even misery and death, synonymous. Were I to report that a man was dead because I knew him to be suffering in much misery, it would be looked upon as trifling—solemn mockery. With a cessation of life every condition of life must cease.

Before leaving the subject of the penalty for transgression we will compare with *the announcement* of the penalty to Adam, *the explanation* of it by the Lawgiver himself. When man was created and placed on probation, the Lord said to him that if he disobeyed the divine requirement or prohibition he should "surely die." To this all future declarations conformed. Indeed, if there is unity of design in the Scriptures they all must conform to this. Accordingly they say, as already quoted: "The soul that sinneth, it shall die." "The wages of sin is death." Said the Lord to Israel: "I have set before you life and death." The penalty for violation of the divine law is nothing less than "the death penalty." God is the author of life, and man is his creature. "All souls are mine," said the Creator; "as the soul of the father, so also the soul of the son is mine; the soul that sinneth, it shall die." Eze. 18:4. The right both to order and to dispose of life rests with him alone.

There is no surer method of settling the meaning of a penalty than to notice how the proper authority pronounces or executes the sentence upon a transgressor. Adam sinned; he was arraigned, and confessed his guilt. He could not hide it from his Maker. The Judge in this case was the author and giver of the law; it was he who first announced the penalty of death. The sentence or the punishment must be conformable to the penalty. Therefore the sentence will be an authoritative comment on, or explanation of, the penalty. The sentence was pronounced in these words: "Because thou hast hearkened unto the voice of thy wife, and hast eaten of the tree, of which I commanded thee, saying, Thou shalt not eat of it, cursed is the ground for thy sake; in sorrow shalt thou eat of it all the days of thy life; thorns also and thistles shall it bring forth to thee; and thou shalt eat the herb of the field; in the sweat of thy face shall thou eat bread, till thou return unto the ground; for out of it wast thou taken; for dust thou art, and unto dust shalt thou return." According to this sentence, when the Lord told the man he should surely die, he meant that he should be returned to his original element, the dust of the ground, out of which he was taken when he was made a man, a living soul. That is what we call literal, personal, or physical death. Nothing else could be implied, for *the record speaks of nothing else* as pertaining either to the penalty or the sentence. And who shall amend the word of the Lord, or question his decision, in a matter of his own law and of the life and death of his creatures?

On the subject of punishment we will examine but one text, as our limits do not admit of any extended argument on the point. This text is Matt. 25 : 46; and we notice this because it is supposed to conflict in direct terms with the view of the penalty given above. And this being one of the strongest, if not the very strongest, on which an objection is based, an exposition of this will show that the objection itself has no force.

The text reads: " And these shall go away into everlasting punishment; but the righteous into life eternal." The Revised Version says eternal punishment and eternal life. This is strictly according to the original, and no one will object to the rendering.

The whole objection is based upon a misapprehension of the term *punishment*. Many seem to think they have fully sustained the objection when once they have proved that the punishment of the wicked is as eternal as the life of the righteous. Thus Moses Stuart said: " If the Scriptures have not asserted the endless punishment of the wicked, neither have they asserted the endless happiness of the righteous, nor the endless glory and existence of the Godhead."

We admit this, and then our argument has lost nothing, and the objection has gained nothing. The question is not one of *the duration* of punishment, but of *the nature* of it. Of this we say:—

1. The word punishment is not a specific term. Men may be punished by fine, by imprisonment, or by death. The term includes all these, and it may refer to many other things, but it specifies neither of them.

2. This being so, there is only an implied, not a direct, antithesis between the words *punishment* and *life*. When we say a man will be punished, we do not thereby declare what shall be done with or to him. But if we say of two men that one shall be punished and the other shall be suffered to live, the unavoidable conclusion would be that the first would be punished with death, or not suffered to live.

3. If death be punishment, then eternal death, from which there will be no resurrection, is eternal punishment. And this is the destiny of the wicked. "The wages of sin is death." As there will be a resurrection of the unjust, and their punishment is after that, they will suffer a second death, after which there is no more resurrection. The second death is therefore an eternal death.

4. Eternal life and eternal death are complete contrasts. There would be no strong contrast between eternal death and a brief life, or between eternal life and a brief state of death. And there would be no contrast at all between eternal life and eternal imprisonment. The penalty or punishment being death, there is this complete con-

trast between eternal life and the eternal punishment. But it would not exist if the punishment were anything but death.

5. Paul, in 2 Thess. 1: 9, has given a decisive comment on this text. He uses both the terms used by the Saviour, with another term which is specific and therefore explanatory. Of the disobedient he says: "Who shall *be punished* with *everlasting destruction* from the presence of the Lord, and from the glory of his power." The Revised Version reads thus: "Who shall suffer punishment, even eternal destruction from the face of the Lord and from the glory of his might." *Death* and *destruction* are equivalents. Many times the Scriptures say of the wicked that they shall be destroyed. That destruction will be fore ever. They shall die, and never again awake. What a doom! And it may be averted by obedience to God through faith in his Son. But he who dies that death receives the just due of his own works. "The wages of sin is death." It is not the Lord's pleasure that any should be destroyed. "God so loved the world, that he gave his only begotten Son, that whosoever believeth in him should not perish, but have everlasting life." "As I live, saith the Lord God, I have no pleasure in the death of the wicked; but that the wicked turn from his way and live; turn ye, turn ye from your evil ways; for why will ye die, O house of Israel?"

The force of the apostle's words in 2 Thess. 1: 9 is sometimes lost by assuming that it means *banished* from the presence of the Lord, and from the glory of his power. But that could not be, for in the whole universe no one can get beyond his presence and power. See Ps. 129 : 7-12. The destruction of the wicked is by fire; and in Rev. 20 : 9, we learn that when the hosts of Satan compass the camp of the saints and the beloved city, "fire came down from God out of Heaven and devoured them." And thus will the word be literally fulfilled; from the presence of the Lord, from the glory of his power, even from Heaven shall the fire of destruction fall upon the ungodly. "This is the second death." It is their dying a second time. Truly an "everlasting punishment."

Much as we deplore the utter loss of so many of our race, as lovers of order and Government we acquiesce in the decisions of infinite justice. And we rejoice that justice has decreed the utter destruction of the incorrigibly rebellious, rather than that the universe of God should be the scene of eternal blasphemies and misery. Let creation be cleansed from sin, and all be love and peace.

We repeat a declaration before made, that circumstances make the death of the sinner an eternal death. The term die, or the penalty death, as stated to Adam, does not necessarily carry with it any idea of time or duration. To die is to lose life; death is the absence of life. We know of no one thing which more clearly shows the nature of the penalty of the law than the revealed truth that "Christ died for our sins."

CHAPTER III.

THE relation of justification and obedience is precisely the relation of faith and works. The Scriptures make this subject very plain, yet scarcely any doctrine seems to be more misapprehended. The difficulty arises from a widely prevailing and growing desire to put off the law of God, or to plead exemption from its obligation. As law is the foundation of every Government, the divine Government not excepted, we shall have to notice further the nature of our obligation to the law in order to elucidate its relation to justification by faith.

There is a peculiar expression in Isa. 51:6. The Lord says: "My salvation shall be forever, and *my righteousness shall not be abolished.*" That this refers to his attributes or personal character, would appear improbable, even in the absence of any testimony on the subject; for the idea of the abolition of his attributes or of his personal righteousness is too absurd to ever receive a notice. But if it refers to his law, which is the foundation of his righteous government, the expression is reasonable and also necessary as a revelation. And there is proof that it has this application. In Ps. 119:172, it is said, "All thy commandments are righteousness." Now as the character of the divine Lawgiver is best revealed to us through the revelation of his will, and as his attributes must of necessity show forth in his Government, the stability of his character is determined or shown by the stability of his law; for it would be of little account to *declare in words* that he was unchangeable, while he *showed in action* that he was not. Again, this application is confirmed by the connection: "Hearken unto me, ye that know righteousness, the people in whose heart is *my law*." Verse 7. We have quoted the scriptures showing that God's law of ten commandments is a rule of holiness, of justification, condition of life, perfect, the whole duty of man, &c., which identify it as the same law referred to in Isa. 51 : 6, 7, and Ps. 119 : 172, which is the embodiment of righteousness. Hence, they who say that God's law of ten commandments is abolished, directly contradict this scripture, and are vainly contending with God. This view may be strengthened by an examination of the Saviour's words in Matt. 5 : 17–20; but we only invite investigation of that text, and pass to the apostle's argument on justification.

What is the import of the apostle's declaration in Rom. 3 : 28? It reads: "Therefore we conclude that a man is justified by faith without the deeds of the law." Does it mean that we now form our characters in Christian life without works, or without obedience to the law? So many seem to think ; but we cannot. 1. That view is highly unreasonable. We cannot form any character by mere feeling or belief. It is only by actions, by deeds, or by works, that any character can be formed. 2. It is contrary to the whole scope and tenor of the Scriptures, as we shall try to show.

The idea of the text is presented also in verse 21 of the same chapter, which we have considered in another place. It reads: "But now the righteousness of God without the law is manifested, being witnessed by the law and the prophets." There is no difficulty at all if it is borne in mind that the subject is that of *justification to a sinner condemned.* Now it is a truth so evident that no argument is needed in its favor, that *a criminal cannot be justified by the law which he has broken.* Surely there is nothing so strange in this that any need to be troubled to comprehend its force or bearing. It is only by losing sight of the *relations* brought to view in this chapter, and of the *principles* which must characterize the actions of a just Government in dealing with transgressors, that difficulties are found. We are indeed "justified freely by his grace," but on a basis which enables God to be just while he is a justifier of the believer. This must never be forgotten if we would honor his justice and his Government. Pardon *must* have respect to the broken law. And as there can be no condemnation without law, for "sin is not imputed when there is no law," even so justification must be according to law, or else justice will be disregarded. There can be no determination of character, either good or bad, without the law. By the law is the knowledge of sin. This is one direction in which the law imparts knowledge, but not the only one. The law is a witness of the righteousness of God. The apostle says that we are made the righteousness of God in Christ. 2 Cor. 5: 21. This means that our characters are conformed to his revealed will. And the righteousness of God manifested in us, through the faith of Jesus Christ without the works of the law, is just this, that Christ removes our sin and places us before the throne of justice as free, as sinless as though we had never broken the law. The law being the measure of holiness, of perfection, and the only rule of judgment, is of course a witness of the righteousness so effected. This cannot be denied. The expression, "The doers of the law shall be justified," is sufficient proof that the law contains all that is necessary to justify the obedient; and the law witnesses to the righteousness of God which is effected through faith in Christ in the characters of the faithful, because it enforces and demands that righteousness. We can readily understand why a sinner, a carnally-minded man, restive under just restraint, whose heart is enmity against God, should desire the abolition of such a law. But we cannot understand why a man who professes to love God and to be loyal to his Government should desire its abolition; nor can we believe that the God of justice, who will bring every work into judgment, will consent to its abolition. He has said: "My righteousness shall not be abolished," and we respect his word and bow to the rule of his righteous judgment. Eccl. 12 : 13, 14; Rom. 2 : 12, 16.

Many stumble over the gospel plan because they make no difference between *justification* and *salvation*. If we had regard only to *original justice*, there could be no difference; that is, if a man had never sinned he would have been justified, and of course saved, by his obedience. But this original or personal justice no one now possesses. Hence, while the principles cannot change, and the *rule* of justification is ever the same, the *means* are entirely different from what they would be if man had never sinned. Here is where many err. They suppose, or seem to suppose, that if the law ceases to be the means of justification, it ceases also to be the rule. They do not judge of the law by its nature or original object, but from a partial view of the position of its transgressor. The law, as a rule of right, will *form* a perfect character, but cannot *reform* an imperfect one. The rule of the mechanic will determine or point out a right angle on the end of a board he is framing; and if the board is square—if the angle is right, it is justified or proved right by the rule. But if the angle is not right, the rule will point out the inaccuracy, but will not make it right. That must be effected by another tool. But if the saw is the means of making the proper angle on the board, does the saw therefore become the rule of determining angles or measurements? By no means. And there is precisely this difference between the law and the gospel. "By the law is the knowledge of sin;" but the gospel is the remedy. The law points out the errors of character, the gospel reforms them. The law being the only rule of right, "the doers of the law shall be justified." Rom. 2:13. This is but plain justice; for no one can suppose that the man who did the law—who obeyed God in all his life, would be condemned. But Paul also says that there are no doers of the law—that all have sinned; and from this he draws the very evident conclusion, *"therefore,* by the deeds of the law there shall no flesh be justified." Rom. 3:20. So we are justified now "freely by his grace;" entirely by faith; works do not enter into our justification. And why not? Because, as the apostle shows, this justification by faith has respect to "the remission of *sins that are past."* Rom. 3:25. Over these our future acts of obedience can have no influence or control.

It has been thence inferred that the sinner justified is under no further obligation to keep that law by which he cannot be justified. But it cannot be that they who teach thus realize how destructive is that view to every principle of right and justice; how it dishonors the gospel of Christ; how it tends to pervert a holy gospel of love to a mere system of license. Of all the abuse the gospel has ever received at the hands of its professed friends, this is the deepest. It is contrary to Scripture, and to all just reasoning. Ask the advocate of that theory if the law of his State will justify the thief in stealing, or the murderer in killing. He will answer, No; the law condemns such actions. Ask him how the criminal can escape the true desert of his crimes, and he will reply, Only by the governor's pardon. Ask again, If the law condemns the transgressor, and he can be justified only by pardon, does that pardon release him from obedience to the law, so that he may thereafter disregard its claims? Will he affirm this? Will he tell you that that pardon thereafter becomes the rule of life to such a man? And if the pardoned one should again be committed for crime, will the jury try him, and the judge condemn him by the governor's pardon, or by the statute of the State? Could we get any to take the same unreasonable position in regard to the law of the State that many take in regard to the law of God? Not one. If angels ever weep at the blind folly of mortals, it would seem that such teachings furnish an occasion. To see men of talent, of learning, of apparent piety, strip the plan of salvation of every principle of justice, pervert it to a system of license, draw conclusions directly contrary to reason and common sense, and argue on the divine Government as they would be ashamed to argue in respect to the Government of the State, surely, this is enough to fill the heavens with astonishment.

This error is not altogether confined to those who are called Antinomians. All those who teach that Christ did not suffer the penalty of the law, that his death did not meet the full demands of justice, but was *substituted* for its demands, really subvert the law by denying that the gospel has honored its claims. We think that in many cases they are unconscious of the demoralizing tendency of their position. This, however, will be considered more fully when we come to the subject of the vicarious death of Christ.

Had man never sinned, he would have been justified on the ground of obedience—by works. Without sin he could not have been condemned.

This shows that *justification is in works, provided that the works are perfect.* To deny this is equivalent to affirming that man would have been condemned—not justified—if he had continued in perfect obedience. And this is what we have before said, that *justification is in the law,* but man lost it by transgression of the law. It is obedience only that forms a right character. "He that doeth righteousness is righteous." 1 John 3:7. Faith in the blood of Jesus removes guilt, and presents us before the throne as righteous by imputation; but faith, without works, does not build up character. That is to say, that we are justified from past sins by faith without works, but we cannot maintain that justification through future life by faith without works. In this respect, "faith without works is dead." James 2:20. And so Paul instructs the brethren: "Work out your own salvation with fear and trembling." Phil. 2:12.

Justification by faith is not *a final procedure;* it does not take the place of the Judgment, nor render the Judgment unnecessary. It looks to something beyond itself to be accomplished in the future. Of course this remark would not apply where probation was cut off immediately or very soon after justification took place. But it certainly does apply where life is prolonged and probation is continued. Justification by faith, in the plan of the gospel, may be defined in full as that change in man's relations and condition by virtue of which, 1. He is counted just as regards his past life, though in his life he has not been just. 2. The Government and its subjects are guarded against future depredations. And, 3. God may consistently accept his service as that of a loyal subject.

In regard to the first point, there can be no question on the part of anybody. To the second, all must concede that both the Government and its subjects ought to be secured against injury, and, to effect this, it is necessary not only to do a work *for man*, but, also, *in him*. While the act of laying the penalty upon a substitute vindicates the majesty of the law, and is all that can be done in respect to the past, *a change of heart*, a thorough amendment of life, can only give that guarantee which is reasonably and justly demanded for the future. And this we call *conversion*. Justification by faith embraces this. With anything less than this we cannot imagine that any one would stand justified before God.

But the third point will not be so apparent to every one, for some may think it is consistent for God to accept the service of any one, at any time it may be offered, without stopping to consider conditions. But to this we cannot assent.

Suppose a person who was born in a foreign land comes to the United States and proposes to take part in the execution of our laws. Of course his proposal is promptly rejected. But he urges his case in the following manner:—

"In my native land I carefully examined the principles of your Government, and admired them; therefore I am come to this country. I have read your laws; I think they are just. I am anxious to bear a part in executing them. I have an education superior to that of many who hold office in this country. I claim to have as good ability as they, and to love your Government as well as they. Why, then, am I rejected from holding an office?"

The answer is readily given, thus:-

"By birth you are a citizen of another Government which is entirely different from this; and as such you are held under obligation to seek its welfare and to further its interests. We cannot know but you are even now acting under instructions from your sovereign. You must publicly renounce allegiance to him, and declare your allegiance to this Government. *You must be naturalized.* Then you will no longer be regarded as an alien, but as an American citizen, and be entitled to all the privileges of one born in this country."

This all can understand; its reasonableness all can see. Without such a safeguard as this, enemies might come in and undermine our Government by abusing and perverting its laws under pretence of executing them. And it is truly strange that any who love justice and good government, and who know that evil is in the world, and in the hearts of men, should stand in doubt as to the necessity of the gospel, to bring us into acceptance with God, and to fit us by a transformation of heart and life for a place in his service and at last in his kingdom.

In the above illustration, so striking in every feature, we have only used the ideas given to us by the apostle Paul, in his letter to the Ephesians.

8

He had before said to the Romans that of all the world, Jew and Gentile, there is none righteous, no, not one. Destruction and misery are in their ways. All stand guilty before God. In harmony with this he speaks of himself and of his brethren as being "by nature the children of wrath, even as others." Eph. 2. And of the brethren, Gentiles in the flesh, he says: "That at that time ye were without Christ, being aliens from the commonwealth of Israel, and strangers from the covenants of promise, having no hope, and without God in the world. But now in Christ Jesus ye who sometimes were far off are made nigh by the blood of Christ." They who were the children of wrath, aliens and strangers, have their condition entirely changed through faith in Christ and by his blood. "Now, therefore," continues the apostle, "ye are no more strangers and foreigners, but fellow-citizens with the saints, and of the household of God." The gospel of Christ is *the law of naturalization*, by means of which aliens or foreigners are inducted into the household of God, and are made citizens of the commonwealth of Israel,— the Israel of God.

In illustrations it is permitted us to represent spiritual things by those which are natural; we have no other means of making comparisons which our minds can appreciate. But we must always remember that there is a depth to spiritual things which the natural cannot reach. A foreigner, dwelling in his native land, may have a high regard for the principles and the rulers of our Government without disparagement to his loyalty to his own; because the two Governments maintain friendly relations with each other. Each has its own territory, and each has paramount right and jurisdiction in its own dominion. But the very nature of the Government of God forbids that there shall, in it, be any parallel to this condition.

1. His dominion, his right of jurisdiction, is universal. No contrary Government has any right to exist.

2. His law, the rule of his Government, is a moral law. It takes cognizance, not of actions alone, but of motives and intentions.

3. As no contrary rule has any right to exist, there can of right be no neutrality in case of usurpation or rebellion. When war is waged against a Government, every good and loyal citizen is bound to support the Government. A refusal to do so is equivalent to giving aid to the enemy.

Now inasmuch as all have gone astray—all have departed from God—the world is in the condition of a mighty rebellion against its rightful ruler. There is a general disregard of his authority and of the rights of his subjects. And no one is on neutral ground; says the Governor: "He that is not for me is against me." And so far has man fallen from his "first estate," that it is declared that "the carnal mind," the natural, unchanged heart, "is enmity against God; for it is not subject to the law of God, neither indeed can be." Rom. 8:7. Hence, all are by nature the children of wrath, because all are aliens, or more properly, in a state of rebellion against the Supreme Ruler of the universe. Can any doubt the necessity of naturalization, or of the acceptance of the amnesty offered, that we may be brought into friendly and loyal relations to the one Lawgiver? Can any deny the reasonableness of the declaration, " Ye must be born again "?

No one, we think, can now fail to see the correctness of our proposition that God cannot consistently accept or approve of the action of any one in his natural state, or in carnal mindedness. Such a state being one of enmity against God, every action springing from the carnal or natural heart is an act of rebellion, because it is done in utter disregard of the authority of our rightful Sovereign. Every act has its spring in self-will; it proceeds from a spirit, which, if it could have undisputed sway, would dethrone Jehovah and substitute its own will for his.

The acceptance of man as the servant of God involves the duty in man to serve God. Instead of justification by faith releasing man from works, or from obedience to the divine law, it brings him to work; it obligates him to work; it fits him to work. Some seem to doubt whether the acknowledged principles of right and justice, which are incorporated in human Governments, will be exacted in the divine Government; whether the gospel does not supersede them to some extent. To this the Scriptures give a sufficient answer: " Shall mortal man be more just than God? Shall a man be more pure than his Maker?" God himself has planted this regard for justice in our hearts, and shall not he regard it? There is truly a vast difference between God and us in this respect, but it is all in favor of strict justice on his part. His justice is infinite.

We have remarked that justification by faith does not supersede the Judgment. And the Judgment is not on the basis of faith alone. In this is shown the imperative necessity of obedience. The following declarations of Scripture are conclusive on this point, and very impressive:—

" Fear God, and keep his commandments; for this is the whole duty of man. For God shall bring every work into judgment." Eccl. 12: 13, 14.

" As many as have sinned in the law shall be judged by the law, in the day when God shall judge the secrets of men by Jesus Christ." Rom. 2 : 12, 16.

" For we must all appear before the judgment-seat of Christ; that every one may receive the things done in his body, according to that he hath done, whether it be good or bad." 2 Cor. 5 : 10.

" For the Son of man shall come in the glory of his Father with his holy angels; and then he shall reward every man according to his works." Matt. 16 : 27.

" And, behold, I come quickly; and my reward is with me, to give every man according as his work shall be." Rev. 22 : 12.

Others to the same intent might be quoted. And by these it is seen that not faith, but works. are the sole basis of determination and of reward in the Judgment. Then the question may be asked, Of what benefit is faith, if it does not appear in the Judgment? We answer, It is an auxiliary to works; it enables us to work: it appropriates the strength of Christ by which alone we can work, for without him we can do nothing. John 15 : 5. But faith without works is dead, and of what benefit is dead faith?

Is this inconsistent with grace? No; it is free grace that has opened the way for our escape from eternal ruin. Grace has made our salvation possible. Grace guides and assists us every step on the way. Grace opens the way and assists us, but grace does not insure our salvation without our availing ourselves of its provisions, any more than favor and good will would prevent a man starving if he refused to eat the food which was freely provided for him, and freely offered to him. Grace does not destroy the power of choice, nor release us from the duty and necessity of choosing. Grace will assist us in the work of overcoming, but grace will not release us from the necessity of overcoming. Grace will clothe us with an invincible armor; but grace will not fight our battles for us if we sit still and do nothing. It is now as of old: "The sword of the Lord, and of Gideon." Grace threw down the walls of Jericho; but they would not have fallen if the children of Israel had neglected to compass the city as they were commanded to do. Grace saved Noah from the flood but it would not if he had not built an ark. God has done and will do all that is necessary to make full provision for our salvation. He will fulfill all his promises, *if we will fulfill their conditions.* But he will never do for us that which he has commanded us to do. Grace encourages *trust;* it does not tolerate *presumption.*

They who suppose that we teach justification by the law, because we enforce the obligation of the law, cannot have looked deeply into the word of God, nor have considered the principles of Government. If Jesus takes away the sinful disposition, renews us or gives us a new heart, and brings us in subjection to the law of God, all our obedience to that law is by virtue of that change of heart effected by him; therefore, while he grants to us all the virtue of his blood for the remission of past sins, he is entitled to all the glory of our obedience in the future. So it is all of grace, and we have nothing of which to boast in any respect, nor anything to claim on our own account, for all that we do is by strength imparted by him. Here we have a system which is *all grace*, and no license to sin; a gospel worthy of Heaven -imparting mercy freely, and maintaining law and justice strictly. Here we see that without him we can do nothing; though we shall work out our own salvation with fear and trembling, "it is God that worketh in us to will and to do of his good pleasure." We are justified by faith, yet so that we must add to our faith virtue; patiently continue in well-doing; keep the commandments of God; fulfill the righteousnes of the law, &c.

So far from teaching justification by the law, we emphatically assert that a moral duty, whatever men may call it, whether law or gospel, cannot justify a sinner. That law which points out sin, which is therefore the rule of right, must of **necessity con**demn the sinner, but it will not and cannot justify. This is the teaching of Rom. 3 : 20, 21. And it is singular, but true, that they who teach that the law is abolished, and declaim against it as being insufficient to justify, &c., and who say that the commandments of the original law which are now binding are incorporated into the gospel, really teach justification by law,--by the same precepts which convict of sin. And they are the only ones who do teach justification by law. We say that justification of a sinner by law is impossible; it is contrary to reason, and to the words of the apostle in Rom. 3 : 20. If the law were incorporated into another system, and called by another name, that would not change its nature; it would not cause it to justify the sins which it forbids, nor the sinner who had violated it. The difference between the law and the gospel is as distinct now as it was in the days when the gospel was preached to the sinners in the wilderness. Heb. 4 : 1. The law is a moral rule; sin is immorality; and the gospel is the remedy. The gospel upholds the law, and enforces it upon the conscience, and incorporates it into the life of the believer. But it does not abrogate law nor does it release the believer from obligation to obey the law; neither does it incorporate law into itself, for the two cannot be blended into one.

The correctness of our position may be tested by the following plain statement: The blood of Christ, the blood of the covenant, is that whereby we have remission of sin. Heb. 9 : 22; Rom. 3 : 25. The gospel is a system of remission; it is good news of salvation from sin unto eternal life. The blood of Christ is a free gift; the gift of God's undeserved grace. Hence, baptism may be a *gospel condition* of justification, because it is not any part of original obligation, or of moral duty. If it were a moral duty it *could not* be a part of a system of remission of sin, because as such it would be required on its own account. The commandment which says, "Thou shalt not steal," *cannot* become a part of the gospel; it cannot be incorporated into a system of remission, or a remedial system, because it is of a moral nature. It is obligatory without any regard to a sinful condition. It is reasonable that a remedial plan should say, "Repent, and be baptized for the remission of sin," for baptism is not a moral duty; it is not of obligation on its own account. But it were highly absurd to say, Thou shalt not kill for the remission of sin; or, Honor thy father and thy mother for the remission of sin. And the absurdity is not removed if you change their position, and call them gospel; you cannot change their nature. And they who teach the abolition of the decalogue, and the incorporation of these precepts into the gospel, are responsible for this absurdity. It belongs to their theory.

We have seen that in speaking of justification by faith, cr of the exercise of grace through the blood of Christ for the remission of *sins past*, the apostle clearly divides between faith and works, and excludes works entirely. It is faith only—works not at all. But when he speaks of the *future life* of the justified, he speaks in a different manner. Then he teaches to " work out your own salvation with fear and trembling." Phil. 2:12. This is evangelical truth as well as the other; but it is an order which could not be given or obeyed relative to justification for past offenses, of which he is speaking in Rom. 3; for no one could work out a justification for a past offense.

But can it be that God regards *future sin* with any more favor than he does *past sin?* We think not. And if he does not, it would be reasonable to expect that his plan of salvation contemplated *prevention* as well as *cure;* and so we find it. Jesus saves from sin; puts away sin by the sacrifice of himself; says to the justified one, Go, sin no more; he is not a minister of sin, but of righteousness; therefore we shall not continue in sin that grace may abound. Both are in the gospel plan. Thus, man is under condemnation for sin; he also has a carnal mind, which is enmity against God, and not subject to the law of God; Rom. 8:7; by position, a sinner—in disposition, sinful. It would not be sufficient to forgive past transgression and leave the sinful disposition, as we should become again involved in sin and brought under condemnation. Nor would it be sufficient to remove the sinful disposition and leave the burden of past sin upon us, for that would condemn us in the Judgment. Therefore Christ becomes a Saviour to us in both respects. He freely forgives our past sins, so that we stand free and justified; and he takes away the carnal mind. which is enmity against God, and not subject to his law, and makes us at peace with God—subject to his law; he writes it in our hearts so that we may delight in it. Then "the righteousness of the law" is "fulfilled in us, who walk not after the flesh," the carnal mind, "but after the Spirit." Rom. 8 : 4.

The following remarks by Andrew Fuller are pointed, and worthy of careful consideration:—

"An atonement has respect to justice, and justice to the law or rule which man has violated

"If the doctrine of the atonement leads us to entertain degrading notions of the law of God, or to plead an exemption from its preceptive authority, we may be sure it is not the Scripture doctrine of reconciliation. Atonement has respect to justice, and justice to the law, or the revealed will of the Sovereign, which has been violated; and the very design of the atonement is to repair the honor of the law. If the law which has been transgressed were unjust, instead of an atonement being required for the breach of it, it ought to have been repealed, and the lawgiver have taken upon himself the disgrace of having enacted it. Every instance of punishment among men is a sort of atonement to the justice of the country, the design of which is to restore the authority of good government, which transgression has impaired. But if the law itself is bad, or the penalty too severe, every sacrifice made to it must be an instance of cruelty. And should a prince of the blood royal, in compassion to the offenders, offer to suffer in their stead, for the purpose of atonement, whatever love it might discover on his part, it were still greater cruelty to accept the offer, even though he might survive his sufferings. The public voice would be, There is no need of any atonement; it will do no honor, but dishonor, to the legislature; and to call the liberation of the convicts an act of grace, is to add insult to injury. The law ought not to have been enacted, and now it is enacted, ought immediately to be repealed. It is easy to see from hence, that in proportion as the law is depreciated, the gospel is undermined, and both grace and atonement rendered void. It is the law as abused, or as turned into a way of life, in opposition to the gospel, for which it was never given *to a fallen creature*, that the sacred Scriptures depreciate it; and not as the revealed will of God, the immutable standard of right and wrong. In this view the apostles delighted in it; and if we are Christians we shall delight in it too, and shall not object to be under it as a rule of duty, for no man objects to be governed by laws which he loves." —*Atonement of Christ, from the works of Andrew Fuller, pub. by Am. Tract Society, pp. 124, 160, 161.*

These remarks are just, and well worthy the consideration of all. We close our examination of this subject by quoting the emphatic language of inspiration as to the effect of justification by faith: "Do we then make void the law through faith? God forbid; yea, we establish the law." Rom. 3 : 31.

CHAPTER IV.

DEATH OF CHRIST VICARIOUS.

THE question, Was the death of Christ vicarious? has received much attention in the theological world, and apparently troubled many minds. It is a question of great importance, as the subject of the efficacy of the Atonement is involved in it. Perhaps we might more correctly say, it involves the possibility of there being any atonement. We think the nature of an atonement is such that it must be effected by vicarious death; vicariousness is an essential element of such a transaction. That which is done for another is vicarious; and as Christ died for us, his death was vicarious. He who suffers for his own sins makes no atonement. True, he satisfies the demand of the law, but he is lost. Had all the world been left to perish, the penalty would have been inflicted and justice honored, but there would have been no atonement. An atonement can only be made by one who suffers for another, or others; and this shows the remark to be just, that there can be no atonement where there is no vicariousness.

Those who deny a vicarious death generally reason thus: Justice would not admit of the penalty being inflicted twice for the same offense; therefore if Christ suffered vicariously, or in our stead, we must be released as a matter of justice, and not of pardon or favor; for where the law takes its course there is no pardon.

But this reasoning is defective in every respect. It might apply if *mercy* were the sole object; but where *justice* and *mercy* unite there must be conditions, whereby we avail ourselves of the benefits of his death. But his death was voluntary, and unconditional; a free-will offering to justice in our behalf. He honors the law whether we will honor it or not;. and if we will not accept him we must bear the consequences. He has made an offering to the divine law. We did not make it, nor will it avail for us unless we accept it, and by faith appropriate the benefits thereof to ourselves. On this point the reader is requested to consider again the remarks on page 47, on the conditions of pardon.

Again, in such reasoning the true nature of substitution is not considered. If a man commits a crime worthy of death, and another dies in his stead, he does not necessarily remove the guilt of the criminal thereby. So the death of Christ makes salvation *possible* by vindicating the law in man's behalf, and opening the way for pardon without infringing on justice. But his death does not make the salvation of any man *necessary*, as will be seen from the fact that *pardon is offered* through faith in him. But if his death was in the nature of the payment of a debt which could not be collected a second time, or of suffering a penalty in such sense that they for whom he died could not justly suffer it, even if they persisted in rejecting him, then there would be no room for pardon. All men might then *demand* their release on grounds of justice! But that is not the system of the gospel. That would amount to an indiscriminate and unconditional pardon which, as we have seen, is subversive of justice and of Government.

But if Christ did not suffer in our stead, how is justice vindicated in case we are pardoned? If he did not suffer the penalty in our behalf, and we do not suffer it because he sets us free, then the penalty is never suffered, and the law is not honored, for justice is robbed of its due. Some affect to think that this is the gospel plan; but only because they lose sight of the great gospel truth that Christ is set forth as a propitiation, that *through faith in his blood* we may receive the remission of sins that are past, *that God may be just*, and the justifier of him that believeth in Jesus. Rom. 3 : 23–26. No one can imagine that Christ bore our sins on the tree except in the sense of suffering in his death the desert of our sins, for death is that desert. "He hath made him to be sin for us"—not that he was a sinner, for he "knew no sin," but he was counted a sinner—sin was imputed to him, if you please, for our sake, "that we might be made the righteousness of God in him." 2 Cor. 5 : 21. We cannot imagine how he was made sin for us, except by his bearing our sins, which he did, and standing *in our stead* before the violated law.

The sacrifices of the Levitical law typified the offering of Christ; and what their death was in type his must surely be in fact. The forms prescribed in that law show plainly their intent. The requirement to lay their hands upon the

heads of their offerings, was peculiarly significant. "If any man of you bring an offering to
the Lord, . . . he shall put his hand upon
the head of the burnt offering; and it shall be
accepted for him to make atonement for him.
Lev. 1 : 2–4. See also 3 : 2, 8, 13. If the priest
sinned, he was required to bring a bullock for a
sin offering; "and he shall lay his hand upon the
bullock's head." Chap. 4 : 4. If the whole congregation sinned, then "the elders of the congregation shall lay their hands upon the head of
the bullock." Verse 15. Also verse 24; chap. 8 :
14, 22.

The object of this action is made clear in chap.
16 : 21, where the same thing is done over the
scape-goat. The high priest was there acting in
behalf of all the people. 'And Aaron shall lay
both his hands upon the head of the live goat,
*and confess over him all the iniquities of the chil-
dren of Israel*, and all their transgressions in all
their sins, *putting them upon the head of the goat.*"
This could be the only object in all like transactions. Thus the sin was transferred from the
sinner to the object or offering upon which his
hands were laid. And this opens to us the full
sense of Lev. 1 : 4, and parallel passages. "He
shall put his hand upon the head of the burnt
offering,"—thereby transferring his sin to the
offering, so that it bore the sin of the man—"and
it shall be accepted for him." Of course it was
accepted as an offering to the broken law, in his
stead, for it had his sin.

While the action of the priest in Lev. 16 : 21

is conclusive as to the object of laying one's hand upon the head of his offering, to put his sins upon the head of the sacrifice, it does not confound the scape-goat with the sin offering, as some have imagined. Of this we shall speak at length in another place.

The same is fully shown by the following: Although the sinner was required to lay his hand on the head of the offering, the priest made the atonement for him; Lev. 4 : 20, 26, 31, 35, and others. The atonement was made with the blood of the offering. It was early revealed to man that the blood was the life. "But flesh with the life thereof, which is the blood thereof, shall ye not eat." Gen. 9 : 4. "Be sure that thou eat not the blood; for the blood is the life; and thou mayest not eat the life with the flesh." Deut. 12 : 23. "For the life of the flesh is in the blood." "For it is the life of all flesh." "For the life of all flesh is the blood thereof." Lev. 17 : 11, 14. Therefore when the Lord said, "Whoso sheddeth man's blood, by man shall his blood be shed," it was equivalent to saying, Whoso taketh man's life, by man shall his life be taken; for he said again, "*Your blood of your lives will I require.*" Gen. 9 : 5.

Now "the wages of sin is death," and "without shedding of blood there is no remission." Rom. 6 : 23; Heb. 9 : 22. That is to say, the sinner has forfeited his life, and the law dishonored cannot be satisfied or vindicated without the shedding of blood, or taking life, for life is its due. This plainly shows that *the penalty of the law* is

9

executed by *shedding blood, or taking life;* and also that the remission of sin, or its penalty, to the sinner, does not relax the claims of the law; for when his sin was transferred to the offering, that was accepted for him, and its blood or life taken for his. " For the life of the flesh is in the blood, and I have given it to you upon the altar to make an atonement for your souls; for it is the blood that maketh an atonement for the soul." Lev. 17 : 11. So the sin was remitted or forgiven the sinner, and laid upon another, who suffered its penalty. With these facts before us, we notice that all those scriptures which speak of *Christ's blood being shed*, are a confirmation of the fact that he died, or suffered the penalty of the law. The wages of sin is death—the life is in the blood; he shed his blood—he died for sin. How plain the truth; how reasonable the plan appears when freed from the perversions and "doctrines of men."

That which is done for another is vicarious. Death suffered for another is vicarious death; but in the preceding cases brought from the Scriptures, the sin offerings *never* were slain or offered for themselves, or for their own wrongs, but *always* for the sins of others. Their blood was shed in the stead of that of others; their deaths were truly vicarious. And if we take away from them all ideas of substitution or vicariousness, we take away the sole reason of their being slain, and all possibility of an atonement consistent with justice.

It needs no more than a mere reference to the Scriptures to show the relation those transactions bore to the gospel of Christ, and that the death of Christ was in truth substitutionary and vicarious. "All we like sheep have gone astray; we have turned every one to his own way; and the Lord hath laid on him the iniquity of us all." Isa. 53 : 6. "Who his own self bare our sins in his own body on the tree." 1 Pet. 2 : 24. "So Christ was once offered to bear the sins of many." Heb. 9 : 28. Thus he bore our sins—they were laid on him—he was made sin for us; standing in that relation to the law in our stead. And the wages of sin being death, because our sin was laid on him, "he was wounded for our transgressions, he was bruised for our iniquities." "For the transgression of my people was he stricken." "His soul" was made "an offering for sin." Isa. 53 : 5, 8, 10. He that doeth not all the words of the law is cursed; but Christ is made a curse for us to redeem us from the curse of the law. Deut. 27 : 26; Gal. 3 : 10–13. "Christ died for the ungodly." Rom. 5 : 6. "Was delivered for our offenses." Chap. 4 : 25. "Christ died for our sins." 1 Cor. 15 : 3. He died for all, for all were dead, or condemned to death, for all had sinned. 2 Cor. 5 : 14. He "suffered for sins, the just for the unjust." 1 Pet. 3 : 18. "Christ hath suffered for us." Chap. 4 : 1. In all these expressions the idea of substitution is prominent, as it was in the type.

Again, the same truth is taught in all those scriptures which speak of Christ having purchased us. He gave "his life a ransom for many." Matt. 20 : 28. To ransom, says Webster, is to redeem from captivity by paying an equivalent. "Who gave himself a ransom for all." 1 Tim. 2 : 6. "Ye are not your own; for ye are bought with a price." 1 Cor. 6 : 19, 20; 7 : 23. "Denying the Lord that bought them." 2 Pet. 2 : 1. "Ye were not redeemed with corruptible things, as silver and gold, . . . but with the precious blood of Christ." 1 Pet. 1 : 18, 19. "Hast redeemed us to God by thy blood." Rev. 5 : 9. "Which he hath purchased with his own blood." Acts 20 : 28. Now the sole idea of redeeming, purchasing, or buying, with a price, is that of substitution by equivalent, or receiving one instead of another.

George Storrs, of New York, in a small work on the Atonement, rejected the idea of Christ dying in the stead of the sinner; and his views ought to be noticed, especially as he represented a class. He said the atonement must correspond to man's nature, and to the demand of the law, for "it is such a satisfaction as justice rightfully demands." The best satisfaction to law is obedience; an atonement is satisfaction rendered for disobedience. It is indeed such a satisfaction as justice demands. But it would be difficult for any one to explain why the Atonement must correspond to man's nature, and to the claim that justice has on man, if the death of the atoner be not substitutionary. How otherwise could it meet the claim? Again he said that "by dying, though death had no claim on him, justice was vindicated." Now if "death had no claim on him," how could justice be *vindicated* in his death?

And is justice ever vindicated in the death of one on whom it has no claim? No; it is rather a perversion of justice. But all admit that death had no claim on Christ, so far as his own actions were concerned; therefore if justice was upheld or vindicated in his death, it was because he died " in the room and stead " of those on whom death had a claim. That there was a transfer of sin all will admit; our sins were laid on him. But death has a claim on the sinner, for the wages of sin is death. And if the sin was transferred, of course the claim of death must also have been transferred. So death had a claim on him; but only as he stood in our stead. He was made sin for us; therefore he was made a curse for us. 2 Cor. 5:21; Gal. 3:14. The idea of vicariousness, or complete substitution, is as plainly taught as language can teach it; and the wonder is that the question was ever raised by Bible-readers, or that the possibility of the negative being true was ever admitted.

We must further notice the objection that if a complete substitute is accepted, justice is satisfied, and the release of the accused is of justice, not of mercy. Many respectable speakers and authors seem to have become strangely confused on this subject. The objection seems, at first glance, to have force; but it is really founded on a very partial and superficial view of the gospel plan. It is mercy to the criminal for the Government to accept a substitute; and mercy to him also for the substitute to offer or consent to stand in his stead. It is nothing but mercy, pardon, free gift, to the sinner, in every part of the trans-action. And it would be so if he had himself procured a substitute; much more when the Governor provides the substitute, and this even the Son of his delight, and invites the sinner to return to his allegiance and obedience, that he may receive pardon and life through his blood. It has been noticed that justice and mercy must unite in order to both honor the Government and spare the sinner. Paul shows that they do unite in the gospel, for therein God can be just and the justifier of him that believeth in Jesus. His justice is shown by maintaining the dignity and honor of his law, even at the expense of the life of his Son; his mercy is shown by justifying us through his blood. But inasmuch as Christ was not a sinner, it would be very difficult to show wherein God was just in the death of his Son, unless he died to meet the just desert of our sin in our stead.

Burge on the Atonement, a work which reflects a somewhat popular view, says:—

" If a man engage to perform a certain piece of work, for a reward which is proposed, it makes no difference whether he do the work himself, or procure another to do it for him. Let the work be done according to agreement, and he is entitled to the reward. So, if Christ has done for believers the work which the law required them to do, God is now bound, on the principle of strict justice, to bestow the promised reward, eternal life. There is no grace, but stern, unbending justice here." Pp. 202, 203.

Barnes takes substantially the same view, and both aver that Christ did not suffer the penalty of the law, but something substituted for the penalty. Did this illustration merely go to show the insufficiency of Christ's obedience to moral law to make an atonement, without the suffering of death, there could be no objection raised against it. But it goes far beyond this. In order for an illustration to be worth anything, there must be some analogy between its main points and the thing illustrated. In this case there is none whatever.

Man is a rebel, condemned to death; the law can only be satisfied with the taking of life. Now in regard to rendering satisfaction to a broken law there cannot possibly be anything existing between sinful man and his Creator, answering to the nature of a contract, as this illustration supposes. But its defect is most plainly seen in this, that man does not, and cannot, *procure* a substitute. If man by his own efforts had *procured* the substitutionary sacrifice of Christ, the Atonement would rest on an entirely different footing from what it now does. Any illustration based on such an utter impossibility, which is so contrary to evident truths, and to the whole revealed plan of the Atonement, cannot aid in a correct understanding of it. God has *set forth* his Son to be a propitiation—to suffer death, the penalty of the law, for us; so that his substitutionary sacrifice is *the gift* of God, even as Christ himself was the gift of God. "For God so loved the world that *he gave* his only begotten Son."

If we take for granted that the death of Christ meets every demand of the law, yet so long as he is the gift of God, there is mercy in the transaction. But Dr. Barnes thinks there was no mercy if it met the requirement of the law. He remarks:—

"If it should be said that there was mercy in the gift of the Saviour, and that so far as that is concerned the transaction is one of mercy, though so far as the law is concerned the transaction is one of justice, it may be replied that this is not the representation of the Bible. The idea of mercy pervades it throughout. It is not only mercy in providing an atonement; it is mercy to the sinner. There *is* mercy in the case. There is love. There is more than a mere exaction of the penalty. There is more than a transfer. There is a lessening of suffering," &c. Pp. 232, 233.

No one doubts that in the Atonement there is mercy to the sinner; but we are not prepared to admit that the transaction (death of Christ) is not one of justice so far as the law is concerned. We think this *is* the representation of the Bible. The death of Christ either met the demand of law and justice, or it did not. If it did, then it was, *so far*, a legal transaction; then "stern, unbending justice" was honored in his death. But if it did not, then we fail to see how divine justice is vindicated in granting pardon through him; how God can be *just* in justifying the *believer* any more than he could have been in justifying an *unbeliever*, seeing that justice had no part in the transaction. We have been accustomed to regard this declaration of the apostle (Rom. 3: 24-26) as positive proof that justice was satisfied in his death, in order that pardon might be granted to the believer without slighting the claims of the law; and it does not seem to be possible to vindicate the system on any other principle than this. And if we only admit that Christ suffered the penalty of the law, which was death, as the Scriptures abundantly show, then there is no difficulty whatever in this view.

And we can only decide that "there is a lessening of suffering" by being able to measure the extent or severity of the sufferings of Christ, which no finite mind can do. Dr. Barnes' statement is made on the supposition that the sufferings of the lost will be eternal. But we have seen that the idea of "eternal punishment" does not embrace eternal suffering, but rather eternal death; "everlasting destruction," as the apostle says. It is possible, and the thought is not at all unreasonable, that the sufferings of Christ, the Son of God, as far exceeded the sufferings of a human being, as he is high in his nature above man, or as his blood is more precious and of more worth than that of man. It is safe to say that that remark of Dr. Barnes was made without due consideration.

The following words of Maclaurin are at once so suggestive and impressive that we are pleased to present them to the reader:—

"Men may paint Christ's outward sufferings,

but not that inward excellence from whence their virtue flowed, namely, his glory in himself, and his goodness to us. Men may paint one crucified; but how can that distinguish the Saviour from the criminals? On each side of him we may paint his hands and his feet fixed to the cross; but who can paint how these hands used always to be stretched forth for relieving the afflicted and curing the diseased; or how these feet went always about doing good; and how they cure more diseases and do more good now than ever? We may paint the outward appearance of his sufferings, but not the inward bitterness or invisible causes of them. Men can paint the cursed tree, but not the curse of the law that made it so. Men can paint Christ bearing the cross to Calvary, but not Christ bearing the sins of many. We may describe the nails piercing his sacred flesh; but who can describe eternal justice piercing both flesh and spirit? We may describe the soldier's spear, but not the arrow of the Almighty; the cup of vinegar which he but tasted, but not the cup of wrath which he drank out to the lowest dregs; the derision of the Jews, but not the desertion of the Almighty forsaking his Son, that he might never forsake us who were his enemies."

But let us further examine the facts of the gospel and see if they will justify the statement of Dr. Barnes that there was *only mercy* in the offering of Jesus Christ for man, as a sacrifice for sin. We do not see how any one can carefully consider the sacrifice, and the reason of its being made, and yet say there was no manifestation of divine justice in the transaction.

Man is a sinner, condemned to death. Justice demands his life. But God loves the world, and gives his Son to die for man. The Son volunteers to die; the plan is fixed and determined. After years of toil, privation, suffering, and scorn, he sees the hour of his death approaching. Alone with his Father he pleads, "Father, if it be possible, let this cup pass from me." Not once only does he cry. His soul is exceeding sorrowful, even unto death. Great drops of sweat, as it were blood, burst through the pores of his skin, so intense is his agony, as he prays again and again, "Father, if it be possible, let this cup pass from me." Soon is he betrayed, mocked, buffeted, spit upon, scourged, a crown of thorns placed upon his head, falsely accused and unjustly condemned, made to bear his own cross till he faints under the burden, and finally, nailed to the cross, a most cruel means of death, in agony he expires. Now, in all candor, let us ask, was there nothing but mercy in this transaction? Was there *any* mercy to the Saviour? It is readily acknowledged that "mercy pervades it throughout," as far as the sinner is concerned; but was it so toward the Saviour? The sinner was not the only one concerned in that transaction. No one can make or indorse this statement of Dr. Barnes unless he looks to the benefit accruing to the sinner, without considering the sufferings and death of the Saviour. And that is surely a very limited consideration of the *nature* and *object* of the death of Christ which leaves his death altogether out of view!

It may be objected here that Dr. Barnes claims an absolute excess of mercy, because the sufferings of Christ were but a small part of the sufferings that were justly due to the guilty world. But that makes not the least difference; for the question of the justice or the injustice of *that part endured by him* must be settled by the same principles that would govern the case had he endured the whole. The objection, however, is wholly inadmissible, involving a material error in itself; for *death* is the penalty of the law, and the just due of the sinner. This Christ suffered, and to deny this were to deny the whole gospel.

Why was this immense sacrifice made? Was man of so great value that the glorious Son of the Most High must come to rescue him from ruin? That is by no means the sole reason. Satan made a bold attempt to frustrate the plan of the Almighty. Man, with the power of reason and of will conferred upon him by his Maker, must be free to act and to form his own character in the sight of the Lawgiver. He yielded to the tempter's wiles and broke the law of his Creator and Benefactor. Not only the life of man, but the honor of God is at stake. Shall Satan be permitted to triumph, and man be utterly ruined and blotted from the earth? Or shall the divine Lawgiver relax the strictness of his law, and so let man escape the penalty which he had incurred? Either would dim the glory of the Most High. Either would cause " the sons of God," who "shouted for joy" when the foundations of the earth were laid, to vail their faces in astonishment and in sorrow. God, whose love and justice are alike infinite, determined to open a way whereby man might be recovered from his fall, and the integrity of the law be maintained, and its claims fully honored. A way, through the sacrifice of his Son, whereby "he might be just, and the justifier of him who believeth in Jesus." And shall we yet say that the sacrifice of Jesus was not an offering to justice? that it had no reference to the dignity of the divine law, which had been dishonored? We cannot see how people can read the sacred Scriptures, and look upon the agonies of the cross of Calvary, and yet say that the Atonement does not answer the demand of justice.

But the views which we have quoted from Barnes and others on this point, are not those which are commonly accepted by evangelical Christians. And we rejoice that they are not. On the other hand we present a few quotations, the sentiments of which, we feel confident, will meet a response in many an earnest Christian heart. The first is from Bishop Baring, in a sermon on "Christ's Death a Propitiatory Sacrifice":—

"It is the constant failing of man's limited intelligence to attempt to exalt one attribute of Jehovah by the surrender of another, and to throw light upon his love by vailing his justice. But the salvation of the gospel, while it immeasurably heightens the glory of each attribute, exhibits them all in perfect harmony; so that each sheds a luster on the rest, and 'mercy and truth are met together; righteousness and peace have kissed each other.' Ps. 85:10. Oh, where can we find set forth in more awful reality the immutability of God's threats, the severity of his justice, his infinite abhorrence of sin, than in the simple narrative of the agony and bloody sweat, the cross and passion of God's coequal Son."

Dr. Chalmers, in a sermon on the "Power of the Gospel," said:—

"That law which, resting on the solemn authority of its firm and unalterable requirements, demanded a fulfillment up to the last jot and tittle of it, has been magnified and has been made honorable by one illustrious Sufferer, who put forth the greatness of his strength in that dark hour of the travail of his soul when he bore the burden of all its penalties."

Robert Hall, in a sermon, "The Innocent for the Guilty," in which he outlines the gospel as "the substitution of Jesus Christ in the stead of sinners, his suffering the penalty of the law in their room, and opening a way for their deliverance from the sentence of condemnation," reasoned as follows:—

"It is highly expedient, or rather necessary, that the person who is admitted as a substitute in the stead of another, should vindicate the law by which he suffered. Otherwise, the more illustrious his character, and the more extraordinary his interposition, the more the sentiments of mankind would be divided between approbation of his character, and disapprobation of the law by which he suffered. It would be dangerous to throw the luster of such a character, the splendor and weight of his sufferings, into the scale opposite to that which contains the law. While he suffered the penalty, had he complained of the law which exacted it, as being too rigid and severe, as having demanded more than was really equitable, all the glory which the law might have derived from such a sacrifice would have been entirely lost. The honor of the law would have been impaired in the estimation of men, in proportion to the impression which his character and example had made on their minds. But so far is this from the case before us, that, on the contrary, we find both his language and his sufferings combine to produce one result.

"Never had justice such an advocate as it had in the doctrine of Christ; at the same time never had it such a victim as in his sacrifice. He illustrated the law in his doctrine, maintained and defended its purity, and rescued it from the pollutions with which the scribes and Pharisees had debased it. He magnified the law, and made it honorable. There was no contrariety between his sufferings and his doctrine; on the contrary, the one afforded the clearest commentary on the equity of the other. Every part of his conduct, and every period of his life, was a practical illustration of the excellence of the precepts which compose that law, the penalty of which he endured on behalf of the offender."

Every one must acknowledge that whatever detracts from the honor of the law, detracts from the glory of the Lawgiver. The law cannot be reproached and its Author be honored. Jesus did not seek his own glory, but the glory of him that sent him; and it was in furtherance of this object that he magnified the law and made it honorable.

The following most impressive language is found in a sermon by John Maclaurin, on "Glorying in the Cross":—

"Here shines spotless justice, incomprehensible wisdom, and infinite love, all at once. None of them darkens or eclipses the other; every one of them gives a luster to the rest. They mingle their beams, and shine with united eternal splendor; the just Judge, the merciful Father, and the wise Governor. No other object gives such a display of all these perfections; yea, all the objects we know give not such a display of any one of them. Nowhere does justice appear so awful, mercy so amiable, or wisdom so profound.

"By the infinite dignity of Christ's person, his cross gives more honor and glory *to the law and justice of God*, than all the other sufferings that ever were or will be endured in the world. When the apostle is speaking to the Romans of the gospel, he does not tell them only of God's mercy, but also of his justice revealed by it. God's wrath against the unrighteousness of men is chiefly revealed by the righteousness and sufferings of

Christ. 'The Lord was pleased for his righteousness' sake.' Rom. 1:17; Isa. 42:21. Both by requiring and appointing that righteousness, he magnified the law and made it honorable. . . Considering, therefore, that God is the Judge and Lawgiver of the world, it is plain that his glory shines with unspeakable brightness in the cross of Christ as the punishment of sin. But this is the very thing that hinders the lovers of sin from acknowledging the glory of the cross, because it shows so much of God's hatred of what they love."

Mr. H. H. Dobney, in his excellent work on "Future Punishment," discoursing on the nature of the law of God, says:—

"The mediatorial work of the Son of God is set forth as that which harmonizes justice and mercy. And we can easily perceive that the authority of law, its motive power, its moral force, is more than preserved by this compensative arrangement, which so wonderfully exhibits both the wisdom and the love of God. For those to whom mercy is shown through the Mediator acquire, by the very means adopted in saving them, a much deeper sense of their guilt in violating law than they would ever have attained; while their gratitude, their admiration, their love exceed the power of language to describe; and sin becomes to them inexpressibly hateful, while holiness—conformity to God—becomes the joy and rejoicing of their heart."

CHAPTER V.

THE SON OF GOD DIED.

SOME affect to think it derogatory to the character of God that his Son should suffer for us—the innocent for the guilty. But all such must have views of the divine Government unworthy of the subject; unworthy of the eternal truth and infinite justice of a holy God. The Lord has said that death was the penalty of transgression, and that his law should not be set aside, nor its penalty relaxed; for he would *by no means* clear the guilty. Ex. 34:7. Was it necessary for God to keep his word? If so, in order to man's salvation, it was necessary to clear man *from guilt* —to save him *from sin;* for, *as guilty, in sin,* he could *by no means* be cleared. Reason attests that the salvation of a sinner can only be effected by providing a willing and honorable substitute. The Bible attests that God gave his own Son, and the Son gave himself to die for us. What reason, in the name of justice and mercy, demands, the Bible reveals in the gift of that holy One in whom infinite justice and mercy unite.

We think that all who have read carefully our remarks upon the requirements of the moral system, pages 32–54, must accept the conclusion, that a substitutionary sacrifice is the only means whereby the broken law may be vindicated, or the honor of the Government maintained, and a way opened for the pardon and salvation of the sinner.

The Scripture plan of atonement has this peculiarity, that it presents one offering for many offences, or, in truth, for many offenders. And this is true whether we consider it in the light of the Old or the New Testament; of the type or the antitype. Their sacrifices under the Levitical law were, indeed, "offered year by year continually" (Heb. 10 : 1), but on the day of atonement, the offerings of which were the heart and substance of the whole system, a goat was offered for all the people. Lev. 16 : 15.

The declaration of the apostle Paul, in Heb. 10 : 4, is too reasonable to admit of any dispute. He says, "For it is not possible that the blood of bulls and of goats should take away sins." A bull and a goat were offered on the day of atonement, on which day the high priest took the blood into the most holy place. To these the apostle refers. His statement is founded on what may be termed the law of equivalents. While the greater may be accepted for the less, strict justice would forbid that the less should be accepted for the greater. A goat is not as valuable as a man. Its blood or life is not as precious, of as great worth, as the blood or life of a man. How much less could a goat answer as the just equivalent of a whole nation! If your neighbor owed you an ounce of silver, you would feel insulted if he offered you in payment an ounce of brass; but, on the contrary, you would consider him both just and generous if he offered to pay you with an ounce of gold. Even so, a man might consider himself demeaned, were he under sentence of death, if the Government should offer to accept the life of a goat in his stead. "Am I," he might inquire, "of so little worth that I can be ransomed by a goat?"

Again, it would not only lower the dignity of a man, but it would give us a mean idea of the justice and importance of the law. If the broken law can be vindicated by the sacrifice of a goat, a dumb animal, the law itself could not be considered of great value or importance.

But how different would the case appear if the Government should announce that the law was so just, so sacred, and its violation so odious in the sight of the lawgiver and of all loyal subjects, that nothing less than the life of a prince royal could be accepted as a substitute for the transgressor. The announcement of the fact that no less a sacrifice would be accepted, without any reason being given, would at once raise the law in the estimation of every one who heard it, and overwhelm the transgressor with a sense of the enormity of his crime. Now he might inquire, "Is it possible that my sin is so great that I can be saved only by such a great sacrifice?" By this it will be seen, as we shall yet more fully consider, that the value of the Atonement—its efficacy as a vindication of the justice of the law and the honor of the Government—consists entirely in *the dignity of the offering.*

And this is by no means a reflection on the requirements or the sacrifices of the Levitical system. If considered as a finality—as having no relation to anything to follow—they do indeed appear insignificant and entirely worthless. But if considered as types of a greater offering yet to be made; as illustrations of man's desert for his transgression, and of God's abhorrence of sin, by which the sinner subjects himself to the penalty of death, they served a useful purpose. And in the prophecies of the Old Testament we find that a greater and more honorable sacrifice was set forth to Israel, as in Dan. 9 : 24–26, where it was announced that the promised Messiah should be cut off, but not for himself; and in Isa. 52 and 53 where he who was to be exalted very high, before whom kings should shut their mouths, was to be " wounded for our transgressions, and bruised for our iniquities." How impressive are the words of the prophet: " Therefore will I divide him a portion with the great, and he shall divide the spoil with the strong; because he has poured out his soul unto death; and he was numbered with the transgressors; and he bare the sin of many, and made intercession for the transgressors."

We insist, and we think with the very best reason, that the Mosaic law reaches its logical conclusion only in the Christian system, even as the prophecies of an exalted sacrifice find their fulfillment in Jesus of Nazareth, the son of David. And the objection raised against the idea of the Son of God dying for man, for the transgression of his Father's holy law, is as contrary to reason as it is to the Scriptures. Were all men thoroughly imbued with a sense of the justice and the just requirements of the law of God, and would accept just conclusions in regard to those requirements, they could not fail to admire, with wonder and with awe, "the mystery of godliness" as presented in the offering of the Son of God as our ransom.

The law of God must be honored and vindicated by the sacrifice offered for its violation; therefore the death of Christ, the Son of the Most High, shows the estimate which he places upon his law. We can have correct views of either, the offering or the law, only as far as we have correct views of the other. Now, as the glory of God was the first great object of the gospel, Luke 1:14, and, as we have seen, the honor of the law must be the chief object of an atonement, we shall best be able to estimate the value of the law of God by having just views of the price paid for man's redemption from its curse. And it is also true that they only can properly appreciate the gift of Christ who rightly estimate the holiness and justice of that law for which he died. They who accuse us of lightly esteeming the Saviour because we highly esteem the law of God, only prove that their study of governmental relations, and of the Bible conditions of pardon, has been exceedingly superficial.

What, then, was the sacrifice offered for us? the price paid to rescue us from death? Did Christ, the Son of God, die? Or did a human body die, and God's exalted Son leave it in the hour of its suffering? If the latter be correct, it will greatly detract from the value and dignity of the Atonement; for the death of a mere human being, however sinless, would seem to be a very limited sacrifice for a sinful race. But, however that might be, we should not question God's plan, if that was the plan. But what say the Scriptures? This must be our inquiry. To these we appeal.

It is by many supposed that the pre-existent being, the Son of God, could not suffer and die, but that he left the body at the moment of its death. If so, the only humiliation the Son manifested was to leave Heaven and dwell in such a body; and so far from the death of the body being a sacrifice on the part of the higher nature, it was only a release and exemption from the state of humiliation. This would hardly justify the Scripture declarations of the amazing love of God in giving his Son to die for the sins of the world.

The Methodist Discipline has a statement concerning the Son of God, which we think is quite in harmony with the Scriptures. "Two whole and perfect natures, that is to say, the Godhead and manhood, were joined together in one person, *never to be divided*, whereof is *one Christ*, very God, and very man, who truly suffered, was crucified, dead and buried." We can only regret that we seldom meet with a Methodist author who takes a position as Scriptural as this of the Discipline.

The view which we call in question supposes that there were two distinct natures in the person of Christ; but we do not so read it in the sacred oracles. But if it be so—if there were two distinct natures united for a season, and separated in death, we must learn it in the revelation concerning him. What, then, are the terms in which this distinction is revealed? What terms express his higher, or divine nature, and what terms express his mere human nature? Whoever attempts to answer these questions will find the position utterly untenable. "Christ" expresses both combined. "Christ, the Son of the living God"—"The man Christ Jesus," both refer to the same person or individual; there are no forms of speech to express his personality higher than the Son of God, or Christ; and the Scriptures declare that Christ, the Son of God, died.

The divinity and pre-existence of our Saviour are most clearly proved by those scriptures which refer to him as "the Word." "In the beginning was the Word, and the Word was with God, and the Word was God. The same was in the beginning with God. All things were made by him, and without him was not anything made that was made." John 1 : 1–3. This expresses plainly a pre-existent divinity. The same writer again says: "That which was from the beginning, . . . the Word of life." 1 John 1 : 1. What John calls the Word, in these passages, Paul calls the "Son," in Heb. 1 : 1–3. "God . . . hath in these last days spoken unto us by his Son, whom he hath appointed heir of all things, by whom also he made the worlds; who being the brightness of his glory, and the express image of his person, and upholding all things by the word of his power." In other places in this letter this same exalted one is called Jesus Christ. In these passages we find the divinity or "higher nature" of our Lord expressed. Indeed, language could not more plainly express it; therefore it is unnecessary to call other testimony to prove it, it being already sufficiently proved.

The first of the above quotations says the Word *was* God, and also the Word was *with* God. Now it needs no proof—indeed it is self-evident—that the Word *as* God, was not *the God* whom he was *with*. And as there is but "one God," the term must be used in reference to the Word in a subordinate sense, which is explained by Paul's calling the same pre-existent person the Son of God. This is also confirmed by John's saying that the Word "was with the Father." 1 John 1 : 2; also calling the Word "his Son Jesus Christ." Verse 3. Now it is reasonable that the Son should bear the name and title of his Father, especially when the Father makes him his exclusive representative to man, and clothes him with such power—"*by whom* he made the worlds." That the term God is used in such a sense is also proved by Paul, quoting Ps. 45 : 6, 7, and applying it to Jesus. "But unto *the son*, he saith, Thy throne, *O God*, is forever and ever, . . . therefore God, even *thy God*, hath anointed thee with the oil of gladness above thy fellows." Heb. 1 : 8, 9. Here the title of God is applied to the Son, and *his* God anointed him. This is the highest title he can bear, and it is evidently used here in a sense subordinate to its application to his Father.

It is often asserted that this exalted one came to earth and inhabited a human body, which he

left in the hour of its death.   But the Scriptures
teach that this exalted one was the identical person that died on the cross; and in this consists
the immense sacrifice made for man—the wondrous love of God and condescension of his only
Son.   John says, "The Word of life," "that
which was from the beginning," "which was
with the Father," that exalted, pre-existent One
"which we have heard, which we have seen with
our eyes, which we have looked upon, and our
hands have handled."   1 John 1 : 1, 2.

This testimony of inspiration makes the Word
that was with the Father from the beginning, a
tangible being appreciable to the senses of those
with whom he associated.   How can this be so?
For an answer we turn to John 1 : 14: "And the
Word was made flesh and dwelt among us."   This
is plain language and no parable.   But these are
not the only witnesses. speaking to the same intent.   Says Paul, "Let this mind be in you, which
was also in Christ Jesus; who, being in the form
of God, thought it not robbery to be equal with
God; but made himself of no reputation, and
took upon him the form of a servant, and was
made in the likeness of men; and being found
in fashion as a man, he humbled himself;" more
literally, *divested himself*, *i. e.*, of the glory he
had with the Father before the world was.   Phil.
2 : 5–8.

Again Paul speaks of him thus: "Forasmuch
then as the children are partakers of flesh and
blood, *he* also *himself* took part of the same."
Heb, 2 : 14.   The angel also announced to Mary,

that her son Jesus should be called the Son of the Highest; and, "That holy thing which shall be born of thee shall be called the Son of God." Luke 1 : 35. Not that the "Son of the Highest" should dwell in and inhabit that which should be born of her, but her son was the holy, pre-existent one, thus by the energy of the Holy Spirit "made flesh." Now if the human nature of Christ existed *distinct* from the divine, the foregoing declarations will not apply to either; for, if that were so, the pre-existent Word was not made flesh; it was not the man, nor in the fashion of a man, nor did the man, the servant, ever humble himself, or divest himself of divine glory, never having possessed it. But allowing that the Word—the divine Son of the Most High —was made flesh, took on him the seed of Abraham, and thus changed the form and manner of his existence by the mighty power of God, all becomes clear and harmonious.

Having noticed the humiliation of the exalted Son of God, we come to the question at issue: Who or what died for man? The answer is, Christ, the Son of the Most High; the pre-existent one that was with God in the beginning; the Word, who was made flesh. Now that the scriptures quoted all refer to the "higher nature" of Christ, the pre-existent Son of God, no one can doubt. Indeed, if the incarnation of the Holy One is not therein revealed, it cannot be revealed at all, and Socinianism is the only resort. But it is therein revealed plainly; and it is equally plain that the same Word, or Son, or Christ, died for our sins. We remarked that the titles of the Father are given to the Son, whereby he is called God. In Isa. 9 : 6, 7, he is called the son given; the child born; Wonderful; Counsellor; the mighty God; the everlasting Father; the Prince of Peace; and he is to sit upon the throne of David.

These expressions clearly identify the anointed of God, even Jesus. And he is evidently called here Prince of Peace in the same capacity that he is called the "King of Peace," in Heb. 7, because "he is our peace," Eph. 2 : 14, or makes peace for us on the throne of his Father; for it is only in his priestly office that he is King of Peace, that is, a priest after the order of Melchisedec. But Paul again says that he is our peace, reconciling us unto God by the cross, we being "made nigh by *the blood of Christ.*" Eph. 2 : 13–16. We have seen the necessity of blood to make an atonement, and that the high priest never entered the holies without it; and Christ, the King of Peace, our High Priest, obtains redemption for us "by his own blood." See Heb. 6 : 20; 7 : 1–3; 8 : 1; 9 : 11, 12. Therefore that exalted one referred to in Isa. 9 : 6, 7, shed his blood or laid down his life for us. Again he is prophesied of under the name Immanuel, which Matthew said means "God with us." The angel said he should "save his people from their sins." Matt. 1 : 21, 23. And Paul said he accomplished this or put away sin by the sacrifice of himself, purging us "by his own blood." Heb. 9 : 11–14, 26.

The gospel according to John, as quoted, takes up the Word, in the beginning, as God, with God, by whom all things were made; says the Word was made flesh and dwelt among us; represents him as saying he came from the Father and returned to him; as praying that the Father would restore to him the glory which he had with him before the world was; relates how he taught and wrought miracles; was falsely accused of the Jews; was put to death on the cross; his blood was shed; he was buried, and rose again from the dead. Now we ask the candid reader to look at this testimony, and answer: Is the history of any other person given in this book than of him who is called the Word, who was in the beginning? And if any other individual or person was referred to, who was that person?

Phil. 2:5-8, as quoted, speaks of Christ as being in the form of God; he thought it not robbery to be equal with God; was made in the likeness of man; humbled himself, and became obedient unto death, even the death of the cross. Again we appeal to the candid: Is not all this spoken of one person? Or did one person humble himself, and another become obedient to death?

Paul, in Col. 1:14-20, uses the same form of expression that he does in Heb. 1. He says of the Son: "In whom we have redemption through his blood, the forgiveness of sins; who is the image of the invisible God, the first-born of every creature; for by him were all things created, that are in heaven, and that are in earth, . . . all things were created by him, and for him; and he is before all things, and by him all things consist. And he is the head of the body, the church; who is the beginning, the first-born from the dead; that in all things he might have the pre-eminence. For it pleased the Father that in him should all fullness dwell; and having made peace through the blood of his cross, by him to reconcile all things to himself." Here is a description of power, of authority, of fullness, of divinity, truly wonderful; yet this exalted one, by whom all things were created, has made peace by the blood of his cross, and was raised from the dead; he is the head of the church, and we have redemption through his blood. Such testimony cannot be avoided; it needs no comment.

Jesus, in his testimony to the churches, takes up the same idea expressed by his apostle in Col. 1, as being creator of all, and first-born of every creature, and says: "I am the first and the last; I am he that liveth and was dead." Rev. 1 : 17, 18. Here it is expressly affirmed that he who is the first and the last, was dead. Thus it is abundantly shown that Christ, the Son of the Most High, the Word, by whom the worlds were made, in whom all things consist, the first and the last, the image of the invisible God, in whom all fullness dwells, was made flesh and laid down his life, to purge us from sin, and to redeem us to God by his own blood.

We have remarked that we should not question God's plan, whatever that might be. But we find that there is a fitness, a conformity to the necessity of things, in God's arrangements. The value of the Atonement is not merely in the *appointment* of God; for, were it so, "the blood of bulls and of goats" might have answered every purpose, had God so appointed. But Paul says it is *not possible* that such blood should take away sin, or purge the conscience. Again, it is not in mere *suffering;* for, were that the case, man might atone for himself were he to suffer long enough. But it is evident from every principle of just government, that a man under the condemnation, to death, of a holy, just, and immutable law, could never make atonement for himself. But, the value of the atonement really consists in *the dignity of the offering.*

As a man under condemnation could not make an atonement for himself, so no one of the race could make atonement for another, all being alike involved in sin. And we may go further than this: Were a part of the human race unfallen, or free from sin, they could make no atonement for the other part, inasmuch as they would still be the creatures of God, and the service of their lives would be due to him. Therefore, should they offer their lives to God for their fellow-creatures, they would offer that to which they had no absolute right. He who owes all that he possesses cannot justly give his possession to pay the debts of another.

And the same reasoning would hold good in the case of the angels. They are but the "fellow-servants" of all on earth who serve God. Rev. 19 : 10; 22 : 8, 9. The life of an angel would be utterly inadequate for the redemption of man, as the angels are dependent creatures as man is, and as really owe to God the service of their lives as man does.

And again, as man has been in rebellion, were it possible for him to extricate himself from his present difficulty, he could give no security—no satisfactory assurance, that he would never again turn from his duty. And of the angels, we must say that sin has entered their ranks; the "Son of the Morning" exalted himself to his ruin. Isa. 14:12-15; the covering cherub lifted up himself against God. Eze. 28:13-17. Any redemption wrought by them, or by beings of that order, would still leave distrust in regard to the security of the Government from any future attempts against its authority.

But there was one Being to whom this reasoning and these remarks would not apply. It was the Son of God. He was the delight of the Father; glorified with him before the world was; adored and worshiped by angels. Prov. 8:30; John 17:5; Heb. 1. All creatures were made by and for him, and he upheld all things by the word of his Father's power. John 1:1-3; Col 1:15-17; Heb. 1:3. Enjoying the glory of the Father, he sat with him upon the throne from which all law proceeded. Now it is evident that he to whom such remarks will apply could make an offering that would meet the necessities of the case in every respect. He possessed the requisite dignity to magnify and vindicate the honor of the law of his Father in suffering its penalty. He was the Truth as well as the Life, and he said the law of his Father was in his heart, which was a guarantee that he would do no violence to the law himself, but would shield it from desecration and rescue it from reproach, even to the laying down of his life in its behalf. He was so far removed by nature and position from the rebellion that he could not be suspected of any complicity with it. He was so well acquainted with his Father's holiness and justice that he c uld realize, as no other could, the awful condition of the sinner, and the terrible desert of his sin. He was so pure and exalted that his sufferings and death would have the desired effect upon the minds of those who were the recipients of his grace, to produce in them an abasement of themselves and an abhorrence of the sins which caused him to suffer, and thus to guard against a future rebellion amongst them whom he redeemed. And he left that throne of glory and of power and took upon him the nature of fallen man. In him were blended "the brightness of the Father's glory" and the weakness of "the seed of Abraham." In himself he united the Lawgiver to the law-breaker—the Creator to the creature; for he was made "sin for us, that we might be made the righteousness of God in him." He was a connecting link between Heaven and earth; with one hand on the throne of God, and the other reaching down to grasp the poor, ruined creatures under the condemnation of a holy law. He "humbled himself" as it is not possible for any other to do. "He was rich" in a sense, and to an extent, that no other was. He had something to offer, of value far beyond our comprehension, and he freely gave it all for us. For our sakes he became poor. He left that glory to take

11

upon himself grief, and toil, and pain, and shame, and to suffer even unto death; a death the most cruel that the malice of his enemies could invent, to save his enemies from well-deserved ruin.

> "O Lamb of God, was ever pain,
> Was ever love, like thine?"

Well might an inspired one exclaim, "Oh! the depths of the riches both of the wisdom and knowledge of God! How unsearchable are his judgments, and his ways past finding out!" Well might he pray that we "may be able to comprehend with all saints, what is the breadth, and length, and depth, and height, and to know the love of Christ which passeth knowledge."

With this clear testimony before us, we are better prepared to appreciate the law of God, to the honor of which such an amazing sacrifice has been offered. If we estimate it according to the price paid for its vindication, we are lost in wonder, and can only pray with David, "Open thou mine eyes, that I may behold wondrous things out of thy law." Ps. 119:18. The law is holy and just, and without a sacrificial offering, man must have perished. And what an offering! the brightest ornament of Heaven, by whom the Eternal Father made all things, who was worthy to receive the worship of angels, became obedient to death to redeem guilty man from the curse of his Father's law, thus showing to a wondering universe that the law cannot be set aside, nor its judgments reversed. Truly has the Lord fulfilled his promise, to "magnify the law and make it honorable." Isa. 42:21. All the statements of the Bible writers are shown by this to be fully warranted, in regard to its perfection, completeness, as containing the whole duty of man, the elements of justification, a rule of holiness, etc.; also the remark previously made, that the holiness of this law, and of course of those who would keep it perfectly, is that which grows out of the attributes of God, as pure and changeless as Heaven itself. And we leave it to the candid judgment of those who lightly esteem and wantonly break the law, if God in justice spared not his Son, his well beloved Son in whom he greatly delighted, but let him suffer its penalty when he took its transgressions upon him, how can they hope to escape his justice and his wrath in the great coming day, if they continue to transgress it? Reader, can you hope that God will be more favorable to you if sin be found upon you in that day, than he was to his Son? True, his death was expiatory; he died for you; but do not therefore presume on his grace, but turn from sin, and live to his pleasure and glory. Do not abuse his mercy, because he grants the "remission of sins that are past," by claiming indulgence for sins in the future. Be warned in time, for Christ is not the minister of sin, but of righteousness. He will not save you *in sin*, but *from sin*. While the carnal mind is enmity against God, and not subject to his law, the Christian can say, "I delight in the law of God." Rom. 7:22; 8:7. May this be your happy experience.

CHAPTER VI.

DOCTRINE OF A TRINITY SUBVERSIVE OF THE ATONEMENT.

IT will no doubt appear to many to be irreverent to speak thus of the doctrine of a trinity. But we think they must view the subject in a different light if they will calmly and candidly examine the arguments which we shall present. We know that we write with the deepest feelings of reverence for the Scriptures, and with the highest regard for every Scripture doctrine and Scripture fact. But reverence for the Scriptures does not necessarily embrace reverence for men's opinions of the Scriptures.

It is not our purpose to present any argument on the doctrine of the trinity, further than it has a bearing on the subject under consideration, namely, on the Atonement. And we are willing, confidently willing to leave the decision of the question with all who will carefully read our remarks, with an effort to divest themselves of prejudice, if they unfortunately possess it. The inconsistencies of Trinitarians, which must be pointed out to free the Scripture doctrine of the Atonement from reproaches under which it has too long lain, are the necessary outgrowth of their system of theology. No matter how able are the writers to whom we shall refer, they could never free themselves from inconsistencies without correcting their theology.

Many theologians really think that the Atonement, in respect to its dignity and efficacy, rests upon the doctrine of a trinity. But we fail to see any connection between the two. To the contrary, the advocates of that doctrine really fall into the difficulty which they seem anxious to avoid. Their difficulty consists in this: They take the denial of a trinity to be equivalent to a denial of the divinity of Christ. Were that the case, we should cling to the doctrine of a trinity as tenaciously as any can; but it is not the case. They who have read our remarks on the death of the Son of God know that we firmly believe in the divinity of Christ; but we cannot accept the idea of a trinity, as it is held by Trinitarians, without giving up our claim on *the dignity of the sacrifice* made for our redemption.

And here is shown how remarkably the widest extremes meet in theology. The highest Trinitarians and lowest Unitarians meet and are perfectly united on the death of Christ—the faith of both amounts to Socinianism. Unitarians believe that Christ was a prophet, an inspired teacher, but merely human; that his death was that of a human body only. Trinitarians hold that the term "Christ" comprehends two distinct and separate natures: one that was merely human; the other, the second person in the trinity, who dwelt in the flesh for a brief period, but could not possibly suffer, or die; that the Christ that died was only the human nature in which the divinity had dwelt. Both classes have a human offering, and nothing more. No matter how exalted the pre-existent Son was; no matter how glorious, how powerful, or even eternal; if the manhood only died, the sacrifice was only human. And so far as the vicarious death of Christ is concerned, this is Socinianism. Thus the remark is just, that the doctrine of a trinity degrades the Atonement, resting it solely on a human offering as a basis. A few quotations will show the correctness of this assertion.

"As *God*, he obeyed all the requirements of the law, and made it honorable in the justification of sinners; as *man*, he bore its curse on the tree, and endured its penalty."—*Manual of Atonement, p. 25.*

"The sufferings of Christ were endured in his human nature. Though possessing a divine nature, yet in that he could not suffer and die. His sufferings were endured in his human nature." *Id., p. 88.*

"It is no part of the doctrine of the Atonement that the divine nature, in the person of the Saviour, suffered."—*Barnes on Atonement, p. 224.*

"It was meet that the mediator should be man, that he might be capable of suffering death; for, as God, he could not die."—*Buck's Theol. Dict., Art. Mediator.*

"Trinitarians do not hold to the sufferings or death of divinity."—*Mattison on the Trin., p. 39.*

"His mediation between God and man is chiefly in his human nature, in which alone he was capable of suffering and dying."—*Scott on 1 Tim. 2:5.*

"I know not any scripture, fairly interpreted, that states the *divine nature* of our Lord to be *begotten* of God, or to be the *Son of* God."—*Clarke on Heb. 1:8.*

" Is it to be wondered that the human body in which this fullness of the Godhead dwelt, and in which the punishment due to our sins was borne upon the tree, should be exalted above all human and all created things?"—*Id. on Phil. 2 : 9.*

Dr. Clarke says the apostle John doubtless directed his first letter against the heretics then abounding. Of them he says:—

" The *Gnostics* even denied that Christ suffered; the Æon, or Divine Being that dwelt in the man Christ Jesus, according to them, left him when he was taken by the Jews," &c.—*Note on 1 John 1 : 8.*

So far as that particular heresy of the Gnostics is concerned, it has become wide-spread and almost all-prevailing in the denominations of the present day. Indeed, we cannot see but Dr. Clarke himself was tinctured with it, according to the quotations given above.

We trust that we have shown to the full conviction of every one who " trembles at the word " of the Lord, that the Son of God, who was in the beginning, by whom the worlds were made, suffered death for us; the oft-repeated declarations of theological writers that a mere human body died are, by the Scriptures, proved untrue. These writers take the doctrine of a trinity for their basis, and assume that Christ is the second person in the trinity, and could not die. Again, they assume that death is not a cessation of life; and between the two unscriptural assumptions they involve themselves in numerous difficulties, and load the doctrine of the Atonement with unreasonable contradictions. We would not needlessly place ourselves in opposition to the religious feelings of any class, but in order to clear the doctrine of the Atonement from the consequences of these assumptions, we are compelled to notice some of the prominent arguments presented in favor of the doctrine of a trinity.

In the "Manual of Atonement," 1 John 5 : 20 is quoted as containing most conclusive evidence of a trinity and of the Supreme Deity of Christ. It is there claimed that he is called "the true God and eternal life." The whole verse reads thus: "And we know that the Son of God is come, and hath given us an understanding that we may know him that is true, and we are in him that is true, even in his Son Jesus Christ. This is the true God and eternal life." A person must be strongly wedded to a theory who can read this verse and not see the distinction therein contained between the true God and the Son of God. "We are in him that is true." How? "In his Son Jesus Christ." The distinction between Christ and the true God is most clearly shown by the Saviour's own words in John 17 : 3 : "That they might know *thee, the only true God, and* Jesus Christ, *whom thou hast sent.*"

Much stress is laid on Isa. 9 : 6, as proving a trinity, which we have before quoted, as referring to our High Priest who shed his blood for us. The advocates of that theory will say that it refers to a trinity because Christ is called the everlasting Father. But for this reason, with others, we affirm that it can have no reference to a trinity. Is Christ the Father in the trinity? If so, how is he the Son? or if he is both Father and Son, how can there be a trinity? for a *trinity* is *three* persons. To recognize a trinity, the distinction between the Father and Son must be preserved. Christ is called "the second person in the trinity;" but if this text proves a trinity, or refers to it at all, it proves that he is not the second, but the first. And if he is the first, who is the second? It is very plain that this text has no reference to such a doctrine.

In seeking an explanation of this text, we must bear in mind the work of Christ as brought to view in this and parallel passages. These words refer to the "child born," the "son given," who, as we have seen, bears the title of God subordinate to his Father. And if an apostle could call himself the father of those whom he had begotten in the gospel (1 Cor. 4:15; 1 Tim. 1:2; Titus 1:4), how appropriately is this title applied to the Prince of Peace, who is, in a peculiar sense, the everlasting Father of all to whom he gives everlasting life. The New Jerusalem is called the Bride, the Lamb's wife (Rev. 21); Christ of course is the Bridegroom, the husband. But Paul says Jerusalem above is our mother. Gal. 4:26. If so, why not her husband, the bridegroom, be our father? Surely there is nothing inappropriate in this. But, as the New Jerusalem is not the mother of the unregenerate, these being reckoned the children of the bondwoman, so Christ is not called their father. They are not his children, and he does not give them everlasting life. Therefore the title is applied to him in a subordinate and restricted sense. In its unrestricted and universal sense it applies only to the Supreme One, "the God and Father of our Lord Jesus Christ." 2 Cor. 11 : 31; Eph. 1 : 3; 1 Peter 1 : 3.

John 12 : 40, 41, has been supposed to prove the Supreme Deity of Christ, and therefore a trinity. "These things said Esaias, when he saw his [Christ's] glory, and spake of him." This refers to Isa. 6, which chapter speaks of "the King, the Lord [Jehovah] of hosts;" and it is thence inferred that Christ is that Lord of hosts. But those who quote this in such a manner should know (and some of them do know) that there are two words in Isa. 6 rendered Lord, just as there are in Ps. 110 : 1, which says: "The LORD said unto my Lord." The first is Jehovah; the second Adonai—the Father and Son. In Isa. 6 : 3, 5, 12, Jehovah is used; in verses 1, 8, 11, Adonai is used. Now John 12 : 40 is a quotation from Isa. 6 : 10, which refers to Adonai, the Son, and not to Jehovah. Many have been misled by a wrong application of this text. Those who know the fact above stated cannot honestly use it as it has been used in theological controversies.

Jer. 23 : 5, 6 is supposed to afford decisive proof of a trinity, in that the "Branch' which is raised up unto David shall be called Jehovah. Clarke, in his commentary, gives the following rendering of this text, from Dr. Blayney: "And this is the name by which Jehovah shall call him, our righteousness." He adds:—

"Dr. Blayney thus accounts for his translation: Literally, according to the Hebrew idiom,—and this is his name by which Jehovah shall call our righteousness; a phrase exactly the same as, 'And Jehovah shall call him so,' which implies that God would make him such as he called him, that is, our righteousness, or the Author and Means of our salvation and our acceptance. So that by the same metonymy Christ is said to 'have been made of God unto us wisdom, and righteousness, and sanctification, and redemption.' 1 Cor. 1 : 30.

" I doubt not that some persons will be offended with me, for depriving them by this translation of a favorite argument for proving the Divinity of our Saviour from the Old Testament. But I cannot help it. I have done it with no ill design, but purely because I think, and am morally sure, that the text, as it stands, will not properly admit of any other construction. The *Septuagint* have so translated it before me in an age when there could not possibly be any bias or prejudice either *for* or *against* the forementioned doctrine—a doctrine which draws its *decisive* proofs from the New Testament only."

On this Dr. Clarke remarks: "I prefer the translation of Blayney to all others. . . . As to those who put the sense of their creed upon the words, they must be content to stand out of the list of Hebrew critics. I believe Jesus to be Jehovah, but I doubt much whether this text calls him so."

We must be careful to distinguish between a *criticism* and an *opinion*. After clearly defining the doctrine of the text, Dr. Clarke tells us what he *believes*, which is not the doctrine of the text.

And we are constrained to question its being the doctrine of the Scriptures. There must be a distinction between the Father and the Son; and that must be precisely the distinction between Jehovah and his Anointed One, Jesus the Christ. We have recently read an argument by a man of undoubted ability, who endeavors to prove that Jesus is Jehovah, by comparing the words of the prophets with those of the New Testament. Thus, the prophets say that Jehovah is the Saviour of men, and the New Testament says that Jesus is the Saviour; therefore Jesus is Jehovah.

That is apparently, but not really, an argument. They who speak thus seem to forget the teachings of the New Testament, that *God was in Christ*, reconciling the world unto himself." 2 Cor. 5:19. "For God so loved the world that *he gave* his only begotten Son, that whosoever believeth in him should not perish, but have everlasting life." John 3:16. And again Jesus said: "My doctrine is not mine, but his that sent me." "He that sent me is with me; the Father hath not left me alone; for I do always those things that please him." "The words that I speak unto you I speak not of myself; but the Father that dwelleth in me, he doeth the works." John 7:16; 8:29; 14:10. God hath indeed spoken unto us in these last days, but it is "by his Son." Heb. 1:1, 2. It is very true, "that God hath given to us eternal life, and this life is in his Son." 1 John 5:11. The Son comes in the name of the Father; he represents the Father to the world; he accomplishes the will and purpose of the Father in redemption. As Christ is the Son of God, and the only representative of the Father, it could not be considered strange that he should bear the name and title of his father; "for it pleased the Father that in him should all fullness dwell." Col. 1:19. But *the Son is not the Father;* and therefore it cannot be that Christ is Jehovah, but was sent of Jehovah to do his will and work, and to make known the counsels of his grace.

As before remarked, the great mistake of Trinitarians, in arguing this subject, is this: they make no distinction between a denial of a trinity and a denial of the divinity of Christ. They see only the two extremes, between which the truth lies; and take every expression referring to the pre-existence of Christ as evidence of a trinity. The Scriptures abundantly teach the pre-existence of Christ and his divinity; but they are entirely silent in regard to a trinity. The declaration, that the divine Son of God could not die, is as far from the teachings of the Bible as darkness is from light. And we would ask the Trinitarian, to which of the *two natures* are we indebted for redemption? The answer must, of course, be, To that one which died or shed his blood for us; for "we have redemption through his blood." Then it is evident that if only the human nature died, our Redeemer is only human, and that the divine Son of God took no part in the work of redemption, for he could neither suffer nor die. Surely, we say right, that the doctrine of a trinity degrades the Atonement, by bringing the sacrifice, the blood of our purchase, down to the standard of Socinianism.

But we are not the only ones who see this difficulty in the Trinitarian views of the atoning sacrifice. Their own expressions betray a sense of the weakness of their position, and of the necessity of something more than a human offering for the redemption of man. Dr. Barnes, as quoted, says that "the divine nature in the person of Christ" could not suffer, nor die; yet, in speaking of the nature of the Atonement, he says:—

"If it be a part of the doctrine of the Atonement, and essential to that doctrine, that the Redeemer was divine, that he was 'God manifest in the flesh,' that there was in a proper sense an incarnation of Deity, then it is clear that such an incarnation, and the sufferings of such an one on a cross, were events adapted to make an impression on the universe at large, deeper by far than would be done by the sufferings of the guilty themselves." "All must feel that it was appropriate that the Eternal Father should command the sun to withdraw his beams, and the earth to tremble, and the rocks to rend—to spread a universal pall over the world—when his Son expired on the cross." "He had descended from Heaven, and had taken upon himself the form of a servant. He had subjected himself voluntarily to poverty, shame, and contempt; he had been bound, and scourged, and publicly rejected; he had submitted to a mock trial and to an unjust condemnation; he had borne his own cross to the place of crucifixion, and had voluntarily given himself up to be put to death in a form that involved the keenest torture that man could inflict." Pp. 255-7.

If it were true that the divine nature—that which "descended from Heaven"—could not suffer and die, such remarks as the above are only calculated to mislead; and it must appear to all that they betray a consciousness, on the part of the writer, that if the sacrifice was only human, as he had elsewhere said, the offering lacked in dignity, and the Atonement in efficacy.

The Manual of Atonement, as quoted, says he could only die as man; that in his divine nature he could neither suffer nor die; and yet uses the following words:—

"It was sin that drew Christ from the skies, and influenced him to lead a life of suffering in this world. It was sin that wounded his sacred head—that agonized his soul in the garden—that led him to Calvary—that nailed him to the cross, and drew out his heart's blood as a sin-atoning sacrifice." P. 138

Who would not suppose from the above that the very Christ that came "from the skies" died on the cross? Why is this language used? Evidently to make an impression of the enormity of the sin, and the value of the sacrifice, which could not be made by the death of a human being. That object might be accomplished without any contradiction, by allowing what the Scriptures plainly teach of the death of the Son of God.

Dr. Scott, who says his death was only in his human nature, further says:—

"'I am he that liveth;' the ever-living, self-existent God, to whom as mediator it was given to have life in himself, and to be the life of men; and who had also been obedient to death for sinners; but behold he was alive as the first-fruits of the resurrection, to die no more."—*Note on Rev. 1 : 18.*

"This same person, who created and upholds all worlds, as the high priest of his people, purged away the guilt of their sins, *by himself*, and the sacrifice of his death upon the cross."—*Note on Heb. 1 : 3.*

If it was *given* to the "self-existent God" to have life in himself, *by whom was it given?* Here is a plain declaration that "the ever-living, self-existent God" died for sinners, which we *cannot* believe, and Dr. Scott did not believe, for he contradicted it elsewhere. The self-existent God could not purge away our sin "by himself," but the Son of God could "by himself" (as Paul says, Heb. 1 : 3), and the self-existent God could *by his Son;* for God was in Christ reconciling the world to himself.

Dr. Clarke, in his Commentary, says:—

"Considering him (Paul) as writing under the inspiration of the Holy Ghost, then we have from the plain, grammatical meaning of the words which he has used, the fullest demonstration (for the Spirit of God cannot lie) that He who died for our sins, and rose again for our justification, and in whose blood we have redemption, was *God over all*."—*Clarke on Col. 1.*

In view of the remark from the same author,

which we before quoted, that the suffering or punishment due to our sins was borne in the human body, the above is a most remarkable statement. In the former quotations he said that the divine nature was not the Son of God; that the Godhead dwelt in a human body, and it was the human body that endured the punishment due to our sins; and in the latter quotation he says that "he who died for our sins, and rose again for our justification, and in whose blood we have redemption, was God over all." Can it be possible that he thought that the human nature, in distinction from the divine nature which dwelt therein, is God over all? We very well know that he thought the divine nature which dwelt in the human was God; and if the human nature, which died for us, was also God, then he certainly has presented to us two Gods, namely, a divine God and a human God! And each one is God over all. We think he has fallen into the same inconsistency which was manifested by the Manual of Atonement, by Dr. Scott, and by Dr. Barnes. Each said that divinity or the divine nature could not suffer nor die, and each said that the pre-existing divinity suffered and died. Dr. Scott even said that the self-existent God died as our mediator. We believe that the doctrine of the trinity lies at the foundation of these errors on the part of these able authors. The Bible is not, and should not be made, responsible for such inconsistencies. They are not at all necessary to an understanding of the Bible or the doctrine of the Atonement. On the contrary, they prevent

12

an understanding of the truth, and cause the teachings of the Scriptures to appear confused and uncertain in the eyes of all who trust in the wisdom of the wise of this world.

Dr. John Harris, in his first volume on Theological Science—the Pre-Adamite Earth—has very forcibly stated the truth concerning the pre-existence and manifestation of the Redeemer. He says:—

"For εν αρχη [in the beginning] even then He already ην [was]. The assertion of his pre-existence is included alike in αρχη and in ην. For when every created thing had yet to be, He already was. He comprehends every being in himself." P. 31.

And of the manifestation of this pre-existent one he further says:—

"His disciples subsequently declared that the life had been manifested, and that they had seen it; that that which was from the beginning they had handled and seen, even the Word of Life." P. 34.

Now, when the disciples also declare that that Word which they saw and handled was put to death on the cross, and rose from the dead, we cannot avoid the conclusion that that which was from the beginning, which was before all things, actually died for man. Of course we cannot believe what men say about his being co-equal with God in every respect, and that the divine Son of God could not suffer nor die. These are mere human words. But that the Word, or Logos, was the Son of God, that he was before all things, that he was made flesh, that he was seen and handled of men, that he was put to death, that he was raised from the dead—these are the words of inspiration. "What is the chaff to the wheat? saith the Lord."

"The mystery of godliness," the **mystery** of the incarnation, is great indeed. It is to be doubted whether a finite mind will ever be able to comprehend it. This does not speak against it as a fact; for we may accept a fact revealed, when we cannot comprehend the nature of the fact. We may believe that a certain star is thousands of millions of miles from the earth, but the human mind can have no just conception of such a distance. We believe in the being of the omnipotent God, but we cannot comprehend his being. We believe that he who was glorified with the Father before the world was, was made flesh, and dwelt among men; in whom, as the Methodist Discipline justly expressed it, were two natures joined together in one person, never to be divided; who truly suffered and died for us. What a sacrifice for guilty man! What an offering to the immutable law of Jehovah! What a vindication of the mercy and justice of the Father!

> "Here's love and grief beyond degree;
> The Lord of glory dies for men!"

"O the depth of the riches both of the wisdom and knowledge of God! How unsearchable are his judgments, and his ways past finding out!" See 1 Cor. 2:8; Rom. 11:33.

CHAPTER VII.

In Part First we considered the moral in distinction from the natural system, and certain principles of Government which are universally accepted, and arrived at the conclusion that substitutionary sacrifice is the only means whereby a sinner can be relieved from condemnation. And from this conclusion, if the principles are carefully considered, we cannot see how any one can dissent. But a substituted sacrifice is the basis of all atonement; and hence we conclude that *an atonement is consistent with reason.* The principles of Government and the recognition of divine justice, demand an atonement or the entire destruction of a sinful race, confronted as it is with the declaration, "The wages of sin is death."

In Part Second we have, thus far, examined the principles of the divine Government as revealed in the Bible, in behalf of which the Atonement must be made. For, an atonement is a vindication of justice by an offering to the broken law. And we have examined the nature of the offering made for man's redemption. That "the Son of God died" there can be no doubt, except with those who prefer their own theories to the plain testimony of the word of God. That in his death he suffered the penalty, the full penalty, of the law, there seems to be no ground to dispute, unless the scripture is directly denied which says. "The wages of sin is death." That he died for "the world," "for all," that he "tasted death for every man," is expressly declared; and of the sufficiency of the offering there can be no doubt, admitting the declarations of the Scriptures concerning the actual death of that exalted being who is called the Word, who "was in the beginning," who was in glory "with the Father" before the world was. According to the most commonly received views these points about exhaust the subject, it being taken for granted that the death of Christ and the Atonement are the same thing. But they are not identical. True, there can be no atonement without the death of a sacrifice; but there can be the death of the sacrifice without an atonement.

While we have endeavored to vindicate the truth that the death of Christ was vicarious—a truth which we cannot see how any can deny and yet profess to believe the Scriptures—we have avoided using the common term, "vicarious atonement." That which is done by substitution is vicarious; and as Christ makes atonement for others, not for himself, it is also called vicarious. But the word is properly used in a stricter sense, as of substitution only; as that Christ does for us just what the law requires of us. The law requires the life of the transgressor, and Christ died for us; therefore his death was truly vicarious. But the Atonement is the work of his priesthood, and is not embraced within the requirement upon the sinner; for it is something entirely beyond the limit of the sinner's action. A sinner may die for his own sins, and thereby meet the demand of justice; but he is then lost, and we cannot say any atonement is made for him. The action of the priest is not in the sinner's stead, for it is beyond that which the sinner was required or expected to do; and in this restricted sense it is not vicarious, as was the death of Christ. By this it is seen that there is a clear distinction between the death of Christ and the Atonement, and as long as this distinction is lost sight of, so long will the term "vicarious atonement" convey a wrong impression to the mind. Many diverse views of the Atonement exist; and there are many whose views are vague and undefined; and we believe that both confusion and error arise on this subject from a disregard of the above distinction, more than from all other causes combined.

We have seen (pages 127–129) that when a man brought an offering, he was required to lay his hand upon its head; if the people had sinned, the elders of the congregation were required to lay their hands upon the head of the offering; but in every case *the priest made an atonement.* See Lev. 4: 20, 26, 31, 35; 5: 6, 10, 16, 18; 6: 7; 16: 30, 32, and others. "When a ruler hath sinned . . . he shall bring his offering, a kid of the goats, a male without blemish; and he shall lay his hand upon the head of the goat, and kill it in the place where they kill the burnt offering before the Lord; it is a sin offering. . . And the priest shall make an atonement for him." Lev. 4: 22–26. Three things in this work we notice in their order: 1. He shall lay his hand upon the head of the offering. 2. He shall kill it. 3. The priest shall make an atonement. Here it is plainly seen that the killing of the offering and making the atonement are distinct and separate acts; and we shall find that in every case where a sin offering was brought to the priest, he took the blood to make an atonement, according to the word of the Lord: "For the life of the flesh is in the blood; and I have given it to you upon the altar to make an atonement for your souls; for it is the blood that maketh an atonement for the soul." Lev. 17 : 11.

In regard to the ceremony of laying hands upon the head of a sin offering, Rollin, in his remarks on the Religion of the Egyptians, says: "But one common and general ceremony was observed in all sacrifices, viz., the laying of hands upon the head of the victim, loading it at the same time with imprecations, and praying the gods to divert upon that victim all the calamities which might threaten Egypt." Thus we see that the idea of substitutionary sacrifice, or vicarious death, was not confined to the Hebrews, but was recognized wherever the efficacy of sacrifices was acknowledged, which must have been revealed immediately after the fall of man.

Passing over many instances of the use of the word, we turn to Lev. 16, to the prescribed order on the day of atonement, which specially typified the work of our High Priest and Saviour. On the tenth day of the seventh month, the high priest made an atonement for all the people. The Lord fixed it as a statute, "to make an atonement

for the children of Israel, for all their sins once
a year." Verses 29, 34. First, he made an atonement for himself and for his house, that he might
appear sinless before God when he stood for the
people. But this first act did not typify anything
in the work of Christ, for Paul says he was separate from sinners, and therefore need not offer for
himself. Heb. 7 : 26, 27. As the high priest entered the most holy place on the day of atonement, it will be necessary to take a brief view of
the sanctuary to understand this work.

The book of Exodus, commencing with chapter
25, contains an order from the Lord to make him
a sanctuary, with a full description thereof, together with the formula for anointing the priests
and inducting them into their office. The sanctuary was an oblong building, divided into two
parts; the first room was called the holy, which
was entered by a door or vail on the east side.
The second part was called the most holy, which
had no outside entrance, but was entered by a
door or vail at the back or west end of the holy,
called "the second vail." The articles made and
placed in the sanctuary were an ark of wood over-
laid with gold, and a mercy-seat, which was the
cover of the ark. On the mercy-seat were made
two cherubim of gold, their wings shadowing the
mercy-seat. In the ark were placed the testimony, or tables of stone, containing the ten commandments. See Ex. 25 : 16-21; 31 : 18; 1 Kings
8 : 9. The ark was put into the most holy place
of the sanctuary, and was the only article put
therein. In the holy place, or first room, were

the table of show-bread, the golden candlestick, and the altar of incense.

When the commandment was given to make the sanctuary, the object was stated by the Lord, that he might dwell among them. A holy dwelling-place, or dwelling-place of the Lord, is given as the signification of the word sanctuary. In accordance with this design, the Lord said he would meet with the high priest above the mercy-seat, between the wings of the cherubim, there to commune with him of all things that he would give him in commandment unto the children of Israel. Ex. 25 : 22. But by other scriptures we learn that he would meet with them in the most holy place only once a year, on the tenth day of the seventh month, which was the day of atonement.

He promised also to meet with them at the door of the tabernacle of the congregation, or holy place, where there was a continual or daily offering. Ex. 29 : 42, 43; Heb. 9 : 6, 7. Let it be borne in mind that although the glory of God was to abide in the sanctuary, it was manifested only in two places as specified: at the door of the holy where the table and candlestick were set, and in the most holy, above the ark, over the wings of the cherubim. Sometimes the glory of God filled the whole sanctuary; but when that was the case, the priests could not go in to minister. See Ex. 40 : 34, 35; 1 Kings 8 : 10, 11; 2 Chron. 5 : 13, 14; 7 : 1, 2. These few facts are sufficient to guide us in our examination of the atonement; and the reader is requested to ex-

amine them with care, and get them all well fixed
in the mind.

Having made an atonement for himself, the
high priest took two goats from the people, and
cast lots upon them, one to be chosen for a sin
offering, the other for a scape-goat. The goat
upon which the Lord's lot fell was then slain, and
the priest took its blood and went into the sanctuary and sprinkled it upon the mercy-seat and
before the mercy-seat, in that manner making an
atonement for the children of Israel, by *blotting
out their sins and removing them from the presence
of God*. That this was the true idea and intent
of that work, we learn from Lev. 16 : 15–19,
wherein it is not only said that the priest made
atonement for the children of Israel, but that he
also made atonement for the holy places, cleansing
them and hallowing them from the uncleanness
of the children of Israel. The uncleanness or
sins of the children of Israel could never come
directly in contact with the holies of the sanctuary, but only by proxy; for they (the people)
were never permitted to enter there. The priest
was the representative of the people; he bore
their judgment. Ex. 28 : 30. In this manner the
sanctuary of God was defiled; and as the blood
was given to make atonement, the priest *cleansed
the sanctuary* from their sins by sprinkling the
blood upon and before the mercy-seat in the
divine presence. That this process is called the
cleansing of the sanctuary we learn in the plainest
terms from this scripture. We quote as follows:—

"Then shall he kill the goat of the sin offering,

that is for the people, and bring his blood within the vail, and do with that blood as he did with the blood of the bullock, and sprinkle it upon the mercy-seat, and before the mercy-seat. And he shall make an atonement for the holy place [*Heb.*, the sanctuary], because of the uncleanness of the children of Israel, and because of their trans-gressions in all their sins; and so shall he do for the tabernacle of the congregation, that remaineth among them in the midst of their uncleanness. . . . And he shall sprinkle of the blood upon it with his finger seven times, and cleanse it and hallow it from the uncleanness of the children of Israel." Lev. 16:15–19. From this language there can be no appeal.

It has been seen that the sinner brought his offering; that it was slain; and that the priest took the blood and made the atonement; and here it is further established that the atonement was made in the sanctuary. This most clearly proves that the killing of the offering did not make the atonement, but was preparatory to it; for the atonement was made in the sanctuary, but the offering was not slain in the sanctuary.

These things, of course, were typical, and have their fulfillment in the work of the Lord Jesus Christ, the Son of God. That he is a High Priest, and the only mediator in the gospel, will be readily admitted; but the order and manner of his service must be determined by the Scriptures. The apos-tle states that he is a priest after the order of Melchisedec, that is, a kingly priest, on the throne of the Majesty in the Heavens, a minister of the sanctuary and true tabernacle which the Lord pitched, and not man. Heb. 8:1. Of course this is the antitype of the earthly sanctuary, of the tabernacle pitched or made by man. He also affirms that if he were on earth, he would not be a priest for the evident reason that the priests of the earthly sanctuary were of the tribe of Levi, while our Lord sprang out of Judah, of which tribe Moses spake nothing concerning priesthood, and of which no man gave attendance at the altar. Heb. 7:13, 14; 8:4. This will correct a mistake very often made, that the priesthood of our Lord commenced on earth. If he had entered on the work of his priesthood at his baptism, as has been said, he would have acted with those who were types of himself; and if as a priest he had officiated in the temple, it would have been to make offerings typical of his own.

That Christ was a "prophet, priest, and king," many of us have learned from our early childhood; but comparatively few ever learn the true relation these offices sustain to each other. He was "that prophet" while on earth; and Paul's testimony given above shows that he filled no other office. Many suppose that his priesthood is connected with that kingdom which is given to him as the Son of David. But this is utterly forbidden by plain Scripture declarations. Aaron had no kingship, and David had no priesthood; and Christ is not a priest after the order of Aaron (Heb. 7:11), so is he not a king on the throne of David (*i. e.*, during his priesthood). It is "after the order of Melchisedec," who was both king and priest, that Christ is a priest on his Father's throne. At different times, he occupies two different thrones (See Rev. 3:21); and the throne of his Father in Heaven, which he now occupies as priest, "he shall have delivered up" at his coming. 1 Cor. 15:23–28. Then, in subjection to his Father, he will take his own throne, called also the throne of David, on which he will reign forever—without end. Luke 1:32, 33. But then he will no more be a priest, his priesthood being altogether on the throne he now occupies. The reader is requested to examine these points carefully, as a misunderstanding of them has given rise to much confusion in the "theological world."

Having shown the distinction between the earthly and heavenly sanctuaries, Paul proceeds to set forth the relation which the ministrations in each sustain to the other, saying of the priests on earth: "Who serve unto the example and shadow of heavenly things." Heb. 8:5. As the earthly is the shadow and example, we may compare it with the heavenly, the substance, by which we may gain a clearer idea of the latter than is afforded us by any other means. Indeed, the comparison is made to our hand by the apostle. Note the following text, in which the distinction here claimed between the death of Christ and his work as priest to make atonement, is clearly recognized: "For the bodies of those beasts *whose blood is brought into the sanctuary by the high priest for sin*, are burned without the camp. Wherefore Jesus also, that he might sanctify the people with his own blood, *suffered without the gate.*" Heb.

13 : 11, 12. Thus we learn definitely that, as priest, he makes atonement; but his priesthood is not on earth, but in the sanctuary in Heaven; and that he did not suffer in the sanctuary where atonement is made. It *was not* necessary, in the type, for the priest to slay the offering (see Lev. 1 : 4, 5); but it *was* necessary for the priest to take the blood and with it enter the sanctuary of the Lord to make an atonement. Jesus did not shed his blood as priest; it was shed by sinners. But he did by "his own blood" enter "into the holy places" not made with hands, of which the earthly were figures, "to appear in the presence of God for us." Heb. 9 : 12, 24.

We might quote much to show the prevalence of the error, that the Atonement was made on the cross, but that is not necessary. The "Manual of the Atonement," from which we have before quoted, says:—

"When he had completed his mediatorial work, he meekly yielded himself up into the hands of his heavenly Father, saying, 'Into thy hands I commit my spirit.'"

So far from his "mediatorial work" being completed when he was on the cross, it had not yet commenced. The mediatorial work is the work of the priest, which he had not entered upon when he died. Paul says he entered into Heaven "by his own blood," "now to appear in the presence of God for us." But if his mediatorial work was completed when he was on earth, even before his death, as the above quotation would have it, then he cannot be a mediator now! and all that the Scriptures say of his priesthood on the throne of his Father in Heaven, there making intercession for us, is incomprehensible or erroneous.

By thus confounding the sacrifice or death of Christ with the Atonement, the latter is supposed to be a general work, made for all mankind. With this we cannot agree. That Christ died for all, is distinctly stated, but we have seen that that was only preparatory to the Atonement, and it is in the Atonement that application is made of the blood to the full removal of sin. This is shown also in the type. The goat of the sin offering was slain for the people, and, of course, was offered to meet the wants of all; but while the priest made the atonement, they were required to "afflict their souls," or come as humble penitents before the Lord, and whosoever did not should be cut off from among the people. Lev. 16:29; 23:27-29. This, then, was required of them individually, in that day, in order that their sins might be atoned for by the priest; for we cannot suppose that *they* would be cut off whose sins were actually blotted out, or removed from the presence of the judge, by the blood of the offering with which the sanctuary was cleansed from sin.

The same is also taught by Peter, who says that God exalted Jesus, who was slain, to be a prince and Saviour, to grant repentance and forgiveness of sins. Acts 5:30, 31. Now that "he died for all" there can be no question; and his death is absolute and without condition. But not so the Atonement; for Peter says again, "Repent ye, therefore, and be converted, *that your sins may be blotted out*, when the times of refreshing shall come from the presence of the Lord," &c.   Acts 3 : 19.   We have found that, when the priest made the atonement, he took the blood and cleansed the sanctuary of God from the sins wherewith it had been defiled; and this is the only act which will answer to the expression of blotting out the sins, for blood was the only thing that would remove them.   Hence, while the blood of Christ was shed for all, the efficacy of that blood in atoning for, or blotting out, sin, is contingent, it availing only for those who will repent and be converted.   He died for the world—he died for all; and he is able to save to the uttermost *them that come unto God by him*.   Heb. 7 : 25.   But he will save no others.

Another cause of confusion is this, that reconciliation and the Atonement are often supposed to be the same; and where the distinction is recognized their relation is not always observed, a disregard of which tends to about the same result as a denial of the distinction.   Thus it has been said: "The Atonement may exist without reconciliation, but reconciliation cannot exist without the Atonement."   This is exactly the reverse of the true order, and the error is the result of confounding the death of the offering with the Atonement.   It is quite true that reconciliation has the Atonement in view, but it must precede the Atonement.   The death of Christ opens the way for reconciliation to all, but no one can have his sins actually atoned for or blotted out who rejects the offering of Christ, or who is not reconciled to God.

It is admitted that there is a close relation between the two; but nearness of relation does not argue identity. The death of Christ, the offering of his blood, opens the way for reconciliation. Reconciliation secures an interest in the Atonement; and this in turn is made with the blood previously shed. The offering of Christ is the corner-stone of the whole work, for " without the shedding of blood there is no remission." It is for this reason that we are so constantly directed to the cross of Christ. Without this, there could be neither reconciliation nor atonement. But that the relation and order of the work is as we here state, namely, that his death, and reconciliation through his blood, look forward to his priestly work of atonement, is proved by the words of Paul in Rom. 5:10. "For if when we were enemies, we were reconciled to God by the death of his Son, much more, being reconciled, we shall be saved by his life." Reconciliation first; salvation as the result.

Two views are held by different classes of theologians on the subject of reconciliation. One, that reconciliation is on the part of man only; the other, that reconciliation is mutual—that God is reconciled to man as well as man to God. It very frequently happens that controversy arises between men from a misapprehension of each other's meaning, and this is doubtless much the case on this subject. If it be shown that reconciliation must be on the part of an enemy or of the offending party only, then the first-named

13

view is correct. But if by reconciliation is also meant that the justice of God must be appeased in behalf of the offender, the last view is the true one. We might say that both are correct, according to the two constructions put upon the word; and reasons can be given for both, as most words allow of different shades of meaning. On this subject Dr. Barnes makes a very strange statement. He says:—

"Reconciliation is in fact produced between God and man by the atonement. God *becomes* the friend of the pardoned sinner."—*Atonement, p. 268.*

Passing over his reversion of the actual order, we remark that this is equivalent to saying that God is not the friend, but the enemy, of the sinner before he is pardoned. But how, then, is pardon effected? The Saviour said that "God so loved the world that he gave his only begotten Son." Did he, as our enemy, love us? as our enemy, give his Son to die for us? was he, as our enemy, in Christ, reconciling us to himself? and does he, as our enemy, pardon us? and does he only *become* our friend after he has pardoned us? Now as Dr. Barnes was what is termed a "representative man," it would be natural for any one, on reading such remarks from him, to judge that the doctrine itself was absurd.

While it is beyond denial that God loved the world and gave his Son to die for the world, it is equally true, and very evident, that *the death of Christ does not take anything from our actual guilt.* We are as deserving of punishment as if he had never died. And, if we are not reconciled to God; if we do not so accept the offering of Christ as to appropriate it as our own, and to cease our violations of the divine law, that offering avails nothing for us. The justice of God stands arrayed against us as really as if his Son had never died. His death is an offering to the divine law—a vindication of the integrity and justice of the divine Government, but not so as to make our pardon inconsistent with free grace. Andrew Fuller, the eminent Baptist author, says:—

"Free grace, according to Paul, requires a *propitiation*, even the shedding of the Saviour's *blood*, as a medium through which it may be honorably communicated."

And again, speaking of sacrifices for sin, he says:—

"All agree in the idea of the displeasure of the Deity being *appeasable* by an innocent victim being sacrificed in the place of the guilty."

This must be the correct idea. The justice or displeasure of the Deity is rendered *appeasable* by the sacrifice, but is really *appeased* by the mediation of our High Priest. If reconciliation may be used in this sense, then our version of Eze. 16:63 may be allowable: "And I will establish my covenant with thee; and thou shalt know that I am the Lord; that thou mayest remember, and be confounded, and never open thy mouth any more because of thy shame, when I am *pacified* toward thee for all that thou hast done, saith the Lord God." Though we think it would admit of a translation somewhat different, we see no reason for objecting to this, considering that God's justice must be appeased (pacified); in other places represented as the turning away of his anger from the violator of his law.

We have no disposition to find fault with the "Authorized Version," that is, the commonly received translation, of the Scriptures. We have great reason to be thankful for it, and for the great blessing it has proved to the world. But all must admit that it has defects, and these are in some cases of such a nature as to obscure a truth which might be made plain by a more judicious rendering. On the subject before us we must commend the Revised Version of the New Testament as giving much the clearer view. Thus, in Rom. 5 : 11, the A. V. translates *katallagee*, atonement, which is incorrect. The Revision properly renders it, reconciliation. In Heb. 2 : 17, the A. V. renders *hilaskomai*, to make reconciliation, which is also incorrect. The Revision renders it, propitiation; it might properly be rendered, atonement. Whiting's Translation so renders it. Other translations agree with the Revision in both texts. In both Testaments the reader will find some difficulty in understanding this subject if guided by the translation only, as it is not always easy to express the various shades of meaning in a translation; and in this matter it appears evident that the translators of the A. V. did not closely mark distinctions which clearly exist. As evidence of this, we notice that the word "atonement" occurs but once in this version of the New Testament, Rom. 5 : 11, and there by a mistranslation, as has been noticed. Neither it nor its relative, expiation, properly occurs in the version. But the fact, the thing expressed by these terms is referred to directly by the writers of the New Testament. Nothing but a careful study of the Levitical law can give us a clear understanding of the doctrine. It is for this reason, as we believe, that the closing words of the Old Testament, in a prophecy referring to the very last times of the present dispensation, say, "Remember the law of Moses." The law of Moses gives us a faithful "pattern," or "shadow and example" of the work of our High Priest in Heaven, so important for us to understand who live in the time when his work is soon to close, and his coming is near, to save all "who look for him," and to take vengeance upon them who know not God and obey not the gospel. Heb. 9 : 28; 2 Thess. 1 : 7–10.

Whatever may be thought of the application of the word "reconciliation," all must admit that there is a vast difference in the position of the parties. Man is a rebel, an enemy to his Maker. God, though he loves man in his ruined condition, is a just Governor. His love can certainly go no farther, and grant no more, than justice can permit. Justice must be *appeased;* and while *the offering makes it possible to pardon* consistent with justice, it leaves us guilty, worthy of the condemnation under which we rest. A complete vindication of the righteousness of the law is found in the sacrifice of the Son of God; but, as concerns the sinner, personally, he rests under condemnation still, until the mediation of Christ brings him into such harmonious relations with the divine Government that it will not endanger its principles, nor reflect dishonor upon the Governor, to freely forgive him and take him back into his favor.

When we consider that the sacrifice is the means whereby the Atonement is made, we can readily understand how *hilasmos* is used in 1 John 2:2, defined by Liddell & Scott, a means of appeasing, an expiatory sacrifice. Jesus Christ is the propitiation—the sacrifice to divine justice, for all. It is by means of his intercession, his pleading his blood, that probation is given and mercy offered to the whole world.

But it cannot too often be pressed upon the mind of the impenitent that probation, and the offer of mercy through the blood of Christ which was shed for all, does not secure the salvation of all. Says David, "Blessed is he whose transgression is forgiven, whose sin is covered. Blessed is the man unto whom the Lord imputeth not iniquity." Ps. 32:1, 2. This blessing does not come upon all, but it is placed within the reach of all by the death of Christ. And whose sins will be covered? Evidently theirs who have confessed and forsaken their sins, or who have been reconciled to God. This is exactly the order of the work described by Peter in Acts 3:19. "Repent ye, therefore, and be converted, that your sins may be blotted out when the times of refreshing shall come from the presence of the Lord." This blotting out is by the blood which the High Priest brings into the sanctuary to cleanse it from sin. We cannot, for a moment, suppose that the sin of any will be blotted out or covered, who still maintains his opposition and enmity to God; but he who confesses and forsakes shall find mercy; that is, he who is reconciled shall have his sins forgiven and blotted out. "If we confess our sins, he is faithful and just to forgive us our sins, and to cleanse us from all unrighteousness." 1 John 1:9. "He that covereth his sins shall not prosper; but whoso confesseth and forsaketh them shall have mercy." Prov. 28:13.

As the work of the high priest under the law in making atonement for all the people, was but the work of one day, a short time compared to the continual work of intercession, and that day clearly specified, so is the atonement by our High Priest, Jesus Christ, in the antitype. It is accomplished just before his second coming. If this be made to appear it will be another and a strong proof that reconciliation is distinct from it, and must precede it. But this will be examined in a separate chapter.

CHAPTER VIII.

THERE are no isolated, independent truths in the great plan of salvation, even as there is no special "saving" duty in Christian life. It takes the sum of all the graces to make a perfect Christian character; and so also it takes all the truths and doctrines of the gospel to make the one complete system of salvation. The great foundation of the whole is the sacrifice of Christ; the shedding of his blood for the sins of the world. Heb. 9:22. To us belongs reconciliation through his death. Rom. 5:10; 2 Cor. 5:20. As the work of the priests under the law only reached its ultimate object when the high priest went into the most holy place with the blood of the sin offering, and cleansed the sanctuary of God from the sins of the people, so the result of the gospel of remission is fully accomplished, not by the death of the sacrifice; not by our repentance and reconciliation to God; but, by the action of our great High Priest, who appears in the presence of God for us; in blotting out our sins and removing them forever from the presence of the throne of the Most High.

The subject of the Judgment may be considered a continuation of the subject of the preceding chapter, namely, the Atonement. The word "Judgment" may, however, cover or include much more than the word "Atonement." The latter has to do solely with the people of God, for the Atonement is made only for those who are reconciled to God by the death of his Son; whereas the Judgment has to do with all mankind, for "God shall bring every work into judgment, with every secret thing, whether it be good, or whether it be evil." But the subject of this chapter is not thus extensive, as it will be confined to the judgment of the righteous.

The prevailing ideas of the Judgment are vague and indefinite. Probably a majority, certainly many, look upon it in the following light: That the Lord shall appear in the clouds of heaven; that all the dead, both the righteous and the wicked, will be raised, and the Judgment will then sit upon the whole human race. Another view, and a popular one, is that each one is judged immediately after death. Both these views are forbidden by the Scriptures, which say that the saints shall judge the world, 1 Cor. 6:2, and that God hath appointed a day in which the Judgment shall take place. Acts 17:31; see also 2 Peter 2:9, and 3:10. Now it is not reasonable to suppose that the saints will judge the world in their present state, or previous to the time when themselves are judged. The following from Bliss' review of Prof. Bush on the Resurrection is more reasonable and scriptural than the views which are generally entertained:—

"We are inclined to the opinion that the judgment is after death, and before the resurrection; and that before that event the acts of all men will be adjudicated; so that the resurrection of the righteous is their full acquittal and redemption

—their sins being blotted out when the times of refreshing shall have come (Acts 3:19); while the fact that the wicked are not raised proves that they were previously condemned."

Eld. Josiah Litch, in a work entitled "Prophetic Expositions," said:—

"The trial must precede the execution. This is so clear a proposition that it is sufficient to state it. . . . But the resurrection is the retribution or execution of judgment, for they that have done good shall come forth to the resurrection of life. . . . There can be no general Judgment or trial after the resurrection. The resurrection is the separating process, and they will never be commingled again after the saints are raised, no matter how long or short the period to elapse between the two resurrections."

That the judgment of the saints is fully accomplished while the Saviour is in the sanctuary in Heaven, before his coming, and therefore before the resurrection, is evident; for (1) Their judgment must be closed while Jesus is their advocate, that he may procure their acquittal. And (2) They are raised immortal, which is the evidence of their acquittal. The judgment of the wicked must be subsequent to the redemption of the righteous (for the saints will take part in that transaction; see 1 Cor. 6:1–3), and yet previous to the second resurrection. It is quite reasonable to consider that the wicked are merely rejected while Christ is a priest, their cases being passed over for future consideration; indeed, this is the only view that will harmonize all Scripture; and as the resurrection of the righteous to immortality and eternal life is the announcement of the *decision* of the judgment to them, so the wicked are raised to condemnation and the second death, which is the *execution* of the judgment before determined in regard to them.

While none would deny the typical nature of the sacrifices and the work of the priests under the Levitical law, there are few, comparatively who ever trace the subject to its logical conclusion. By this we would not have any understand that we favor that system of speculation which holds it necessary to find a spiritual meaning in every loop and fold, every pin and tenon of the tabernacle. Such a system of interpretation subverts the truth by leading into a field of conjecture which is always unprofitable, and has a tendency to turn away the mind from the things which are plainly revealed. What we do mean is this: There are few who endeavor to learn all that the type teaches of the antitype as presented in the words of the Scriptures. The New Testament gives some very clear explanations of the types; but these are often overlooked, especially by those who disregard the plain declarations of the word, and are only satisfied when the words of the Scriptures are "spiritualized." And this spiritualizing process becomes a pleasing one, because it gives license to the imagination, and each investigator feels at liberty to put that construction upon the sacred text which best suits him. But what a sad use is this to make of Heaven's message to fallen man!

In a careful study of the book of Revelation we have found that a knowledge of certain other portions of the Bible is indispensable to an understanding of many of its symbols. These are, the law of Moses, the prophecy of Daniel, and Paul's letter to the Hebrews. Or we may say, which amounts to the same thing in fact, that a solution of the types in the law of Moses is found in the study of the prophecy of Daniel, the letter to the Hebrews, and the book of Revelation.

It has been noticed that, although the work of the priests was "continual," or daily, in the holy place, which may properly be considered an intercessory work, the atonement was the work of *an appointed day*, occupying but a short period of the yearly service. And when this work was completed,—when the sanctuary was "cleansed and hallowed from the uncleanness of the children of Israel," Lev. 16 : 19, then the people stood acquitted; then the high priest put their sins upon the head of the scape-goat, and they were borne far away from the camp; then the high priest could pronounce the heavenly benediction upon the waiting people of God, who had "afflicted their souls" before the sanctuary. As Kitto says: "On this day the high priest gave his blessing to the whole nation." The work of this day was not for a few individuals; it was for the nation,— for the whole people of Israel.

This was a type of the "day of Judgment" for God's people. We have been informed by learned Jews that they looked upon it in this light; they considered it their day of Judgment. The Talmudists say: "Penitence itself makes atonement for slight transgressions; and in the case of grosser sins it obtains a respite until the coming of the day of atonement, which completes the reconciliation."

As that day was appointed, announced, and well known to all the people, so is provision made in the antitype that God's people may understand their true relation to the great day of atonement. In Rev. 14 : 6, 7 is presented one of the most interesting and important proclamations found in the sacred word. It reads as follows:—

"And I saw another angel fly in the midst of heaven, having the everlasting gospel to preach unto them that dwell on the earth, and to every nation, and kindred, and tongue, and people, saying with a loud voice, Fear God, and give glory to him, for THE HOUR OF HIS JUDGMENT IS COME; and worship him that made heaven, and earth, and the sea, and the fountains of waters."

Related to the fact of this proclamation are several points of great interest to the student of the Bible.

1. By reading the chapter we discover that this message is given *before the second advent*, and during the probation of man. Verse 8 makes an announcement concerning Babylon, which is supplemented by another on the same subject in chapter 18. In verses 9–12 of chapter 14 is given yet another message, containing a most solemn warning against false worship, and a call to keep the commandments of God and the faith of Jesus. Of course this message is given before the close

of probation. In verses 14–20 the second advent of Christ, the Son of man, is presented, together with the object of his coming—to reap the harvest of the earth,—and a description of the terrible fate of those who are not his. Compare 2 Thess. 1:7–10. This is in perfect harmony with the view that is presented in these pages, that the Judgment must precede the resurrection; and this, the resurrection, takes place at Christ's appearing. 1 Cor. 15:51–54; 1 Thess. 4:13–18.

2. We say that the Judgment precedes the resurrection, but it does not follow that all the saints will be in the grave when the judgment of the righteous takes place; for some are found keeping the commandments of God and the faith of Jesus —that is, they are heeding the warning of the "third angel"—when Christ appears. And Paul says that "we shall not all sleep;" that some will be "alive and remain" at the coming of the Lord. Of course their judgment takes place while they are living; for as the sleeping saints are raised immortal, proving that they have been fully acquitted in the great assize above, so the living saints at that time will be changed, translated, "in a moment, in the twinkling of an eye." Upon them, in the same instant, will be conferred the same immortality which is given to the resurrected saints.

3. In Rev. 11:15–18 is shown that the dead are judged—not through the whole dispensation, but—under the sounding of the seventh trumpet. This is the last of a series of trumpets covering the whole period of the gospel dispensation.

Under this trumpet the dead are judged, and reward is given to the saints. Compare Matt. 16: 27; Luke 14 : 14; Rev. 22 : 12. Under this trumpet are destroyed the wicked—those who corrupt the earth. See 2 Peter 2 : 9. Under this trumpet Christ receives dominion over the kingdoms of the earth, which is given at the close of his priestly work on his Father's throne. Please read Ps. 2 : 6–9; 110 : 1; Heb. 10 : 12, 13.

4. This message of Rev. 14 : 6, 7 is called "the everlasting gospel," though it is different from any proclamation made in the ministry of Christ and his apostles. Paul reasoned of judgment to come; Acts 24 : 25; he said God has appointed a day in which he will judge the world. Acts 17 : 31. He did not and could not say that that day was then present—that it had come.

5. Yet it is not "another gospel," but an essential part of the same gospel which they preached; a part which could not be preached in their day, as the Judgment had not then yet come. In further proof of this, compare Isa. 61 with the facts of the New Testament. The first two verses of that chapter of the prophecy read thus:—

"The Spirit of the Lord God is upon me; because the Lord hath anointed me to preach good tidings unto the meek; he hath sent me to bind up the broken-hearted, to proclaim liberty to the captives, and the opening of the prison to them that are bound; to proclaim the acceptable year of the Lord, and the day of vengeance of our God; to comfort all that mourn," etc.

Jesus went to Nazareth, and, "as his custom

was," he went into the synagogue on the Sabbath day, and stood up for to read. The book of the prophet Isaiah being given to him he turned to chapter 61, as the book is now divided, and read the words quoted above as far as to the sentence, "to proclaim the acceptable year of the Lord," and abruptly stopped, not reading the words which follow—"and the day of vengeance of our God." As Christ sat down, he said to the people assembled: "This day is this scripture fulfilled in your ears." That day the acceptable year, or season, or time, of the Lord was preached to them. Paul made the same declaration in 2 Cor. 6 : 2: "Behold, now is the accepted time; behold, now is the day of salvation." This was as far as Jesus could read in the prophecy and say it was fulfilled in their ears; this was all that the apostle could declare. The "time accepted" (2 Cor. 6 : 1) had come; it could be then proclaimed; the day of vengeance—the day of Judgment—had not come; it had to be reserved for a future proclamation. See our text, Rev. 14 : 6, 7.

The day of vengeance is equivalent to the day of Judgment, for men are not only judged in that day, but in that day rewards are given to all. Rev. 11 : 18 says the dead are judged and reward given to the saints in that time; 2 Peter 3 : 7 calls it "the day of judgment and perdition of ungodly men." This earth is reserved unto fire against that day. As "the day of salvation" or "the accepted time" has now continued nearly two thousand years, so "the day of Judgment" is a period more than one thousand years in length—

how much more is not revealed,—covering the judgment of investigation of the cases of all the righteous, and the giving of reward to them; followed by the further investigation of the cases of the wicked (in which the saints take part, 1 Cor. 6:1-3; Rev. 20:1-4), and their final overthrow or entire destruction.

There are two thoughts, of solemn importance which present themselves on this subject:—

(1) This message must be given before the second coming of Christ. If it were not given, then the Scriptures would fail; the word of the Lord thus far would not be fulfilled. But sooner would heaven and earth pass away than one jot fail of the word of the Lord. Many prophecies point to the fulfillment of this message. See the following:—

"Blow ye the trumpet in Zion, *sound an alarm* in my holy mountain; let all the inhabitants of the land [or the earth] tremble, for the day of the Lord cometh, for it is nigh at hand. A day of darkness and of gloominess, a day of clouds and of thick darkness, as the morning spread upon the mountains." Joel 2:1, 2.

Other scriptures to the same intent might be quoted, confirming the truth that a warning will be given to the world before the day of the Lord, or the time of the Judgment, commences.

(2) As this warning is called "the everlasting gospel," being a part of the gospel which the Saviour was anointed to preach, *it must be heeded.* It makes not a particle of difference when or by whom it is proclaimed; for whosoever proclaims

14

it does it under Heaven's sanction and super-
vision. That it will be opposed, and even by the
professed servants of Christ, is also a matter of
prophecy. The "evil servant" will say, "My
Lord delayeth his coming." But he cannot stay
the message of warning, nor hinder the coming
of that day. His opposition will only work ruin
to his own soul, for Jesus said: "The Lord of
that servant shall come in a day when he looketh
not for him, and in an hour that he is not aware
of, and shall cut him asunder, and appoint him
his portion with the hypocrites." It will avail
him nothing that he has been called as a servant
of the Lord, or that he has confessed or claimed
that the Lord is his Lord. The prophecy is given
by inspiration, and he who turns away from it
or neglects it does so at his own peril.

But, in order to sound the alarm effectively,
or to so proclaim "the hour of his Judgment is
come" that it shall produce the desired result,
they who preach it must be able to determine
when it is timely; when the proclamation ought
to be made. If they could not know, the trumpet
would give an uncertain sound, if, indeed, it were
sounded at all.

In the prophecy of Daniel are three chains
of prophetic symbols, each giving information
whereby we may know when the end is near.
In chapter 2 is the image seen by Nebuchadnezzar
in his dream, which gives a brief history of the
great kingdoms of the world from the time of
Babylon to the dividing or breaking up of the
Roman Empire. In chapter 7 is a series of sym-

bols consisting of wild beasts, which covers exactly the same ground as that of chapter 2, but supplementing that chapter with later events, reaching down to the very close of the eighteenth century. The same symbols are presented in Rev. 13, with still later events, reaching down to the last message, and the advent of the Lord. Compare Rev. 13:11–18 with chapter 14:9–14. By studying these prophecies, and the history of the nations which shows the progress of their fulfillment, we may learn definitely where we are in the chain of events which reaches down to the coming of the Lord. True, we cannot tell how long it will take to complete the fulfillment; we cannot learn from the prophecies the time of the Lord's coming; but we may learn from these, and also from other scriptures, when "he is near, even at the doors," as Jesus himself has given assurance in his own words. Matt. 24.

Another series of symbols is given in the 8th chapter of Daniel, and to this we must give more particular attention. It relates more particularly to our subject than do the others, and the interpretation is given in plain and unmistakable terms The first symbol is a ram having two horns; this was explained by Gabriel to mean the kingdom of the Medes and Persians. Verse 20. The ram was succeeded by a he-goat, having a notable horn between his eyes. When that was broken four horns came up for it, and these in turn were succeeded by a little horn which "waxed exceeding great." It became stronger than all the king dcms which preceded it. And of this Gabriel said: "And the rough goat is the king [kingdom] of Grecia, and the great horn that is between his eyes is the first king [Alexander]. Now that being broken, whereas four stood up for it, four kingdoms shall stand up out of the nation, but not in his power." Grecia was divided into four kingdoms upon the death of Alexander. But a power came up, small in its beginning, which conquered the world and held all in its iron grasp. The Persian and Grecian Empires appear before us, great by sudden conquest. Not so with Rome. She gradually became exceeding great by successive conquests. It was this power that "magnified himself even to the prince of the host" of heaven; verses 10–12; or stood up against the Prince of princes. Verse 25.

Daniel said he heard one holy one ask another how long this vision should be, even "to give both the sanctuary and the host to be trodden under foot." The answer is made to Daniel in these words: "Unto two thousand and three hundred days; then shall the sanctuary be cleansed." Now it has been seen, by Lev. 16, that the cleansing of the sanctuary, and making the atonement, mean precisely the same thing; for the atonement was made by the high priest sprinkling the blood upon the mercy-seat and altar, and cleansing them from the sins of the people. Hence, this expression of Dan. 8:14 is equivalent to saying, "Unto two thousand and three hundred days, then shall the atonement be made." And again, to understand this time is to understand the fulfillment of the message of Rev. 14:6, 7, "the hour of his judgment is come," for the Judgment sits when the Atonement is made. Thus we see *that the time was appointed and announced for making the Atonement.* This is in conformity to the type, where the tenth day of the seventh month was set apart to that work. While this text stands as a part of that "scripture" which is "profitable for instruction," it is both interesting and profitable to inquire where these two thousand and three hundred days terminate. But to understand this, we must trace the connection between chapters 8 and 9 of Daniel; for chapter 9 is in part explanatory of chapter 8, the explanation of the time (2300 days) being given in the latter, not in the former. Note the following points:—

1. Gabriel was commanded to make Daniel understand the vision.

2. He explained in chapter 8 the symbols of the kingdoms represented therein.

3. He did not explain the time of verse 14.

4. Daniel said he did not understand the vision, which, of course, refers to that part not explained —the time.

5. In chapter 9, Gabriel said he had come to give him understanding, and commanded him to "consider the vision."

6. No vision had been mentioned since chapter 8, which shows that Gabriel had reference to the same vision which he was commanded to make him understand in that chapter.

7. In chapter 9, he commenced instructing Daniel on *time,* the only thing in the "vision" not hitherto explained.

8. He said, Seventy weeks are determined (Heb. literally *cut off*) upon thy people.

9. The seventy weeks commence with the commandment to restore and build Jerusalem, B. C. 457. See Ezra 7.

10. The seventy weeks are evidently "cut off" from the 2300 days, the only period given in the vision. Therefore the time of the going forth of the commandment to restore and build Jerusalem must be the commencement of the 2300 days. And if the seventy weeks are not cut off from the 2300 days, that is, if the seventy weeks do not mark the beginning of those days, then no explanation of the days was given, and Gabriel never did what he was commanded to do. But such a supposition will not be urged. Therefore, we must admit that in Dan. 9 we have a clue to the 2300 days of Dan. 8, and to understand the seventy weeks of Dan. 9, is also to understand the 2300 days of Dan. 8, the two periods commencing together.

In regard to the nature of these "days" no argument can be needed. The "seventy weeks" of Dan. 9, marking the manifestation of the Messiah, which took place at the time of his baptism, see Matt. 3:16, 17; John 1:32–34; Mark 1:14, 15, were not weeks of days, but weeks of years. To deny this were to unsettle one of the clearest evidences in favor of the Messiahship of Jesus of Nazareth. But as the seventy weeks are part of the 2300 days of the vision of Dan. 8, those "days" were not solar days of twenty-four hours, but year-days, "each day for a year," according to a well-known method of counting time. Eze. 4:6.

As the Messiah was to be cut off, and cause the sacrifice and oblation to cease in the midst of the last week of the seventy, which was in A. D. 31, and the time that the apostles turned to the Gentiles marks the close of that period, which was in A. D. 34, it is easy to see that the 2300 days would extend 1810 years beyond that time, or to A. D. 1844. And as the angel said the sanctuary should be cleansed at the end of that period, this must refer, not to the typical sanctuary which was destroyed by the Romans in A. D. 70, but to the antitypical "sanctuary and true tabernacle, which the Lord pitched, and not man." Heb. 8:1, 2.

Some are ready to object to this view, that the heavenly sanctuary where our High Priest officiates cannot need cleansing—that there is nothing impure in Heaven. The zeal of such to vindicate the honor of heavenly things is parallel with that of Peter, who rebuked the Lord for speaking of his ignominious death; he thought a victor's crown only was becoming his Master. But God has a plan appointed, and the death of his Son was in that plan; and the mistaken zeal of his servants must not be suffered to interfere with it. In that plan is also the Atonement which God's now exalted Son as priest makes in the sanctuary in Heaven; and it has been sufficiently shown that the Atonement is made by cleansing the sanctuary. That this expression of the angel refers to the heavenly, and not to the earthly, sanctuary, may be proved by several considerations. The following we think is conclusive on this point.

1. The sanctuary was not cleansed from any impurity of its own, nor from any defilement from use, as ordinary habitations are cleansed, but from sin. Therefore it was cleansed by blood. By referring further to Lev. 16, it will be seen, and will be noticed hereafter, that the design was to take away the sins from the presence of God, and remove them from the throne of judgment. But Paul declares in Heb. 10:4, that "it is not possible for the blood of bulls and of goats to take away sin;" but that was all the blood the priests had to offer in the worldly sanctuary; therefore, as that blood would not remove sin, it follows that *the earthly sanctuary was never cleansed at all,* except in figure, and never could have been had it remained and the priests still officiated therein till the end of the 2300 days. Nevertheless, the necessity existed; for the people were actual sinners, and needed to have their sins remitted or blotted out.

2. The sanctuary, as before noticed, was defiled by the sins of the people, though the people never came in contact with it. The high priest stood as their representative; he bore their judgment. Ex. 28:30. And as he alone went into the most holy place, it follows that it was defiled by his bearing their sins. Now it is plainly stated that Christ bears our sins—they were laid upon him— he is our representative before his Father. And it seems evident that one of the following positions is true: That Christ has taken the sins of

his people, or his people have their sins yet upon them. It will be admitted that the former is true; that as the representative and substitute of his saints, he takes their sins. But if he takes them, where does he take them? Certainly where he is. Now it is by virtue of his priesthood that he bears the judgment of the people; but his priesthood is in the heavenly sanctuary. Heb. 8:1-4. There, according to the type, is where our sins are taken. To show this is the object of the type.

3. That the heavenly sanctuary is cleansed, is proved by direct declarations of the New Testament. Paul, in writing to the Hebrews respecting the types and their fulfillment in the priesthood of the Son of God, says: "It was therefore necessary that the patterns of things in the Heavens should be purified with these [*i. e.*, with the blood of calves and goats]; but the heavenly things themselves with better sacrifices than these." Heb. 9:23. Accordingly he says that Christ entered into the holy places, into Heaven itself, "by his own blood." Verse 12. This is the better sacrifice, or blood, by which the heavenly things are purified or cleansed.

This point being settled, another question arises: Are there two holy places in the heavenly sanctuary? and if so, did not Christ enter the most holy when he ascended on high? In answer to this notice,

1. When Moses was about to make the tabernacle, he was admonished to make all things according to the pattern shown him in the mount. Heb. 8:5; Ex. 25:40.

2. This tabernacle and its officers served "unto the example and shadow of heavenly things." Heb. 8 : 5.

3. The two holy places in the earthly sanctuary are termed "figures of the true" [holy places], and pattern of things in the Heavens. And they could not be patterns of the heavenly. and be made in "all things according to the pattern" shown to Moses, unless the heavenly had also two holy places.

4. That there are two holy places in the heavenly temple is shown by the book of Revelation, in which prophecy has unfolded various events in this dispensation immediately concerning the position and work of our High Priest.

When the living creature (one of the cherubim) called John up "in the Spirit" into Heaven, he said he saw a throne set, and described its appearance, and him that sat thereon; and said there were seven lamps of fire burning before the throne. Rev. 4 : 2–5. The order given to Moses, in erecting the earthly sanctuary, was to set the candlestick with its seven lamps on the south side of the door of the tabernacle of the congregation, which was the holy place. Ex. 29 : 33–35; 40 : 24. As this was a shadow and example of heavenly things, we learn by this text in the book of Revelation, that John's vision of the throne of God was in the holy place of the heavenly temple. where were the seven lamps of fire or golden candlestick. Therein the Lord said he would manifest his presence; Ex. 29 : 42, 43; and there was our Saviour at the time of John's vision, officiating as priest. In this, a continual or daily offering was made, that judgment might be stayed, and the sinner spared, until the time of the cleansing of the sanctuary, or making atonement, which was the blotting out and entire removal of sin from the sanctuary of God. According to the type, this work of propitiation or intercession the Saviour had first to fulfill, in order to give man an opportunity to be reconciled to God, or converted, that his sins might be blotted out in the appointed time.

But we look down the stream of time still further; when the dispensation is drawing to a close, and the seventh trumpet is sounded.* The third woe comes upon the earth, and great voices are heard saying, the kingdoms of this world are become the kingdoms of our Lord and his Christ; the elders before the throne of God announce that "the nations were angry, and thy wrath is come, and the time of the dead that they should be judged, and that thou shouldest give reward unto thy servants the prophets, and them that fear thy name, small and great." Rev. 11:15–17. Here is a series of events, the connection and location of which cannot be mistaken, showing that this trumpet closes up this dispensation. By this we would not be understood to say that it covers no time beyond the close of this dispensation, but it

---

*Keith, on the prophecies, quoted largely from Gibbon, to show that the first four trumpets noted events connected with the downfall of Western Rome. Mr. J. Litch, following Keith, traced the history of the next two, showing their connection with Eastern Rome. In this he gave conclusive evidence that the sixth trumpet ceased to sound in 1840. A pamphlet on the subject of the trumpets can be obtained where this work is published.

certainly does cover the last days of this dispensation. Our Saviour says, "Behold, I come quickly, and my reward is with me, to give every man according as his work shall be." Rev. 22:12. Paul says the saints shall have rest when the Lord Jesus is revealed, taking vengeance on the wicked. 2 Thess. 1:6-10. And Jesus told his disciples they should be recompensed at the resurrection of the just. Luke 14:14. Thus it is shown that the judgment of the dead, the coming of the Lord, and the resurrection of the just, are events transpiring under this trumpet.

It does not seem to admit of a doubt that the judgment of the saints, the blotting out of sin, the making of the atonement, and the cleansing of the sanctuary, are identical. And we have seen that in the type the atonement was made— the sanctuary cleansed, when the high priest went into the most holy place before the ark; and the most holy was opened only on the day of atonement. This fact is also referred to in the scripture under consideration. Under the sounding of the seventh trumpet it is said, "The temple of God was opened *in Heaven*, and there was seen in his temple *the ark of his testament*." Rev. 11:19.

It has been noticed that John was shown a door opened in Heaven; a throne set; and seven lamps of fire before the throne. Rev. 4. But it was not till the seventh trumpet sounded that the temple of God in Heaven was opened where the ark of his testament is seen. By reference to "the example" of the heavenly things—to "the figures of the true"—we learn that the seven lamps, or candlesticks, were in the holy, and the ark of the testament in the most holy place of the sanctuary. And further, that the work of intercession was continual in the holy place, but the most holy was not opened except on the day of atonement.

From this we learn that the work of intercession of our High Priest *in the holy place* in the heavenly sanctuary extended from the commencement of his ministry in A. D. 31, to the sounding of the seventh trumpet (1844), when the antitypical day of atonement commenced, in which the sanctuary is cleansed.

There are differences in the work of the priest in the two holy places of the sanctuary. The intercession, or work of the priest in the holy, is general, for the whole world; and herein is shown the benefit that the whole world receives from the death of Christ. Every sin deserves its punishment, which is death; and without a mediator this would be the unavoidable and universal consequence. But through the pleading of the Saviour, sentence against the evil work is not speedily executed; Eccl. 8:11; the sinner is granted an opportunity to repent; a time of probation is given in which he may return to God through Christ. In this sense Jesus is the propitiation for the sins of the whole world. He has prepared a covering beneath which all may find refuge. By virtue of his death for sin, wherein mercy is exalted and justice honored, the transgressor is spared and invited to accept the blood of Jesus as his substitute, and be reconciled to God. And herein is shown the correctness of the apostle's declaration that God is the Saviour of all men; but there is a special salvation to them that believe. 1 Tim. 4:10. The benefits of probation which all enjoy, are by the blood and intercession of Christ. And surely these are no slight benefits. Though the sinner may pass them by unheeding; may scorn the warning voice, and despise the precious blood; the countless multitude of the redeemed who are all reconciled by these very means, forever attest the value and fullness of those means so blindly disregarded by the impenitent.

On the other hand, the Atonement, made in the most holy place, is specific and limited. By this it is not to be understood that repentance and reconciliation are not granted in the day of atonement, as some have inferred. To uphold that view it would be necessary to show that the penitent would not have been received, according to the type, on the day of atonement. But that cannot be shown; it was not the case. The offering on that day was made for all the people; but they only received the benefit of it who "afflicted their souls," as the Lord commanded. "For whatsoever soul it be that shall not be afflicted in that same day, he shall be cut off from among his people." Lev. 23:29. The reception of benefit from the work of the priest was conditional upon that day, as upon any other day; but upon this day it was complete and final. For incorrigibility upon this day there was no extension of time.

And so it will be in the antitype. As Christ closes his priestly work in Heaven before he comes to earth, and when he comes he will find both righteous and wicked ones living on the earth, it follows that the Atonement will be completed *and probation ended* before he comes. And thus it will be, that they who do not "afflict their souls;" who do not repent and leave their sins while our Advocate is doing that last work, will be cut off without remedy. Crying for mercy after he puts aside his priestly robes will be of no avail. How necessary that we be fully in harmony with the work of God in his last warning message (Rev. 14: 9–12) in order that that day shall not come upon us as a thief.

It is a very solemn thought that the last generation of men, living upon the earth just before the Lord appears, and up to the hour of his appearing, will remain here, busied with the things of this world after probation has closed. The great majority having turned away from the alarm which has been sounded; having rejected the warning which has been given by the servants of the Lord, will not understand the great change which has taken place in the position of the Son of God; they will scoff at the idea of his coming being near, and become bolder in sin as the restraining influence of God's Spirit leaves them.

Our Saviour has given a lesson upon this subject which demands the careful consideration of all. He said: "But as the days of Noe were, so shall also the coming of the Son of man be. For as in the days that were before the flood they were eating and drinking, marrying and giving in marriage, until the day that Noe entered into the ark, and knew not until the flood camo and took them all away; so shall also the coming of the Son of man be." Matt. 24 : 37–39.

In Gen. 6 we learn that Noah and his family were commanded to enter into the ark seven days before the flood of waters came. "And the Lord shut him in." But when Noah was shut in, *all others were shut out.* They had neglected the warning too long. They said as will be said in the last days, "All things continue as they were from the beginning of the creation." 2 Peter 3 : 4. Even after Noah entered into the ark, and the Lord had closed the door, they saw no change; they were emboldened in their hardness of heart because the judgment was delayed. Each day confirmed them in their ideas of their own wisdom, as day after day passed and the flood did not come. Poor souls! they knew not that their destiny was sealed; that there was no chance for them to enter the ark; that they had recklessly passed beyond the offer of mercy. "So shall also the coming of the Son of man be."

The testimony of Jesus after he was glorified teaches the same thing. When he is soon to come the second time he announces: "He that is unjust, let him be unjust still; and he which is filthy, let him be filthy still; and he that is righteous, let him be righteous still; and he that is holy, let him be holy still. *And, behold, I come quickly; and my reward is with me, to give every man according as his work shall be."* Rev. 22 : 11, 12.

This decision is not made when he comes, nor after he comes, but when he is quickly coming. This is further proof that it will be as it was in the days of Noah, and that every case must be decided before the Son of man is revealed, "taking vengeance on them that know not God.'

The relation of justification and obedience has been fully discussed in Chapter Three. But the relation of justification to the Judgment demands consideration. Peter said: "Repent ye therefore, and be converted, that your sins may be blotted out, when the times of refreshing shall come from the presence of the Lord; and he shall send Jesus Christ, who before was preached unto you; whom the Heavens must receive until the times of restitution of all things," &c. Acts 3:19-21. It is evident that Peter did not think their sins would be blotted out *when* they were converted, but at some future time; and the Scriptures clearly show that that time is when the sanctuary is cleansed and the Atonement made.

But in thus using this text it becomes necessary to vindicate the translation. Some affirm with much assurance that "*when* the times of refreshing shall come" is an incorrect rendering, and that it should be—"*so that* times of refreshing shall come." Liddell & Scott give as one definition of the original: "Of the time of a thing's happening, *when, as soon as.*" Pickering says: "*When*, as to time." Barnes, while he admits that the objection has in its favor the more usual use of the word, says: "Others have rendered it, in accordance with our translation, *when*, meaning

15

that they might find peace in the day when Christ should return to judgment, which return would be to them a day of rest, though of terror to the wicked. Thus Calvin, Beza, the Latin Vulgate, Schleusner, etc. The grammatical construction will admit of either."

Thus it is seen that the claim that the Authorized Version is wrong, is far from being established. We have no doubt that "when" should be retained in the text; that the expression, "the times of refreshing," refers specially to the blessing of the Spirit which will be given to the saints when they are sealed with the seal of the living God (Rev. 7), which will enable them to stand when Jesus ceases his priestly work, and during the time of pouring out the seven last plagues.

And yet another question has been raised, on which some minds have been perplexed. If the blotting out of sins is done in the closing work of the priest, when the sanctuary is cleansed, that is to say, in the Judgment, then the sins of all the saints must stand on record till that time. Now it has been shown (Chapter Three) that justification by faith and salvation are not identical; the former is a fact of experience at the present time, while the latter is contingent on "patient continuance in well-doing" on the part of the justified one. As was remarked, "justification by faith is not a *final procedure;* it does not take the place of the Judgment, nor render the Judgment unnecessary. It looks to something beyond itself to be accomplished in the future."

The same perplexity has arisen over the Apostle's words in Acts 2 : 38, " Repent, and be baptized every one of you, in the name of Jesus Christ for the remission of sins." From this it has been inferred, but without sufficient reason, that sin is remitted in the act of baptism. Such an idea is not expressed in the text. Evidently the terms signify *in order to* the remission of sins; and it is too much to claim that in laboring to gain a certain object, that object is obtained in the very act of laboring. God told his people that they should have life—eternal life—if they kept his commandments, which, to the faithful, will be fulfilled "when Christ who is our life shall appear," and not till then. The declaration above quoted, from Acts 2 : 38, points to the same fact as that in chapter 3 : 19. The remission of sin is the work of the Judgment; and the believer must stand justified by faith, looking to the priest for the accomplishment of his hope.

But that the sin is not really blotted out, or atonement made at baptism, or at any other period in probation, is proved by the word of the Lord to Ezekiel, 18 : 26: "When a righteous man turneth away from his righteousness, and committeth iniquity, and dieth in them; for his iniquity that he hath done he shall die." Again, in chapter 32 : 13: "All his righteousness shall not be remembered." That is, he shall be treated as though he had never been righteous. Now the righteousness of the righteous is by faith; therefore if he turn and commit iniquity he shall be treated as if he never had faith; his justification is annulled—he falls from grace.

For a demonstration of the truthfulness of this view, we look to the cases of the faithful who lived before the time of Christ. Were it admitted that the Atonement was made at the death of Christ, it would still remain a fact in the cases of the patriarchs and prophets that their sins were not atoned for, not actually blotted out till the blood was shed by which they are blotted out. But they were justified by faith, and died in that justified state, looking forward to the work of Christ when the object of their faith should be realized; when his blood should take away the sins of which they had already repented; or, in other words, when the Atonement should be made. This is decisive on the point. It proves beyond dispute that it is possible for a person to be justified by faith, accepted of God, and die in hope, without actually having his sins yet blotted out when he dies. And if the patriarchs and prophets could thus rest in hope, waiting for the blood of the coming Messiah to be shed to blot out their sins, so can the saints of a later age take hold of that blood by faith, waiting for Jesus our High Priest to blot out their sins when the times of refreshing shall come.

We think that our position is fully proved by the Scriptures, that, however closely justification and reconciliation are allied, the Atonement is subsequent to both. And this because *it is the Judgment.* If we are justified or reconciled, and so *continue to the end*, we may hope that our sins will be blotted out when the times of refreshing shall come from the presence of the Lord. This work is effected in the most holy place, where the ark of the testament is; this place is opened in Heaven under the sounding of the seventh trumpet; and this trumpet ushers in the judgment of the dead, the coming of Christ without sin unto salvation to them that look for him; the giving reward to all his servants, and the destruction of them that corrupt the earth. These events pass beyond the bounds of human probation, and close up the dispensation of the gospel.

Having traced this subject thus far; having found what the Atonement is; by whom and where it is made; and also for whom; we may turn back to "first principles" and again consider the law of God, and the position it occupies under the gospel. In the type, the testimony—the law —was put into the ark, in the most holy place; and it was over the law that the blood of the covenant was sprinkled by the high priest on the day of atonement. The glory of God was above the cherubim; these were upon the mercy-seat, and this was upon the ark in which was the law. As God looked down upon his law, the very basis of his Government, his justice was aroused, for his law was violated. But mercy interposed; the high priest entered with the blood that brings remission, that had been offered to vindicate the majesty of the law. The blood was sprinkled "upon the mercy-seat and before the mercy-seat."

Again the Lord looks down upon his law, but between him and the law is the mercy-seat sprinkled with the blood of the victim; the law is honored; its penalty has been enforced; a substitute has been accepted; and the penitent sinner is pardoned. We notice that here was a real law, taking hold of the moral relations of God's creatures; that here was actual transgression; on the part of the creatures a disregard of moral obligations. But under the Aaronic priesthood there was no actual taking away of that sin; it remained to be taken away by the blood of Christ. Therefore Christ officiates in behalf of that same law, as Paul shows in Heb. 9:15; and therefore the ark of his testament in Heaven contains that same law, where Jesus offers his own blood. Our High Priest has declared that he delighted to do the will of God, yea, the law was in his heart; he magnified the law and made it honorable; he upheld it in his life; he honored it in his death by suffering its penalty to vindicate its justice; he pleads his blood in Heaven in behalf of those who have broken it.

You who claim that God's law is abolished: look to his heavenly temple where Jesus our great High Priest is, and behold it there safely lodged in the ark. You who say that the law is changed—behold the original in Heaven, of which a copy only was given to Israel. Did not God speak it with his own voice? Did he not write it with his own finger? Did he not give it as a rule of holiness of life? Was it not perfect? Did it not contain the whole duty of man? Yes; and by it God will bring every work into judgment. Here is that justice and judgment which are the habitation of his throne. Ps. 89:14. What evidence have you that the heavenly record of God's immutable will has been changed? Men may mutilate the copy he has given them; they may strike out the name of the Holy One, and insert a term of reproach in its stead, but with him is neither variableness nor shadow of turning.

Peter says that Government is "for the punishment of evil doers, and for the praise of them that do well." All rights and privileges are protected by Government—by law. To subvert the law is to destroy the security of our rights. The law-making power has the sole right to change or abolish laws. Yet in the case of the fourth precept of the law of Jehovah men have not only changed its terms, but they now claim that it is their right to determine whether they shall keep it as the "one lawgiver" proclaimed it, or make changes in it, and observe it according to their own amendments! God said, "The seventh day is the Sabbath of the Lord thy God," and gave the reason, that he rested the seventh day when he created the heavens and the earth. But men say, "The seventh day is the old Jewish Sabbath," and substitute in its place another day which was not the rest-day of God, upon which he never bestowed his blessing, which he never sanctified, and which he never commanded men to keep. They have so long pursued this course that they think it a small matter to make such a change. But how must it look in the sight of Heaven? How must God regard the slight put upon his authority?

CHAPTER IX.

THE SCAPE-GOAT.

In commenting on the position of certain authors on the relations of the death of Christ, it was remarked that pardon, during probation, is not absolute, but relative. It is conditional, as the Scriptures clearly show. God never disregards the claims of his law—of justice. In forgiving the sinner so that he escapes the penalty he has deserved, God does not overlook the crime, or treat it as a matter to be lightly passed over. But he transfers the sin to another who bears it in his stead, and suffers for him. The sin was counted as still existing—an offense against Heaven's King. This is further shown by the action of the priest on the day of atonement. His service did not end with cleansing the sanctuary, or in blotting out the sins of the people from the book of judgment. The sin still existed, though they were cleansed; and it was removed from the presence of God to another object.

Two goats were presented before the Lord, and lots were cast upon them; one to be a sin offering, to be slain, the blood of which was sprinkled in the sanctuary; the other for a scape-goat, which was not slain, and *concerning which the priest took no action till after the Atonement was made.* Let not the reader mistake the import of this expression. We do not say that the priest took no action with the scape-goat until after the sin offering was slain. The statement reaches far beyond that; he took no action concerning the scape-goat until after he had taken the blood of the sin offering into the sanctuary and exercised his priestly office there in blotting out the sins of the people. If this distinction be well considered it may prepare the mind to see the truth concerning the object and antitype of the scape-goat. It has been supposed that this goat was also a type of Christ; but that is a supposition for which the Scriptures give not the least warrant.

Some authors consider that, as the sin offering typified the crucified Saviour, so the scape-goat presented alive before the Lord typified the Lord as risen for the justification of his people. But this view is inadmissible from the order of the service. We notice that,

1. The goat was slain as a sin offering; this typified the death of Christ on Calvary.

2. The priest took the blood and went into the sanctuary for the people; this typified the risen Saviour going into "Heaven itself, by his own blood, to appear in the presence of God for us."

3. After he had made an end of reconciling the holies, that is, after the atonement was fully made in the sanctuary, then the priest brought the live goat and laid both his hands upon the head of the goat, and confessed over him the sins of the children of Israel, putting them upon the head of the goat. This must certainly typify something in the future to be performed after the sanctuary in Heaven is cleansed. But the sins placed on the scape-goat can be of those only who have "afflicted their souls," and are accepted

of God, for they who are impenitent and continue to transgress the law of God, bear their own sins —their sins are on their own heads. And when the sins of God's people have been transferred through the priest to the sanctuary of God, and from thence removed to the head of the scape-goat, the goat is then sent away to "a land not inhabited," and there "let go," or caused to remain. And by this it is clearly seen that the pardon of sin is relative; that the sin is removed from the penitent believer only by transfer; but such transfer does not destroy or put out of existence the sin, as a future action in reference to it is appointed by the Lord.

There is something analogous to this in the New Testament, and it accords with the meaning of Lev. 16:8, as given by reputable authorities. The Hebrew word for scape-goat as given in the margin of Lev. 16:8, is *Azazel.* On this verse, Jenks in his Comprehensive Commentary remarks, "'Scape-goat.' See different opinions in Bochart. Spencer, after the oldest opinions of the Hebrews and Christians, thinks Azazel is the name of the devil; and so Rosenmuller, whom see. The Syriac has *Azzail,* the angel (strong one) who revolted." The devil is evidently here pointed out. Thus we have the definition of the Scripture term in two ancient languages, with the oldest opinion of the Christians in favor of the view that the scape-goat is a type of Satan.

Charles Beecher in his work, "Redeemer and Redeemed," makes an argument that the name Azazel refers to Satan, from which we extract as follows:—

"The use of the preposition implies it. The same preposition is used on both lots, La-Yehovah, La Azazel; and if the one indicates a person, it seems natural the other should, especially considering the act of casting lots. If one is Jehovah, the other would seem for some other person or being; not one for Jehovah, and the other for the goat itself.

"What goes to confirm this is, that the most ancient paraphrases and translations treat Azazel as a proper name. The Chaldee paraphrase and the targums of Onkelos and Jonathan would certainly have translated it if it was not a proper name, but they did not. The Septuagint, or oldest Greek version, renders it by αποπομπαιος [apopompaios], a word applied by the Greeks to a malign deity, sometimes appeased by sacrifices.

"Another confirmation is found in the book of Enoch, where the name Azalzel, evidently a corruption of Azazel, is given to one of the fallen angels, thus plainly showing what was the prevalent understanding of the Jews at that day.

"Still another evidence is found in the Arabic, where Azazel is employed as the name of the evil spirit.

"In addition to these, we have the evidence of the Jewish work Zohar, and of the Cabalistic and Rabbinical writers. They tell us that the following proverb was current among the Jews: 'On the day of atonement, a gift to Sammail.' Hence Moses Gerundinensis feels called to say that it is not a sacrifice, but only done because commanded by God.

"Another step in the evidence is when we find this same opinion passing from the Jewish to the early Christian Church. Origen was the most learned of the Fathers, and on such a point as this, the meaning of a Hebrew word, his testimony is reliable. Says Origin: 'He who is called in the Septuagint αποπομπαιος, and in the Hebrew Azazel, is no other than the devil.'

"Lastly, a circumstance is mentioned of the emperor Julian, the apostate, that confirms the argument. He brought as an objection against the Bible, that Moses commanded a sacrifice to the evil spirit. An objection he never could have thought of, had not Azazel been generally regarded as a proper name.

"In view, then, of the difficulties attending any other meaning, and the accumulated evidence in favor of this, Hengstenberg affirms, with great confidence, that Azazel cannot be anything else but another name for Satan." Pp. 67, 68.

Also on the opinion that the scape-goat typified the Saviour after his resurrection, Mr. Beecher has the following:—

"Matthew Henry says: 'The slain goat was a type of Christ dying for our sins, the scape-goat a type of Christ rising again for our resurrection.' But he forgets that the goat was so unclean that its touch rendered the man by whom it was sent, unclean, and necessitated a thorough washing. Was Christ unclean in his resurrection? It is said, 1 Tim. 3:16, that he was 'justified in the Spirit;' and Rom. 4:25, 'He was delivered for our offenses, but raised for our justification.'

Purity is the grand idea associated with Christ's resurrection, and therefore such a view of the type is manifestly impossible."

Irenæus, writing in A. D. 185, quotes an elder's words against Marcus, who was accused of heresy, as follows:—

"Marcus, thou former of idols, inspector of portents, skilled in consulting the stars, and deep in the black arts of magic. Ever by tricks such as these confirming the doctrines of error. Furnishing signs unto those involved by thee in deception, wonders of power that is utterly severed from God, and apostate, which Satan, thy true father, enables thee still to accomplish, by means of Azazel, that fallen, yet mighty angel. Thus making thee precursor of his own impious actions."—*Irenæus against Heresies*, Book 1, chap. xv, p. 68.

This shows that such an opinion was held by Christians at that time.

In the common acceptation of the word, the term scape-goat is applied to any miserable vagabond who has become obnoxious to the claims of justice; and while it is revolting to all our conception of the character and glory of Christ, to apply this term to him, it must strike every one as a very appropriate designation of the devil, who is styled in the Scriptures, the accuser, adversary, angel of the bottomless pit, Beelzebub, Belial, dragon, enemy, evil spirit, father of lies, murderer, prince of devils, serpent, tempter, &c.

In Rev. 20, there is something that bears a striking analogy to the action of the High Priest in regard to the scape-goat, and is, doubtless, a fulfillment of that type. This scripture, ushering in the first resurrection—the resurrection of the just, who are raised at the coming of Christ,—certainly refers to a period beyond human probation, and therefore after the sanctuary is cleansed. An angel is seen to come down from Heaven, and bind the dragon, which is the devil, and cast him into the bottomless pit, where he is shut up a thousand years. By reference to the Scripture use of this term abyss (rendered bottomless pit), we find the very idea of Lev. 16 : 21, 22 carried out, for it is literally a desert waste, void, or land not inhabited. In every place where the term is used in such a manner as to determine a locality, it is connected with the earth, or a part of the earth. In Rev. 9, at the sounding of the fifth trumpet, the abyss was opened, and locusts came out, &c. This describes the action of the Mahometan power. In chap, 11, the beast that ascends out of the abyss is said to make war against the two witnesses and to kill them. By careful expositors of prophecy this is referred to the French Revolution. In chap. 17, the seven-headed and ten-horned beast is said to ascend out of the abyss. Chap. 13 : 1–10 refers to the same beast in another phase of its existence, and these chapters clearly point out European powers. Thus far we find it confined to the earth. Paul, in Rom. 10 : 7, uses this term in the same manner. "Who shall descend into the deep? (that is, to bring up Christ again from the dead)." The abyss, here rendered *deep*, in other places rendered bottomless pit, refers to the grave, or, at most, to the state of death. In Gen. 1 : 2, "and darkness was upon the face of the deep," the abyss points out a void, waste, or uninhabitable state of the earth; and in no case, where it is possible to trace its connection, has it any other location but the earth.

Two facts only need notice to show the perfect fulfillment of the types in the scripture under consideration. (1) Satan is called the prince of the power of the air. By his creation as an exalted angel he has the power of traversing the air as well as the earth. To deprive him of that power and confine him to the earth would fulfill Rev. 20. (2) When Satan is bound, at the coming of Christ, the earth will be desolated, and left without an inhabitant. As a very brief summary of the proof on this point, the following facts and scriptures are offered:-

At the coming of Christ the saints will ascend to meet the Lord in the air, and be taken to those mansions which he has gone to prepare for them. "For the Lord himself shall descend from Heaven with a shout, with the voice of the archangel, and with the trump of God; and the dead in Christ shall rise first; then we which are alive and remain shall be caught up together with them in the clouds, to meet the Lord in the air; and so shall we ever be with the Lord." 1 Thess. 4 : 16, 17. "Little children, yet a little while I am with you. Ye shall seek me; and as I said unto the Jews, Whither I go ye cannot come; so now I say to you." "Simon Peter said unto him, Lord, whither goest thou? Jesus answered him, Whither I go, thou canst not follow me now, but thou shalt follow me afterward." "Let not your heart be troubled; ye believe in God, believe also in me. In my Father's house are many mansions; if it were not so I would have told you. I go to pre- pare a place for you. And if I go and prepare a place for you, I will come again, and receive you unto myself; that where I am, there ye may be also." John 13 : 33, 36; 14 : 1–3. Compare Rev. 4 : 6, and 15 : 2.

The wicked will all be destroyed from the face of the earth at that time. "Seeing it is a right- eous thing with God to recompense tribulation to them that trouble you; and to you who are troubled rest with us, when the Lord Jesus shall be revealed from heaven with his mighty angels, in flaming fire taking vengeance on them that know not God, and that obey not the gospel of our Lord Jesus Christ; who shall be punished with everlasting destruction from the presence of the Lord, and from the glory of his power." 2 Thess. 1 : 6–9. Most decisive proof to the same point is given in Rev. 19 : 11–21. The King of kings, and Lord of lords, who in righteousness judges and makes war, appears to smite the na- tions and to tread the wine-press of the wrath of God. An angel calls to the fowls of heaven to come to the supper which the great God has pre- pared for them; "that ye may eat the flesh of kings, and the flesh of captains, and the flesh of mighty men, and the flesh of horses, and of them that sit on them, and the flesh of all men, both free and bond, both small and great." The armies of earth are then gathered against the Conqueror, and the beast and the false prophet, and their worshipers are slain. "And the remnant were slain with the sword of him that sat upon the horse, which sword proceeded out of his mouth."

And so Paul speaks of "that wicked" at the coming of Christ: "Whom the Lord shall consume with the spirit of his mouth, and shall destroy with the brightness of his coming." 2 Thess. 2 : 8. God, whose voice once shook the earth, when he spoke his law on Sinai, will speak again with a voice which will shake both earth and heaven. Heb. 12 : 25, 26. And we learn that "a great voice out of the temple of Heaven, from the throne," will be heard when the last plague is poured out, as Jesus says, "Behold, I come as a thief. Blessed is he that watcheth." Rev. 16 : 12–21.

Jeremiah describes the drinking by the nations of the wine-cup of God's fury, which "all the kings of the north; far and near, one with another, and all the kingdoms of the world, which are upon the face of the earth," shall drink; and they shall all "fall, and rise no more," because of the sword which the Lord shall send among them. The Lord has a controversy with the nations, he will plead with all flesh. "And the slain of the Lord shall be at that day from one end of the earth even unto the other end of the earth; they shall not be lamented, neither gathered, nor buried; they shall be dung upon the ground." Jer. 25 : 15 to the end of the chapter.

16

Note on these texts: Paul says the voice of the Lord will be heard but once from Heaven. John says this is just before Christ comes as a thief. Joel says it is in the day of the great battle, and the treading of the wine-press of the wrath of God. See also Rev. 14:14–20. Jeremiah says all the nations shall drink of the wine cup of God's fury, and "all the wicked" be given to the sword. Now when the righteous are taken away from the earth, and all the wicked slain, the earth will be left empty, and without inhabitants. Therefore the following scriptures refer to that time. Jer. 4:19–29. Verse 23 says the earth was without form and void; in the same chaotic state in which it was when first created, before the Spirit of God, in formative power, moved upon the face of the deep—the abyss. "Behold, the Lord maketh the earth empty, and maketh it waste, and turneth it upside down, and scattereth abroad the inhabitants thereof." Isa. 24:1; the entire chapter is on this subject.

"I will utterly consume all things from off the land, saith the Lord. . . The great day of the Lord is near, it is near, and hasteth greatly, even the voice of the day of the Lord; the mighty man shall cry there bitterly. That day is a day of wrath, a day of trouble and distress, a day of wasteness and desolation. . . . Neither their silver nor their gold shall be able to deliver them in the day of the Lord's wrath; but the whole land shall be devoured by the fire of his jealousy; for he shall make even a speedy riddance of all them that dwell in the land." Zeph. 1:2, 14–18.

Thus the Scriptures clearly prove that the earth is yet to be desolated, without an inhabitant, broken down, without form and void, even as it was when first created, before man was made to dwell upon it. In this condition it was called "the deep," "the abyss," which in our version is rendered "bottomless pit." He who has been "the prince of the power of the air," will be confined thereon during the thousand years, Rev. 20:4, to behold the desolation which his rebellion has caused. And thus the antitype of the scape-goat will be sent away, with the sins of God's true Israel upon his head, "to a land not inhabited." Lev. 16:22. Of all that God has revealed by his holy prophets, nothing else fulfills, to the letter, the type of the scape-goat upon whom the high priest placed the sins of Israel after the atonement was fully made,— when he came out from the presence of God to pronounce the benediction of Heaven upon his waiting people.

Some have been troubled over Lev. 16:10, where the scape-goat is reserved also "to make an atonement with him, and to let him go for a scape-goat into the wilderness." While, in general, the definition of the original is, to cover, expiate, or forgive, Gesenius gives as one definition, "to do away, or obliterate." Now we have constantly insisted that the forgiveness of sin was *relative;* not *absolute,* as most writers on the atonement affirm. Forgiveness in probation, in our being justified by faith, has reference to the decisions of the future Judgment. And in the final remission, in the atonement, sin is not so "blotted out," as to be counted as no more existing.   Sin is a terrible stain upon the fair universe of God.   It is not a matter to be passed over lightly.   When it is fully forgiven to the penitent ones, and altogether removed from God's people, it still has an existence, and falls somewhere else; in the type, on the scape-goat; in the antitype, on the devil.   And when he is destroyed, sin perishes with him, it is, in his extinction, literally "done away, or obliterated."   But he has nothing to do with the Atonement.   As soon as the sins of Israel are removed from the most holy—the place of judgment—the work is finished for the people, judgment being rendered in their favor; and the priest no longer represents them as a people in danger of condemnation; no longer bears sin as *their sin*, but only to place it on the head of its originator.   Practically, as far as the people of God are concerned, it would not make a particle of difference whether laid on Satan, or disposed of some other way; they are secure when the blood on the mercy-seat has procured release for them, as they are acquitted at the throne of judgment.

Though the conclusion seems unavoidable that Satan is the antitype of the scape-goat, in whose person sin is finally destroyed or obliterated, we cannot yield to the assertion that Satan thereby takes part in the work of atonement for man, or bears sin in the sense of suffering the penalty of our transgressions.   It has been affirmed (page 40), and we think correctly, that *a voluntary sub-*

stitute is necessary to meet the demands of justice. This position our Saviour occupied; but neither Scripture nor reason lead us to suppose that Satan will ever consent to die for us, or for our sins; he is never spoken of as a ransom; never said to die for us; never represented as a means of redemption. And, as quoted by Mr. Beecher, the scape-goat was not considered as a sacrifice. Whatever may be ultimately done with our sins under the appointment of God; whatever may be done with or to Satan in the closing up of the great rebellion against the throne of Heaven; the bearing of our sins, and dying for us, and meeting in his own person the demands of the violated law for our sakes, is clearly and distinctly set forth in the divine word as the work of Jesus Christ, the Son of God; and in this work he stands alone—no one shares it with him to any extent whatever. And to him shall be the glory, and honor, and praise forever. But what is the part that Satan performs? Simply that of receiving upon himself the infinite weight of sins which he has instigated, and being sent away under their intolerable load.

And here we would ask, What could be more fitting than that the author and instigator of all sin should receive the guilt of those transgressions which he has incited mortals to commit, but of which they have repented, back upon his own head? And what could be a more striking antitype of the ancient ceremony of sending away the scape-goat into the wilderness, than the act of the mighty angel in binding Satan and casting him into the bottomless pit at the commencement of the thousand years?

This is a point of transcendent interest to every believer. Then the sins of God's people will be borne away to be remembered no more forever. Then he who instigated them, will have received them back again. Then the serpent's head will have been bruised by the seed of the woman. Then the "strong man armed" (Satan) will have been bound by a stronger than he (Christ), and the house of the strong man (the grave) spoiled of its goods, the saints. Matt. 12 : 29; Heb. 2 : 14. Then will the work of the enemy in sowing tares among the wheat (Matt. 13 : 24–45), be forever remedied, and the tares will have been gathered into bundles to burn, and the wheat gathered into the garner. Then our great High Priest will have come forth from the sanctuary to pronounce the everlasting blessing upon his waiting people. Then shall we have come unto Mount Zion, and unto the city of the living God, the heavenly Jerusalem, and to an innumerable company of angels. Then will the redeemed, placing the foot of triumph upon the world, the flesh, and the devil, raise their glad voices in the song of Moses and the Lamb. Oh, glorious day! May the Lord hasten it in his good time. Who would not, in view of this, take up the petition of the beloved John, "Even so, come Lord Jesus!"

CHAPTER X.

THE doctrine of the kingdom of Christ calls for special attention in this connection; though some may, at a first glance, think that it is not directly related to the subject of the Atonement. Here we may repeat a statement made, that there are no isolated, independent truths in the great plan of salvation. It takes all the truths and doctrines of the Bible to make one complete system; and the Atonement is the great central work, by virtue of which all other parts of the work of salvation and redemption are carried out. But the special reason why the subject of the kingdom should here receive attention is this: There is another class of texts in the Scriptures which speak of *Christ on his throne* which are misapplied by many religious teachers, who refer them also to his kingly priesthood. They seem to take it for granted that every Scripture declaration concerning his kingly authority must refer to him while sitting a priest on his Father's throne in Heaven. But the Scriptures themselves very clearly distinguish between these two classes of texts, and to amalgamate them is only to make confusion and to obscure the light of some precious Bible truths.

In Acts 1:6 it is recorded that the disciples inquired of Christ: "Lord, wilt thou at this time restore again the kingdom to Israel?" On this we first notice, that the term "Israel" primarily was indicative *of character*, and not *of birth*. Jacob was called Israel, and Esau was not, though they were children of the same parents —twin brothers. Afterward the term was applied to all the descendants of Jacob, though it never lost its primary signification. It was by this fact that Paul proved that the promises of God are strictly and literally fulfilled, though the unbelieving nation were rejected which claimed the sole right to that title. They are not all Israel which are of Israel, nor are all heirs of the blessings of Abraham who descended from Abraham. The promise of kingly glory preceded the existence of the nation (See Gen. 17:5–7), and the rejection of any part of the nation, or even of the whole *as a nation*, did not and could not destroy the promises. When Jesus, because of their rejection of the message from Heaven, foretold the rejection of the Jews, he did it in the following language: "Therefore say I unto you, The kingdom of God shall be taken from you, and given to a nation bringing forth the fruits thereof." Matt. 21:43. That was to say, that the kingdom should be taken from *nominal Israel*, and given to the *true Israel*, the faithful overcomers. See also Gal. 3:29.

And with this agree the words of the Lord to David, as recorded in Ps. 89. "I have made a covenant with my chosen; I have sworn unto David my servant, Thy seed will I establish forever, and build up *thy throne* to all generations." Verses 3, 4. And again: "His seed also will I make to endure forever, and his throne as the days of heaven. . . . Once have I sworn by my holiness that I will not lie unto David. His seed shall endure forever, and his throne as the sun before me. It shall be established forever as the moon, and as a faithful witness in Heaven." Verses 29–37. It is not merely a theory that depends upon the true interpretation of these promises. We shall endeavor to show that the truths which they contain are eminently practical, and that a misapplication of them leads to serious perversions of the gospel and of the relations of Christianity to the kingdoms of this present world.

We turn now to the question found in Acts 1 : 6. The opinion largely prevails among commentators of the present day that the disciples were indulging a very erroneous idea respecting the kingdom, which was the cause of their asking such a question. Dr. Barnes says: "They did not ask whether he would do it at all, or whether they had correct views of the kingdom; but, taking that for granted, they asked him whether that was the time in which he would do it." And from this he draws the conclusion that nothing is so hard to remove as "prejudice in favor of an erroneous opinion." It might be suggested that prejudice against the truth is as blind and unreasoning as prejudice in favor of error. But Dr. Barnes thought that, from the teachings of the Saviour in regard to his kingdom, they should have better known its nature than to ask such a question. And his comment doubtless expresses the views of a majority of commentators of the present day.

We say, "of the present day," because the popular view of the present day was not always the popular view held in the Christian Church. But for that we care nothing; our inquiry is, "What saith the Scripture?"

The question of the disciples was solely in regard to *the time* of setting up the kingdom. The answer of the Saviour was in reference to the subject of the question, the time, and it was not at all calculated to correct a wrong impression in regard to the nature of the kingdom, if they were resting in an error on that subject. "It is not for you to know the times or the seasons, which the Father hath put in his own power." This answer was certainly well calculated to confirm them in the view which they held. Not the hint of the correction of an error, but, to the contrary, they were told that the time of which they inquired was not to be revealed to them. The Revised Version says, "which the Father hath set within his own authority." Margin—"appointed by." A careful examination of the whole subject must convince any one that this is parallel with Matt. 24 : 36. "But of that day and hour knoweth no man, no, not the angels of Heaven, but my Father only." The declaration that the time of which they inquired is set or placed within the authority of the Father, known to no others, is quite the reverse of an intimation that the question referred to something which would never take place.

Verse 3 says that, after his resurrection, Jesus was seen of the disciples "forty days, and speaking of the things pertaining to the kingdom of God." Some appear to think that the time and opportunities were rather limited for their gaining instruction on this important subject. But, remembering that "the kingdom" was the burden of all the teaching and preaching of both Jesus and his disciples during all his ministry, insomuch that he called his gospel "this gospel of the kingdom," Matt. 24 : 14, we would rather take the chance which the disciples had of learning the truth on the subject, than to take a "three years' course" in any theological school now in existence.

We have another instance of the Saviour giving instruction on this subject where the question of time was first in their minds. "He added and spake a parable, because he was nigh to Jerusalem, and because they thought that the kingdom of God should immediately appear." Luke 19 : 11. In this parable he spoke of himself as a nobleman who went into a far country to receive for himself a kingdom, and to return. That this represents his going to his Father in Heaven to receive a kingdom, and returning to this earth, is evident, for, he said: "But his citizens hated him, and sent a message after him, saying, We will not have this man to reign over us. And it came to pass, that when he was returned, having received the kingdom," then he rewarded his servants and destroyed his enemies. But this will apply to no other locality but this earth. And it exactly corresponds to his statement of what takes place at his coming, at "the end of the world." Matt. 13:41, 43. "The Son of man shall send forth his angels, and they shall gather out of his kingdom all things that offend and them which do iniquity. . . Then shall the righteous shine forth as the sun in the kingdom of their Father." It must be borne in mind that "the field is the world;" that the workers of iniquity are represented by the tares, which grow with the wheat until the harvest. That the harvest is reaped at the coming of the Son of man is shown in Rev. 14:14-20, and other scriptures.

The kingdom and dominion over this world is given to Christ, the "nobleman," not at or near the beginning of this dispensation, as many believe, but near its close. This is proved by Rev. 11:14, 15. Under the third woe trumpet, which is the last of the seven trumpets, and which introduces the Judgment (verse 18), a voice proclaims: "The kingdoms of this world are become [the kingdoms] of our Lord, and of his Christ; and he shall reign forever and ever." Under this trumpet the dispensation comes to its close.

Also the prophecy of Daniel is decisive on this point. In chapter two, in the dream of Nebuchadnezzar, the king or kingdom of Babylon answered to the head of gold of the image. This kingdom was succeeded by that of the Medes and Persians, see Dan. 5:30, 31, which answered to the breast and arms of the image. And the Persian was succeeded by the Grecian, Dan. 8:3-8, 20, which was represented by the body of brass of the image. Another kingdom, the fourth, was strong as iron—represented by the legs of iron, —stronger than all that preceded it; and it was divided into ten parts, or kingdoms, in the image represented by the feet and toes. This was the Roman kingdom, which was successor to the Grecian, and which bore an iron rule over all the world. It was divided into ten kingdoms. These are the several parts of the image which was seen by Nebuchadnezzar; and such was the interpretation of the dream, as given by Daniel.

But another object was seen in the dream, and it also represented a kingdom. It was "a stone cut out of the mountain without hands." The original is reflexive in form, conveying the idea of self-moving. This stone smote the image "upon his feet, that were of iron and clay." That is to say, that it smote the image *at some time after* the Roman kingdom was divided, for the stone could not smite the feet and toes of the image before they existed. Or, in the fulfillment, the kingdom represented by the stone could not smite the kingdoms represented by the feet and toes of the image until they had arisen—until the Roman Empire was divided into ten parts or kingdoms.

In the dream, the effect of the smiting of the image by the stone, is thus described: "Then was the iron, the clay, the brass, the silver, and the gold, broken to pieces together, and became like the chaff of the summer threshing-floors; and the wind carried them away, that no place was found for them; and the stone that smote the image became a great mountain, and filled the

whole earth." In the interpretation it is thus
stated: "In the days of these kings shall the God
of Heaven set up a kingdom, which shall never
be destroyed; and the kingdom shall not be left
to other people, but it shall break in pieces and
consume all these kingdoms, and it shall stand
forever." Dan. 2: 35, 44. This describes, not the
conversion of earthly powers, but the entire *destruction* of all earthly powers, their places being
filled by the kingdom of God, by which they are
broken in pieces. See the same foretold in Jer.
25: 15–33. In this chapter it is said that "all the
kingdoms of the world, which are upon the face
of the whole earth," shall drink of the wine-cup
of God's fury, "and fall, and rise no more, because of the sword which I will send among"
them. No such destruction as that described in
Jer. 25 has ever taken place; but it will, for the
word of the Lord declares it. Then will the interpretation of the dream of Nebuchadnezzar be
fulfilled.

It is true that Dan. 2 does not definitely give
the chronology of the setting up of the kingdom
of God; but it does definitely place it *after* the
full development of the image, including the divisions of the Roman power. This brings it down
several centuries this side of the days of the
apostles. But in Dan. 7: 9–14 it is located, as in
Rev. 11: 14–18, in the time of the Judgment. In
Dan. 7 is recorded a vision of the prophet, which
was explained by an angel. Under the symbols
of beasts and horns it presents the same kingdoms and the same events which are given in

chapter 2 in the great image. In chapter 7, the Roman Empire and its divisions are represented by a dreadful and terrible beast with great iron teeth, which had ten horns. This chapter contains, however, two important points which are not found in chapter 2. (1) The rise and work of "another little horn," after the rise of the ten, which was quite different from the others, and at length became stronger than all the others. (2) The sitting of the Judgment, which takes place before the kingdoms of the world are given to the Son of man.

The work of the "little horn" was one of persecution. "And he shall speak great words against the Most High, and shall wear out the saints of the Most High, and think to change times and laws; and they shall be given into his hand until a time and times and the dividing of time." This wearing out the saints of the Most High—the most terrible persecution which the church of God ever suffered—was under the Roman power, but principally under its ecclesiastical form. The angel continued: "But the Judgment shall sit, and they shall take away his dominion, to consume and to destroy it unto the end." These words contain a confirmation of the view we have advanced, that the Judgment sits before the end; before the coming of the Son of man; and before the dominion is taken from this persecuting power. And how noteworthy it is that within the last score of years the civil power has been *entirely* taken away from the church of Rome. "United Italy" has literally dethroned the head of the church, who now pays taxes to the Government as any other citizen! And the next event in the angel's interpretation of the vision is this: "And the kingdom and dominion, and the greatness of the kingdom under the whole heaven, shall be given to the people of the saints of the Most High, whose kingdom is an everlasting kingdom, and all dominions shall serve and obey him." Dan. 7 : 25–27. This closes the interpretation. The last event in every line of prophecy is the giving of the kingdom and dominion to Christ and to his people. And, as has been shown, and will be further noticed, this gift is speedily followed by the overthrow and entire destruction of all the kingdoms and dominions of the world.

It may not be objected that these prophecies refer to the introduction of the gospel and to the establishing of the church of Christ, in the present age. The scope of the prophecies forbids it. The events given in the vision of Dan. 7 cover the entire gospel dispensation, and even reach beyond it. If this be denied, we might as well deny the Judgment and future rewards at once. And— which ought to be decisive with all—the New Testament presents the possession of the kingdom as a matter of promise and of hope to the saints. Thus James says: "Hearken, my beloved brethren. Hath not God chosen the poor of this world, rich in faith, and *heirs* of the kingdom which he hath promised to them that love him?" Jas. 2 : 5. In the same manner Peter speaks "to them that have obtained like precious faith with us," and informs them what they must do in perfecting their characters, "for so an entrance shall be ministered to you abundantly into the everlasting kingdom of our Lord and Saviour Jesus Christ." 2 Peter 1:1–11. And Paul also shows to his brethren the mystery of the possession of the kingdom. He says "that flesh and blood cannot inherit the kingdom of God, neither doth corruption inherit incorruption." 1 Cor. 15:50. In the scriptures already quoted it is said the kingdom is to be everlasting—to stand forever. "Flesh and blood" is an expression indicating a mortal, perishable, corruptible condition. A mortal, corruptible man could not inherit an everlasting, incorruptible kingdom; for he would die and leave it to successors. But that would destroy the scripture which says "it shall not be left to other people." In this present mortal state the saints are *heirs* of the kingdom; when they *inherit* it their heirship will cease.

The Lord himself said his people will inherit the kingdom when the Son of man comes in his glory, sitting upon the throne of his glory. Matt. 25:31–34. But when the Son of man comes, the voice of the archangel and the trump of God will be heard, and the saints will be raised from the dead. 1 Thess. 4:15–17. And Paul further says that when that last trump shall sound, "this corruptible shall put on incorruption, and this mortal shall put on immortality." Then death will be swallowed up in victory. 1 Cor. 15:51–54. Then will the saints be prepared to inherit an incorruptible kingdom, as they will never die and leave

17

their inheritance to others. Thus beautifully do the Scriptures harmonize on this subject.

Now we are prepared understandingly to examine the error of those who apply the prophecies we have here noticed to the reign of Christ as a priest on his Father's throne.

The position which Christ now occupies on the throne of his Father, as a priest-king, he will sometime resign. Read 1 Cor. 15:23–28. His priesthood will not last forever. Instead of forever pleading his blood in behalf of sinful men, he will leave that throne and come to earth again, "taking vengeance on them that know not God, and that obey not the gospel of our Lord Jesus Christ." 2 Thess. 1:6–10. Instead of forever enjoying the privileges of the day of salvation, and living under the mercy of the Lamb, the wicked will, in that coming day, pray to be hid "from the face of him that sitteth on the throne, and from the wrath of the Lamb; [saying] for *the great day of his wrath is come;* and who shall be able to stand?" Rev. 6:15–17.

And now in regard to the faith of the disciples, as indicated by their question on Acts 1:6, we confidently affirm that their belief was in perfect harmony with the letter and spirit of the scriptures we have quoted. And we have yet more, and if possible still more conclusive, evidence to produce.

The angel who announced that Jesus should be born, used the following language: "He shall be great, and shall be called the Son of the Highest; and the Lord God shall give unto him the throne of his father David. And he shall reign over the house of Jacob [Israel] forever, and of his kingdom there shall be no end." Luke 1:32, 33. These are the words of a messenger direct from Heaven, and may not lightly be passed over. And with all these scriptures before them, and having so long enjoyed the personal instruction of the Prince himself "of the things pertaining to the kingdom," we think it is altogether unwarranted to assume that the disciples were laboring under "prejudice in favor of an erroneous opinion."

This text last quoted settles the question that the throne and kingdom which he now occupies is not that to which reference is made in the prophecies which have been examined. For, as shown by 1 Cor. 15:23–28, and o.her texts, there will be an end to this reign; his priestly reign will cease. And the throne which he now occupies is not "the throne of his father David." That throne he will occupy in the future; and his reign upon that will have "no end." And so far from the disciples having their errors corrected by the inspiration which they received on the day of Pentecost, as intimated by Dr. Barnes, Peter confirmed their belief, in his sermon on that day. Speaking of David he said: "Therefore being a prophet, and knowing that God had sworn with an oath to him, that of the fruit of his loins, according to the flesh, he would raise up Christ to sit on his throne." And one of the most decisive evidences that Jesus is not yet sitting on the throne of David, the throne which is his by right of his birth, is found in his own words in Rev. 3:21: "To him that overcometh will I grant to sit with me in *my throne*, even as I also overcame, and am set down with my Father in *his throne*." His Father, upon whose throne he is now sitting, is not *his father David*. That throne upon which he is now, is not and never was the throne of his father David. This proof is absolutely incontrovertible. But, as surely as the "Scriptures cannot be broken," he will yet sit upon the throne of his father David; upon that throne will he rule over the house of Jacob forever; of that kingdom and reign there will be no end. And only in this manner can the oath of the Lord to David be fulfilled.

The Scriptures inform us that the position which the Son of God now occupies is one of expectancy. The apostle says he is set down on the right hand of God, from henceforth expecting till his enemies be made his footstool. Heb. 10: 13. This expectation is based on the promise made in Ps. 110:1: "The Lord said unto my Lord, Sit thou at my right hand, until I make thine enemies thy footstool." His enemies were not put under his feet at the beginning of the period of his sitting at the right hand of his Father. Had that been the case Paul's statement in Heb. 10:13 would not have been correct. But they will be put under his feet when the time comes for him to leave that throne, to resign his priestly office, and to come to destroy his enemies. Ps. 2:7–10 informs us what disposition he will make of them when they are given to him.

"Thou art my Son; this day have I begotten thee. Ask of me, and I shall give thee the heathen for thine inheritance, and the uttermost parts of the earth for thy possession. Thou shalt break them with a rod of iron; thou shalt dash them in pieces like a potter's vessel. And 2 Thess. 1: 6–10, already quoted, shows that it will be at his second coming that he will take vengeance on them that know not God, and obey not the gospel. And this again is in harmony with Rev. 11: 15–18, where it is shown that under the seventh trumpet, which closes this dispensation, the kingdoms of this world are given to Christ. And in connection with this gift it is said: "And the nations were angry, and thy wrath is come, and the time of the dead that they should be judged, and that thou shouldest give reward unto thy servants the prophets, and to the saints, and to them that fear thy name, small and great; and shouldest destroy them which destroy [corrupt] the earth." It seems needless to repeat that the reward of the saints will be given when Jesus comes again. Matt. 16:27; Luke 14:14; Rev. 22:12.

It has been fully noticed that the Judgment of the saints must be completed before Christ leaves the throne of his priesthood. But not so of the Judgment of the wicked. In the Judgment which takes place during his priesthood, it will be determined whose names shall have no place in the book of life; but their cases must come up for review that the measure of their punishment may be determined. To properly locate this work has been one object of the present argument, in distinguishing between the two thrones. There is still a work of judgment after Christ resigns his priestly office on the throne of his Father; after his enemies are given to him, and he has dashed in pieces the nations and kingdoms of the world.

An order of events is laid down in Dan. 7 : 21, 22, from which we gain important instruction on this subject. Speaking of that persecuting power, already noticed, which wore out the saints of the Most High, the prophet said: "I beheld, and the same horn made war with the saints, and prevailed against them; until the Ancient of days came, and judgment was given to the saints of the Most High; and the time came that the saints possessed the kingdom." In regard to the time when the saints shall possess the kingdom, we further quote as follows: "In the regeneration when the Son of man shall sit in the throne of his glory, ye also shall sit upon twelve thrones, judging the twelve tribes of Israel." Matt. 19 : 28. These are the words of the Lord himself to his twelve disciples. And by the words of Paul we readily locate the time of this judgment, if, indeed, any further proof can be asked. He said "the saints shall judge the world" (1 Cor. 6 : 2), but he said also: "Therefore judge nothing before the time, until the Lord come." 1 Cor. 4 : 5. Rev. 20 : 1–6 introduces the coming of Christ, the binding of Satan, the resurrection of the blessed and holy—the first resurrection, which is at Christ's coming—and thrones of judgment given to the overcomers.

And it is further a matter of proof that the saints do not and cannot enter upon this work of judgment in the present life or the present state. In 1 Cor. 6:1–4 the apostle reproves the brethren for going to law, and that before the unbelievers, as though they were not competent to settle their own temporal difficulties. "Do ye not know that the saints shall judge the world? and if the world shall be judged by you, are ye unworthy to judge the smallest matters?. Know ye not that we shall judge angels? How much more things that pertain to this life?" Observe that the judgment of which he speaks, that of the world and of angels, is not in "this life."

And there is reason for this; in this life we cannot discern motives and so understand the lives and hearts of the world as to be able to judge them correctly. Much less can we now judge angels. The fallen angels, who sinned, are reserved unto the Judgment of the great day. 2 Peter 2:4; Jude 6. Even over them shall the saints sit in judgment. But no saint, however faithful and exalted, is qualified to judge them in this life. There is a time coming, however, when our partial knowledge shall pass away; when we shall know even as we are known. 1 Cor. 13: 8–12. Paul had the Spirit of Christ, the Spirit of prophecy; but only so as "to know in part" and to "prophecy in part." But a clearer light is to burst upon his vision when the Lord comes; when this mortal puts on immortality. "When that which is perfect is come, then that which is in part shall be done away." "For now we see through a glass, darkly; but then face to face; now I know in part; then shall I know even as also I am known." All these scriptures leave no room for doubt that the work of the judgment of the world, in which the saints shall take part, is after the priesthood of Christ is ended; after his second coming; after the saints are immortalized and glorified.

But the question may still be asked: If it shall already have been decided who are the lost ones; if their names are not in the book of life, wherefore a further judgment in their cases? To this question the Scriptures afford an easy solution.

In the rewards of the righteous there will be degrees of glory. "For star differeth from star in glory; so also is the resurrection of the dead." 1 Cor. 15:41, 42. One is made ruler over ten cities; another over five cities. Luke 19:17–19. "*They that turn many to righteousness* [shall shine] as the stars forever and ever." Dan. 12:3. And so in the punishment of the wicked, there will be recognized degrees of demerit. Some shall be beaten with many stripes, and others with few stripes. Luke 12:45–48. For some it will be more tolerable in the day of Judgment than for others. Matt. 10:15; 11:22–24.

Dr. Bloomfield says of 1 Cor. 6:2:—

"Upon the whole, there is, after all, no interpretation that involves less of difficulty than the *common one*, supported by some Latin Fathers, and, of modern divines, by Luther, Calvin, Erasmus, Beza, Cassaubon, Crellius, Wolf, Jeremy Taylor, Doddridge, Pearce, Newcome, Scott, and others, by which it is supposed that the faithful servants of God, after being accepted in Christ, shall be in a certain sense, *assessores judicii*, by concurrence, with Christ, and being partakers of the judgment to be held by him over wicked men and apostate angels; who are, as we learn from 2 Peter 2 : 4; Jude 6, reserved unto the judgment of the last day."

And Dr. Barnes observes:—

"Grotius supposes that it means that they shall be *first* judged by Christ, and then act as *assessores* to him in the judgment, or join with him in condemning the wicked."

Certainly this view has a most respectable array of authors in its favor; and well it may have, for we cannot see how any other view of the text can, with any show of reason, be taken. In speaking of the judgment of the righteous, it was remarked that when Christ comes his elect will be translated or raised to immortality in a moment, in the twinkling of an eye. And this act of glorifying them will prove that they have already been judged and acquitted; accepted of the Judge of all. But as there are two resurrections, one of the just and one of the unjust, the fact that the unjust are not raised at that time is conclusive proof that they will have been already rejected, or judged unworthy of eternal life. But it is one thing to determine that a person is guilty, and quite another thing to determine the degree of his guilt and the measure of punishment which he should justly receive; whether he should be beaten with few or many stripes. The first is done before the throne of the Most High while Jesus, as Priest, is blotting out the sins of his people, as he passes by those who are unjust and unholy. The second is done by Christ and the saints, who, as Bloomfield says, act as *assessores judicii.*

As the judgment of the saints takes place before their resurrection, and they are raised to receive the reward determined in their respective cases, so with the wicked. In Rev. 20 we learn that they who have part in the first resurrection sit upon thrones of judgment for a thousand years. And in the same scripture we learn that "the rest of the dead"—in distinction from the blessed and holy—"lived not again until the thousand years were finished." Thus the *assessing* · judgment—to use the idea presented by many authors—will occupy the one thousand years of Rev. 20, and at the end of that period the wicked will be raised to receive their reward—the second death in the lake of fire.

When we consider the exceeding great multitude of the lost who have lived since the time of Cain, and that every case has to be examined, it does not appear strange that one thousand years are set apart to the work. The saints are represented as kings and priests unto God; but they are not actually kings until thrones are given them, which will not be done until after the second advent. In Rev. 5 : 8–10 the four living creatures and the twenty-four elders present vials of incense before the throne in Heaven, which are said to be "the prayers of the saints." Whatever may be the chronology of this part of the chapter—whether the song is by anticipation or sung when the first part is fulfilled—it is true that there is *a past* and *a future* in the song. They *were* redeemed out of every kindred, and tongue, and people, and nation, which indicates the fullness of the gospel work as then accomplished, and they *were* made kings and priests unto God, and they "*shall reign* on the earth." It seems evident that they were made kings and priests before they reign on the earth. And such we find is the order presented in other scriptures. The only priestly work of the saints is done while they are on thrones of judgment, which is altogether during or within the thousand years.

One important end which will be gained by this examination of the cases of all the wicked by the record of their lives, is the complete vindication of the Government and providence of God. To all of the human race, while they only "know in part," many of the ways of God are dark and mysterious. In the words of the poet:—

"That vice should triumph, virtue vice obey,
  This raised some doubts of Providence's sway."

And this is the case with the righteous, while the wicked have openly murmured and denied both the justice and goodness of God. It was said by the Saviour that even a cup of water given to a disciple in the name of a disciple shall not lose its reward. And who so fitting to plead such an act in behalf of a lost one as the person to whom the kindness was shown?

Paul says: "Therefore judge nothing before

the time, until the Lord come, who both will bring to light the hidden things of darkness and will make manifest the counsels of the hearts; and then shall every one have praise of God." 1 Cor. 4:5. On the last sentence of this text Barnes remarks:—

"The word here rendered *praise* (*epainos*) denotes in this place *reward*, or that which is *due* to him; the just sentence which ought to be pronounced on his character. It does not mean, as our translation would imply, that every man will then receive the divine approbation—which will not be true; but that every man shall receive what is due to his character, whether good or evil. So Bloomfield and Bretschneider explain it."

And this is doubtless the true interpretation of the passage. Greenfield says of the word: "By impl. reward, retribution, recompense. 1 Cor. 4:5." This bringing to light the hidden things of darkness, and making manifest the counsels of the hearts, means that they shall be revealed or made manifest to the saints by their examination of "those things which were written in the books." Rev. 20:12. As there are to be degrees of punishment, it is evident from the scriptures noticed, that the determination of the measure of punishment is the work of the saints, where every mitigating circumstance will be presented and considered. This is the sense in which they will be priests in that judgment.

The objection raised against this view, that this does not conform to the idea of the work of priests according to the Levitical law, cannot lie against it, because we may not draw a parallel between the service of the priests under the law and that of the saints in the Judgment. We must decide by the definition of the word, and the facts of the New Testament. The word *priest* does not necessarily imply a mediator in the sense of one who offers sacrifices. Robinson and Greenfield define it, "One who performs the sacred rites." These rites may pertain to offering sacrifices or to mediation, or they may not. If the saints have the work of determining the degree of guilt, and of fixing the amount of punishment, their office is properly that of a priest. And it must be evident to every one that our ideas of the work of priests, if gathered from that of the Jewish priests, must be greatly modified when we come to consider the office of the saints, as the priesthood of the saints *is on thrones of judgment*, which was not the case with the Jewish priests. We may not reason from one to the other, but must let each class stand in its own place, according to the work ascribed to it in the Scriptures.

But it is not alone the righteous who need to have the mysteries of God's providence opened to them. As we remarked, the wicked have lived and died complaining of the ways of God. The Judgment will be made the means of bringing them to confess their error, and to realize that they alone were responsible for their own ruin. The Lord will "convince all that are ungodly among them of all their ungodly deeds which they have ungodly committed, and of all their hard speeches which ungodly sinners have spoken against him." Jude 15. Myriads have died, glorying in their wickedness—in the success of their selfish plans—unconvinced of the ungodliness of their actions. But they will all be convinced; they will all be brought to see the enormity of their crimes against the Most High God, and to confess the justness of his judgments. As is said by the prophet: "I have sworn by myself, the word is gone out of my mouth in righteousness, and shall not return. That unto me *every knee shall bow*, every tongue shall swear. Surely, shall one say, in the Lord have I righteousness and strength; even to him shall men come; and all that are incensed against him shall be ashamed." Isa. 45 : 23, 24.

The one thousand years of Rev. 20 are but the beginning of the reign of God's dear Son after he resigns his position as a priest on his Father's throne. The angel said that of his kingdom, on the throne of his father David, "there shall be no end." Of the stone, which represented the kingdom of God, it is said in Dan. 2 : 35 that it "became a great mountain, and *filled the whole earth.*" In Dan. 7 : 27 it is said that "the kingdom and dominion, and the greatness of the kingdom *under the whole heaven*, shall be given to the people of the saints of the Most High." All the kingdoms of the world, which are upon the face of the whole earth, are to be destroyed. Jer. 25 : 26–33. The kingdoms of this world are given to Christ, and by him will be broken with a rod of iron and dashed in pieces as a potter's vessel. Ps. 2. They are not to be transformed or merged into the kingdom of Christ, but he destroys them and his kingdom takes their place. It fills the whole earth.

And this makes plain Matt. 25 : 34. "Come, ye blessed of my Father, inherit the kingdom prepared for you from the foundation of the world." When God made the world he said it was "very good." There was every tree which was pleasant to the sight, and good for food. No thorns, no thistles marred the face of the fair creation. No evil was found therein. And to man was given "dominion over the fish of the sea, and over the fowls of the air, and over the cattle, and *over all the earth.*" Gen. 1 : 26. This was "the first dominion, the kingdom [which] shall come to the daughter of Jerusalem." Micah 4 : 8. And this will be the fulfillment of the promise that "the meek shall inherit the earth." Matt. 5 : 5. The psalmist adds a condition which the beatitude of the Saviour only implies: "The meek shall inherit the earth, and shall delight themselves in the abundance of peace." Ps. 37 : 11.

And this is proof that the reign of the saints over the whole earth—under the whole heaven—is not in this present state. "In the world ye shall have tribulation." John 16 : 33. The wheat and the tares will grow together until the harvest, which is the end of the world, or of this age. Matt. 13 : 36–42. The "little horn" will practice and prosper and prevail until judgment is given to the saints of the Most High. Dan. 7 : 21, 22. "That man of sin," the wicked one, will exalt himself until he is destroyed by the brightness of Christ's coming. 2 Thess. 2 : 1–8. These, and many other scriptures to the same intent which might be quoted, prove conclusively that in this world—in this present state—the wicked will enjoy their triumph; and the saints must still remain in expectation of theirs; they are but "*heirs* of the kingdom which God hath promised to them that love him." James 2 : 5. There can be no "abundance of peace" for the meek, while the tares grow with the wheat, which will be until the harvest, or the end of the world; while that man of sin opposes and exalts himself against God, which will be until Christ's coming. Not in this world, but in the world to come, will the saints reign, and the will of God be done on earth as it is done in Heaven. Well has the poet said:—

> "There is a land, a better land than this;
> There's my home, there's my home."

There is not the shade of a contradiction between the two statements, that the saints shall have tribulation in this world, and, the meek shall inherit the earth. If the earth were always to be in its present state and condition, where the wicked prosper and the righteous are oppressed, then it would not be possible that the meek should inherit the earth and delight themselves in the abundance of peace. But the earth is not always to remain under the curse. The thorn and the thistle shall not always mar the face of the dominion which was given to man at first, and which man shall eventually inherit forever. God's original purpose will be accomplished; his counsel shall stand. The work of the Captain of our salvation was not ended when he died upon the cross; when his soul was made an offering for sin. Isa. 53 : 10. His work will not yet be finished when he has cleansed the sanctuary by the sprinkling of his blood upon the mercy-seat. The Atonement has in view the fullness of the glory of redemption. It is necessary to understand what is included in the work of redemption, in order to understand what the blood of Christ has purchased for us; what his Atonement accomplishes for man; and what are the riches of the glory of his kingdom.

This glory is greatly obscured by reason of limited views of the design of the Atonement, and of the work of redemption. "The greatness of the kingdom under the whole heaven," which "shall be given to the people of the saints of the Most High," will not be realized until the work of redemption is fully completed, or until the "restitution of *all things*, which God hath spoken by the mouth of all his holy prophets since the world began." Acts 3 : 21. And especially do they limit the Saviour's work, and rob him of his glory who claim—and many do—that the work of redemption is already completed. It is necessary that we give this subject our careful attention.

CHAPTER XI.

REDEMPTION.

However closely salvation and redemption may be related in the gospel plan, there is a difference between the two. Salvation is a saving or keeping from, and redemption is bringing back from. The great salvation through Christ is from death—the second death. The great redemption is from mortality and death—the first death. The Lord promised to redeem his people from death and the grave. Hos. 13 : 14. But that will not apply, strictly speaking, to Enoch and Elijah, as they were saved from death; from going into the grave. But their redemption from mortality—from that condition which brings mankind to the grave—was the same as that of others. It is true that both these words have a different application from that here noted; as, we are saved from sin, and redeemed from our vain conversation. But such application does not disprove the statement made in regard to the difference of the terms, and of their general application.

The apostle Paul says that we, who have the first-fruits of the Spirit, are groaning for redemption. Rom. 8 : 23. And Jesus instructs us, when we see the signs of his coming, to look up, and lift up our heads; for our redemption draws nigh. Luke 21 : 28. By this we see that the work of redeeming love is not yet done for the saints of God. The grave yet holds in its cold embrace myriads of faithful ones, who died in hope. They rested in the promise of God through Christ, and could say with Job, "I know that my Redeemer liveth;" and with him they looked forward to the "better resurrection." Of the ancient worthies, now sleeping, Paul said: "These all, having obtained a good report through faith, received not the promise; God having provided some better thing for us, that they without us should not be made perfect." Heb. 11 : 35, 39, 40. They are resting and waiting for the redemption for which we are waiting and groaning.

And the same apostle informs us that "the first-fruits of the Spirit" which we have received, is also an assurance, "the earnest of our inheritance until the redemption of the purchased possession." Eph. 1 : 14. When man fell,—when sentence was pronounced upon him, his possession shared with him the curse. At the first he was given dominion over the earth; but the Lord said: "Cursed is the ground for thy sake." And when the seed of the woman undertook to bruise the serpent's head, he not only purchased man with his blood, but he purchased his possession also, and with him it remains to be redeemed. Satan may mar the work of God, but he cannot thwart his purpose. God's work will finally be perfected, and the work of the devil will be destroyed. 1 John 3 : 8. Thus the future work of redemption has two great objects to accomplish. And, as before said, they who say the work of redemption is finished; who deny the great work yet to be accomplished, rob the Redeemer of the glory of his work. It remains for us to examine that work in respect to both these objects. And,

1. THE REDEMPTION OF MAN.

Man was made of the dust of the ground, and placed on probation for endless life. He was told that if he disobeyed his Creator he should die. Of course if he obeyed he would live—live forever. But he disobeyed; he took the fearful risk, and did that which his Creator told him, in the most explicit terms, he should not do. In this transaction man subjected himself to two great losses: 1. He lost his innocence, which was essential to his happiness; 2. He lost his life—his very being.

The plan of salvation and redemption embraced a work of recovery or restoration. Not, however, merely to bring man back to the position which he occupied when he was created and placed in the garden of Eden; but, to place him where God originally designed that he should stand when he had passed his probationary state. In probation he was subject to temptation; free to fall. In his final state he will be placed beyond the reach of temptation, fixed in his integrity, no longer in danger of falling; no more exposed to the liability to die. We cannot imagine that the gospel of Christ will do less for man than was embraced in the original purpose of his Maker.

The method of restoring man to a state of innocence and of complete happiness we have fully considered in remarks on Justification, and on the Atonement itself. This embraces the forgiveness of sin, and the renewal of his moral nature; a transformation of his will and affections. This is a recovery from *the first* of the losses which he sustained in his departure from the path of right.

The second loss was entirely different in its nature. It took hold on man's physical being, and reduced him to his original elements; it returned him to the dust of the ground. By this we would not be understood as saying that either man's moral or physical nature can be seriously affected without affecting the other. When man perverts his moral powers he degrades his physical system, and subjects it to untold evils. All the suffering that exists and that ever has existed in the world, had its spring in that source. And, when man abuses his physical system he weakens his moral powers. These propositions will not be denied. But it is equally undeniable that that which directly affects one may only indirectly affect the other. A man may pervert his ways, and despise his Maker, and sear his conscience, and yet live many years; though the end of these things is death. And justification from sin may be received, with a purified conscience and a renewed heart, while yet the physical system is subject to decay and death; though continuance in that justified state—perseverance in the right —certainly leads to eternal life. It is true that the first step toward recovering man from the consequences of the fall, looks forward to the complete recovery in all things; but there are progressive steps in the work; one is taken before another.

For reasons purely theoretical, many in this age deny that death—the death of the physical man—is the result of sin. They say that the man which was made of the dust of the earth would have died if he had never sinned; that, being made of perishable material, he must have perished, from the very nature of his being. But this statement is defective and erroneous. (1) The material universe, the earth, is not necessarily perishable. It may undergo great changes, but we cannot believe it was ever made in vain, or to go out of existence. When it was created it was pronounced very good, and over it "the morning stars sang together, and all the sons of God shouted for joy." Nor is there any evidence that man, who is "fearfully and wonderfully made," would have perished if he had not sinned. At the best it is only a bare assumption, and not sustained by reason. But, (2) It is directly contrary to the word of Jehovah himself, who said, as a sentence upon the sin of man, *because* he had partaken of the tree of which he was forbidden to eat, the earth from which he was taken, over which he was given the dominion, should be cursed, and he should return unto it. And, to carry out this sentence, man was shut out from the tree of life, lest he put forth his hand and take and eat (a purely physical act), and live forever. If we regard the word of the Lord we must admit that death, the death of the whole man, was the result of his disobedience. And no other death but a literal or physical death was threatened or could be inflicted. For, as we have already considered, spiritual death is not an infliction, but a crime; it is not a penalty, but it incurs a penalty. See page 94.

This is an important point, for the breadth of the work of redemption is involved in it. The redemption must be as extensive as the loss; otherwise it would not be complete. If the loss involved the death of the physical nature of man, then redemption must take hold of his physical nature. And this we shall see that it does. We consider then,

1. Christ, our substitutionary sacrifice, died a physical death. This is certainly a good reason for believing that the gospel takes hold of physical relations. We cannot see how otherwise the method or nature of the sacrifice can be accounted for.

2. After death and burial, and remaining in the grave the time allotted by prophecy, he had a physical resurrection. Some have even gone so far as to deny this. Concerning the resurrection the following words are copied from a sermon preached in an orthodox church:—

"The resurrection is typical of the life of the soul; the figure of a spiritual body teaches, not the resurrection of the material body, but the immortality of the soul."

This is the view held by many teachers who are considered orthodox. In harmony with this, a writer, who was a Spiritualist, and professed to be a believer of the Bible, expressed his faith as follows:—

"At death the real man, that is to say his soul and spirit, rise *from* or *out of* his dead body; that in the New Testament this is denominated *anastasis*, or the resurrection."

These quotations are made that the reader may see the necessity of the argument we frame on the literal or physical resurrection of Christ. All who hold to such views place the "resurrection" or rising of the immortal spirit at the time of the death of the body. But the resurrection of Christ did not at all correspond to such a view.

a. The resurrection of Christ was not the rising of his spirit out of his body; for he did not rise until the third day after his death. And they will hardly contend that his spirit did not leave his body until he had been dead three days! yet they must to be consistent with that theory.

b. That which arose was placed under the guardianship of Roman soldiers. But no one can believe that after Jesus had been some hours dead, the soldiers were put on guard to prevent the escape of his spirit, and thence the report of his resurrection.

c. His enemies denied his resurrection, and reported that his disciples had stolen him. Did they mean to deny that his spirit left his body, and to affirm that his disciples came and stole away his spirit while they slept?

d. The angel said to those who came to the sepulcher: "He is not here; for he is risen, as he said. Come, see the place where the Lord lay." Matt. 28 : 6.

e. When his followers went to the sepulcher, after his resurrection, they "found not the body of the Lord Jesus." Luke 24 : 3.

f. When he met with his disciples after his resurrection, he told them to handle him, to examine the wounds in his hands, and feet, and side, and see that it was he himself; and he took food and did eat before them. Luke 24:36–43.

g. In his sermon on the day of Pentecost, Peter proved the resurrection of Christ by the promise of God to David, that of the fruit of his loins according to the flesh, he would raise up Christ to sit on his throne." Acts 2:30, 31. This is positive proof of a bodily resurrection.

We might go farther and prove by the Scriptures that neither believers nor unbelievers, Jews nor Greeks, had any idea of such a mythical resurrection as is now taught by men of various faiths in these days. But it is not at all necessary, for if a bodily or physical resurrection is not proved by the points here noticed, then language cannot be framed to teach it. We now notice,

3. That Jesus, in his resurrection, was "the first-fruits of them that slept." 1 Cor. 15:20. This language is significant of kind as well as of order. We have seen that, in the New Testament, in the case of the Saviour, his resurrection was of a material body. It is also said that the bodies of many saints left the graves at the time of his resurrection. And this is an assurance that the resurrection of all the saints will be that of the body also.

We say the first-fruits indicates *kind* as well as order. The first-fruits of any product was paid from that product, and not from something else. A sheaf of barley would not be the first-fruits of a field of wheat. A measure of wheat would not be the first-fruits of an olive orchard. Such a reckoning or rendering of first-fruits would be considered only absurd. But that would be no more absurd than to make the resurrection of Jesus from a physical death and a burial in the grave, the first-fruits of immortal souls, which never died and could not die! No greater incongruity could be presented. Surely, they who teach such fanciful theories cannot have well considered the result of their action. "They know not what they do." Nothing but the literal resurrection of physical or material bodies will answer to the first-fruits presented in the resurrection of our Saviour.

4. We will briefly present some direct proofs of the resurrection; we shall select such as have a bearing on its nature.

(1) "Thou wilt not leave my soul in hell; neither wilt thou suffer thy holy one to see corruption." Ps. 16:10. This is one of the last texts which would be selected by those who spiritualize the Scriptures, to prove the resurrection of the body; but to that it refers, for inspiration says it is a prophecy of the resurrection of Christ "according to the flesh." Acts 2:30, 31.

(2) "Thy dead men shall live, together with my dead body shall they arise. Awake and sing, ye that dwell in dust; for thy dew is as the dew of herbs, and the earth shall cast out the dead." Isa. 26:19.

(3) "Thus saith the Lord, Refrain thy voice from weeping, and thine eyes from tears; for thy work shall be rewarded, saith the Lord; and they shall come again from the land of the enemy."

Jer. 31:16. We learn from Matt. 2:16–18 that this language was spoken to those mothers whose little children were slain by Herod. Death is the enemy (1 Cor. 15:26) from whose land they will be brought.

(4) "Thus saith the Lord God: Behold, O my people, I will open your graves, and cause you to come up out of your graves, and bring you into the land of Israel." Eze. 37:12. The vision of the valley of dry bones is often spoken of as a prophecy of a spiritual reviving. But the words quoted above are from the Lord's *explanation* of the vision; and no one should presume to explain the Lord's explanation. It is plain, and in harmony with the other scriptures.

(5) "And many of them that sleep in the dust of the earth shall awake, some to everlasting life, and some to shame and everlasting contempt." Dan. 12:2.

(6) "I will ransom them from the power of the grave; I will redeem them from death; O death, I will be thy plagues; O grave, I will be thy destruction." Hos. 13:14.

(7) "But if the Spirit of him that raised up Jesus from the dead dwell in you, he that raised up Christ from the dead shall also quicken your mortal bodies by his Spirit that dwelleth in you." Rom. 8:11.

(8) "For we know that the whole creation groaneth and travaileth in pain together until now. And not only they, but ourselves also, which have the first-fruits of the Spirit, even we ourselves groan within ourselves, waiting for the

adoption, to wit, the redemption of our body."
Rom. 8 : 22, 23.

(9) "We shall not all sleep, but we shall all be
changed, in a moment, in the twinkling of an
eye, at the last trump: for the trumpet shall
sound, and the dead shall be raised incorruptible, and we shall be changed. For this corruptible must put on incorruption, and this mortal must put on immortality." 1 Cor. 15 : 51–53.

If every word shall be established in the mouth
of two or three witnesses, there is no need that
this line of proof should be carried any farther.
Not one of these declarations can fail, for "the
Scriptures cannot be broken." And we rejoice
in the assurance. We do indeed "groan within
ourselves;" our sicknesses and pains are evidences
of our mortality. We long for the day when this
mortal shall put on immortality; when death shall
be swallowed up in victory; when redemption's
work for the suffering saints shall be complete.

On *the nature* of the resurrection we are willing
to submit the foregoing to every candid, reverent
reader of the pages of divine inspiration. On
the importance of the resurrection we must give
a few testimonies.

When Jesus was instructing his disciples concerning their duty to the poor, he said: "For
they cannot recompense thee; for thou shalt be
recompensed at the resurrection of the just."
Luke 14 : 14. Let it be remembered that the resurrection takes place when the Lord Jesus comes
the second time; it cannot take place before, and
if he should never come there would then be no

resurrection of the dead. And, therefore, any text which introduces the resurrection of the just, of necessity introduces also the coming of Christ. And, in like manner, any text which speaks of the coming of Christ, introduces to our minds the resurrection of the just, as they are inseparably connected. See the following decisive proof: "For the Lord himself shall descend from Heaven with a shout, with the voice of the archangel, and with the trump of God; and the dead in Christ shall rise first. Then we which are alive and remain shall be caught up together with them in the clouds, to meet the Lord in the air; and so shall we ever be with the Lord. Wherefore, comfort one another with these words." 1 Thess. 4: 16–18. Notice the points introduced in connection:—

1. The Lord himself shall come; it will be a personal, actual coming.

2. The voice of the archangel (the Son of God, compare John 5 : 27–29), and the trump of God will be heard.

3. The dead in Christ shall rise.

4. The living saints will be caught up with them, translated, to meet the Lord.

5. So—in this manner—shall we ever be with the Lord.

6. These are words of comfort to the saints.

In Luke 14 : 14 are the words of Jesus that we shall be recompensed at the resurrection of the just. In this last text we learn in what manner, and under what circumstances, the reward will be given. Closely related to this, in its several circumstances, is the instruction given in 1 Cor. 15. The whole chapter is an argument on the resurrection, but especially verses 42–54, which speak directly of the resurrection of the righteous.

1. They shall be raised in glory.

2. We shall not all sleep; some will be translated.

3. The trumpet shall sound; the last trump.

4. We shall put on immortality, or, death will be swallowed up in victory.

The coming of Jesus is not spoken of, but it is well understood, for not one of these events can transpire before he comes.

And so the following: " When Christ, who is our life, shall appear, then shall ye also appear with him in glory." Col. 3 : 4. We shall .appear with him in glory at that time, because the saints are "raised in glory," immortalized, at that time. Another apostle testifies to the same thing. " We know that, when he shall appear, *we shall be like him;* for we shall see him as he is." 1 John 3 : 2.

" And when the chief Shepherd shall appear, ye shall receive a crown of glory that fadeth not away." 1 Peter 5 : 4. This is a parallel text, and one of great clearness and force. And yet several times more we find the Son of God pointing to the advent and, of course, to the resurrection of the just, as the time of conferring the reward. " For the Son of man shall come in the glory of his Father, with his angels; and then he shall reward every man according to his works." Matt. 16 : 27. " Behold, I come quickly; and my reward is with me, to give every man according as his work shall be." Rev. 22 : 12. See also Matt. 25 : 31–34.

The infinite importance of this subject to the saints, as the time when and the means whereby they shall be glorified, fully justifies the apostle Paul in calling it "the blessed hope." "Looking for that blessed hope, and the glorious appearing of the great God and our Saviour Jesus Christ." Titus 2 : 13. More literally: "And appearing of the glory of the great God, and our Saviour Jesus Christ." Compare Matt. 16 : 27, quoted above.

We cannot forbear quoting a few words from the comments of Dr. Clarke on 1 Cor. 15. On verse 32 he says:—

"What the apostle says here, is a regular and legitimate conclusion from the doctrine that *there is no resurrection;* for if there be no resurrection, then there can be no judgment; no future state of rewards and punishments; why, therefore, should we bear crosses, and keep ourselves under continual discipline! Let us eat and drink, take all the pleasure we can, for to-morrow we die; and there is an end of us forever."

Very few theological writers of the present time, recognized as eminent and orthodox, would use the language here used by Dr. Adam Clarke. A great change has come over the minds of the Christian world, on this subject. Dr. Clarke said that, in his day, early in the present century, the faith and preaching of the church differed much, on this subject, from that of the apostles and the early church. And in no part of the Christian era has the popular sentiment, concerning the nature and importance of the resurrection, changed as fast as from Dr. Clarke's time to the present. The following are his words:—

"One remark I cannot help making; the doctrine of the resurrection appears to have been thought of much more consequence among the primitive Christians than it is *now!* How is this? The apostles were continually insisting on it, and exciting the followers of God to diligence, obedience, and cheerfulness, through it. And their successors in the present day seldom mention it! So apostles preached; and so primitive Christians believed; so we preach, and so our hearers believe. There is not a doctrine in the gospel on which more stress is laid; and there is not a doctrine in the present system of preaching which is treated with more neglect!"

The doctor inquires, "How is this?" It is not difficult to give the reason: the church has accepted *a substitute* for the coming of Christ and the resurrection. The Bible says that immortality is brought to light by Christ in the gospel. The schools of Christian theology teach that it was most forcibly brought to light by Plato— shown to be inherent in the nature of man The Bible says we are to seek for immortality. "What a man seeth, why doth he yet hope for?" Why seek for that which we already possess? The Bible says we shall put on immortality at the resurrection. Theology teaches that, if there is any bar to the fullness of our immortality, it is removed by death! by means of which we are ushered into a state of immortal joy. The Bible says we shall appear in glory when Christ, our Life, appears. But theology teaches that we are glorified by death, which opens the pearly gates to the soul set free from the clogs of our physical natures. The contrast may be carried much farther, but none who read the Bible can fail to see it. And to show that our presentation of the contrast is strictly just, we quote the following paragraph from one of the most influential religious papers in the United States. It was part of a comment on 1 Thess. 4:13–18, which teaches us to comfort one another with the facts that the Lord is coming, the dead in Christ will be raised, and the living saints will be translated. Thus it speaks:—

" For all practical purposes of comfort the doctrine of the blessed immortality of the righteous, the immortality of the soul, takes the place for us of any doubtful doctrine of the Lord's second coming. At our death the Lord comes for us. That is what we are to wait and watch for. The dead are already passed into glory. They do not wait for the trump for their judgment and blessedness."

How *can* the church highly appreciate the coming of Christ and the resurrection of the dead, while holding to such views? The inquiry may be raised, If the immortality of the soul and glorification at death "takes the place *for us*" of the advent and the resurrection, why did it not take their place for Paul and his brethren? Has "that blessed hope" really been displaced for another in the gospel plan, or is the church proving recreant to the truths of divine inspiration? This is a matter of the highest importance; it concerns our loylaty to the truth of the Most High, and the honor of our Saviour, whose plans and appointments are being disparaged before the world.

Life is the greatest gift that can be conferred upon a creature. All enjoyments, all hopes, all possibilities, are centered in life. The loss of life is the aggregate, the sum total, of all losses. Man may lose many things in life; when life is lost, he has no more to lose. Death is the extreme penalty of law. It is *the* penalty of the transgression of God's law. This penalty—this loss of all—man incurred by disobedience to his Maker. Jesus, the Son of God, came to seek and to save that which is lost; he came to open a way whereby man might escape death and have everlasting life. He is the great Restorer to life; he is "our Life." Col. 3:4. "God hath given to us eternal life, and this life is in his Son." 1 John 5:11:

It must be apparent to every reader of the Bible that when man was placed on probation it was for his life. When he sinned, he incurred the penalty of the law which said he should die. The sentence against his transgression was that he should return unto the ground out of which he was taken. The means employed to execute the sentence, was depriving him of access to the tree of life lest he should eat and live forever. But one contrast is presented throughout the Bible: it is of life and death.

Death is an enemy, which Jesus came to overcome and to destroy. 1 Cor 15 : 26; 2 Tim. 1 : 10.. The race of man is literally a dying race; without Jesus there is no hope. The earth has become a vast charnel house, marked with its graves from one end to the other. Death severs the dearest ties of earth; it bereaves hearts, and brings the keenest anguish to loving ones. Its conquests are well-nigh universal; it holds in its gloomy prison-house the untold millions of our ill-fated race. But, as an enemy to the saints of God, death itself is doomed. The rapacious grave shall be robbed of its spoil. "But I would not have you to be ignorant, brethren," said an inspired apostle, "concerning them which are asleep, that ye sorrow not, even as others which have *no hope*." He then proceeds to remove all occasion of ignorance, and give them the ground of gospel hope concerning their loved ones sleeping in death. He bases all on the fact "that Jesus died and rose again." And then rehearses in order the future facts in which the hope of the Christian may rest. 1. The Lord, "the Lord himself, shall descend," and the trumpet shall sound. 2. The sleeping ones, "the dead in Christ shall rise." 3. We that are alive and remain shall be caught up together with them, and so ever be with the Lord. His conclusion is: "Comfort one another with these words." And this, said the apostle, "we say unto you by the word of the Lord." Here is no conjecture; faith rests here without a doubt.

Let the mourning, bereaved ones look up; redemption draws near. Oh, the glory of that day

when Jesus shall come to gather his ransomed
ones home. The voice of the archangel shall open
the graves of the righteous ones, who once felt
the sting of death. In the bloom of immortal
youth they rise to meet their Lord. Remembering the pains of death which they once endured,
and conscious that, for them all pains and tears
have forever passed away, they shout in triumph,
" O death, where is thy sting ? " Looking down
upon those dusty beds where they have long
slumbered, they exultingly ask: " O grave, where
is thy victory?" And the translated ones join
with them in one rapturous song: "Thanks be to
God, who giveth us the victory through our Lord
Jesus Christ." Well might the lamented Bliss
anticipate the triumph of that day when he
sung:—

> " All joy his loved ones bringing,
> When Jesus comes;
> All praise through Heaven ringing
> When Jesus comes;
> All beauty bright and vernal,
> When Jesus comes;
> All glory, grand, eternal,
> When Jesus comes."

" When this corruptible shall have put on incorruption, and this mortal shall have put on immortality," and God shall wipe away all tears from
the eyes of his people; and there shall be no more
death, neither sorrow nor crying, then we shall
realize, as we cannot now, the value of the blood
of Jesus and the glory of his Atonement. Then,
and not till then, can the church sing her song of
complete victory; then, for the saints, love's redeeming work will indeed be done.

CHAPTER XII.

THE recovery of man from the effects of the fall of Adam, and of the sins incident to our fallen condition, is by forgiveness of sin and the resurrection of the dead. These means of divine grace have been quite fully noticed. But the work of grace is not completed in these, even as the curse of the transgression did not fall on man alone. Having been made of the dust of the ground, he was closely allied to the earth over which he was given dominion, and the earth was cursed for his sake. It is not necessary here to inquire into all the reasons why the earth was cursed for man's sake; it is sufficient to our present purpose to accept the fact as revealed in the word of God.

To carry out the original counsel or purpose of the Creator, the work of redemption must include more than the recovery of man from sin and death; it must include the restoration of the earth. The curse must be removed, and the earth be restored to that state of freedom from evil in which it was when God pronounced everything "very good." Without the redemption of the earth, creation would never be entirely recovered from the foul blot brought upon it by sin. Satan would triumph thus far, that a reproach and a stain would not only be cast upon the work of the Creator, but it would be perpetuated;

the evil would be immortalized.   Or, to prevent
that, the work itself would have to be destroyed.

Destruction is but an act of justice where it
falls upon an intelligent probationer, who chooses
his own destiny, and refuses to fulfill the will of
his Maker, and the object of his being.   God can
consistently *permit evil*, both moral and physical,
for a season, in order that an intelligent agent
may develop his character, with the provision for
a Judgment wherein justice and truth shall be
fully and certainly vindicated.   And he may consistently destroy the willful transgressor of the
divine law.   But to destroy the work of his own
hands, which had no volition in suffering the
curse, would be a final victory for the enemy.   To
permit evil without reference to a Judgment, to
perpetuate and immortalize it in the universe,
would be an eternal reproach on the plan and
work of the Creator.   It would forever mar the
beauty and purity of his work; forever prevent
the carrying out of his original purpose, unless
sin and misery were in his original purpose, which
we cannot admit.   It would not vindicate justice,
because the eternity of evil bears no relation to
the penalty of transgression originally announced.

God's counsel shall stand.   Whatever he may
temporarily permit for the purposes of probation
and of judgment, we cannot suppose that his original purpose will be finally thwarted, so that
that which originated in the will of Satan and
in rebellion, shall eternally prevail, and obscure
that which originated solely in the will and mind
of Jehovah.   But, reasonable as is our proposi-

tion, we are not left to reason out the conclusion. The revelation of the mind of God in respect to man and to his inheritance is clearly made, and we therefore proceed to examine the Scriptures in regard to

2. THE REDEMPTION OF THE EARTH.

It was remarked that the redemption of man did not contemplate merely a restoration to that state which he occupied when he was created; as he was then placed upon probation for life. But they who are redeemed from sin and death have passed through probation; they have secured eternal life; they are brought into that condition which God purposed that man should occupy when he had faithfully fulfilled his period of trial and received the boon of immortality. In like manner, the earth will be more than restored to its primitive condition. When man was created his dominion was not in the condition for which it was designed. He was told to "multiply, and replenish the earth, and *subdue it*." The Lord "planted a garden eastward in Eden," and man was appointed "to dress it and to keep it." Had he remained innocent, and retained his position in the garden, as his descendants multiplied they would have extended the garden in the process of subduing the earth, until its surface had become one vast garden—a scene of surpassing loveliness. But sin at once arrested the work. The ground was cursed; the garden was removed; the tree of life was taken away; and in its stead thorns and thistles sprung up to increase man's cares and labors. The curse upon the earth, the growth of thorns and thistles, the absence of the tree of life, were no more a part of God's original purpose concerning the earth, than sin and misery were in his original purpose concerning man. And, of course, the full accomplishment of his original purpose will bring the whole earth to a state of beauty; when the desert shall rejoice and blossom as the rose, and the wilderness be like Eden, even as the garden of the Lord. Isa. 35 : 1; 51 : 3. Both man and his dominion must and will be placed beyond the reach of the curse; beyond the power and the danger of moral and physical evil.

The wondrous mercy and love of God in providing a way of salvation at such an immense sacrifice as the gift of his own dear Son, was not appreciated by the fallen race. As men multiplied upon the earth they corrupted their way before God, and the land was filled with violence and iniquity. When they had gone astray almost without exception, the Lord determined to check this career of crime, and destroy the wicked generation. Noah alone, of all the millions living, had maintained his integrity. The purpose of mercy to the race was carried out in him.

After the flood, as the inhabitants of the earth again increased, instead of humbling themselves before the Most High, who had so wondrously made known his justice and his power, they made the flood an excuse to justify their insane ambition, and they set themselves to build a tower by means of which they might defy the power of the Almighty! In this they showed as little regard for his authority and might, as they had faith in his promise of which the bow in the cloud was a token. But the Lord is not straitened in resources to frustrate the purposes of the rebellious. He confounded their language so that they could no longer plan and labor in concert, and they, of necessity, "left off to build it."

As the people on the earth were now divided into nations, and all going astray from the Lord, it became necessary to separate one family, one people, to preserve the knowledge of God, and by whom to develop the plan of salvation and to identify the promised seed of the woman who was to bruise the head of the serpent. In the midst of all this perverseness, Abraham stood alone, a man of singular integrity and steadfastness in the right, insomuch that he was favored with the remarkable title of "the friend of God." He was constituted the father of all the faithful who should live upon the earth, even to the end of time; and to the promise made to him we are directed to look for our hope. See Heb. 6 : 11–20.

Also it is said, "And if ye be Christ's then are ye Abraham's seed, and heirs according to the promise." Gal. 3 : 29. Our heirship is, therefore, directly related to the promise made to Abraham. What is the promise? Of what are we heirs? It has been said by some that the only promise given to Abraham in which we have any interest is that of "the seed," or of Christ.

But that cannot be so, for the apostle in this same chapter, Gal. 3 : 16, says that the promises were made to Abraham and *to Christ;* not *of Christ.* If we are Christ's we are heirs of the same promises. This is further proved in Rom. 8 : 17, where it is said that if we are the children of God we are "heirs of God, and *joint-heirs with Christ.*" Thus it appears that certain promises were made to Abraham and to his seed; that the seed is, primarily, Christ, and secondarily, they that are Christ's; heirs with him of the promises.

According to the Scriptures it is an important consideration for us to be acknowledged as the seed or heirs of Abraham. Now it cannot be an important matter to be proved an heir of him who has nothing to bestow. What, then, was the promise, what the inheritance, which we may expect to receive from Abraham, our father? That the promise was of an inheritance, of a possession, or, so to speak, of a homestead, is abundantly proved in both Testaments. Thus Paul said of Abraham: "By faith he sojourned in *the land of promise* as in a strange country, dwelling in tabernacles with Isaac and Jacob, heirs with him of the same promise." Heb. 11 : 9. And further in verse 13: "These all died in faith, not having received the promises, but having seen them afar off, and were persuaded of them, and embraced them, and confessed that they were strangers and pilgrims on the earth."

As strangers and pilgrims they dwelt in the land of promise; although it was to be their inheritance, they dwelt in it as in a strange country, and died in faith of the promise yet to be fulfilled. This language is unmistakable in its import. In its obvious import it is fully sustained by the words of Stephen. The Lord said unto Abraham: "Get thee out of thy country, and from thy kindred, and come into the land which I shall show thee. . . . And he gave him none inheritance in it, no, not so much as to set his foot on; yet he promised that he would give it to him for a possession, and to his seed after him, when as yet he had no child." Acts 7 : 3-5. And we learn by Heb. 11 that he died without receiving it; therefore the promise remains to be fulfilled; and if to be fulfilled to him, of course "to his seed,"—all that are Christ's.

When we come to examine the original promises in the Old Testament, to which the writers in the New Testamemt refer, we shall find that "the land" is their chief burden. When the Lord called Abraham at the first he told him to go into *a land* which he would show him. And when he came into Canaan the Lord appeared unto him and said, "Unto thy seed will I give *this land;* and there he builded an altar unto the Lord." Gen. 12 : 1, 7. After Lot was separated from him the promise was renewed. That the prominence of this point may be seen, we copy in full what was said to him on this occasion.

"And the Lord said unto Abram, after that Lot was separated from him, Lift up now thine eyes, and look from the place where thou art northward, and southward, and eastward, and westward; for all the land which thou seest, to

thee will I give it, and to thy seed forever. **And
I** will make thy seed as the dust of the earth;
so that if a man can number the dust of the
earth, then shall thy seed also be numbered.
Arise, walk through the land in the length of
it and in the breadth of it; for I will give it
unto thee." Gen. 13 : 14–17.

At the next repetition of the promise this point
is made especially prominent, as follows: "And
he said unto him, I am the Lord that brought
thee out of Ur of the Chaldees, to give thee
this land to inherit it." Gen. 15 : 7. And again,
"I will give unto thee, and to thy seed after
thee, the land wherein thou art a stranger, all
the land of Canaan, for an everlasting possession,
and I will be their God." Gen. 17 : 8. Thus
the Lord has spoken the word that he brought
Abraham out of his native land to give him
the land that he would show him, and to his
seed, for an everlasting possession. This was his
purpose; but this purpose was never fulfilled;
Abraham, with his posterity, died in faith of its
fulfillment, and as God is faithful it will certainly
be brought to pass.

That this promise of *the land* was deeply impressed upon the minds of the patriarchs is proved
by their references to it. When Abraham sent
his servant to take a wife for Isaac, he said:
"The Lord God of Heaven, which took me from
my father's house, and from the land of my kindred, and which spake unto me, and that sware
unto me, saying, Unto thy seed will I give this
land; he shall send his angel before thee, and

thou shalt take a wife unto my son from thence."
Gen. 24 : 7.

The Lord also appeared unto Isaac in Gerar, as
he was on his way to Egypt, and said unto him:
"Go not down into Egypt; dwell in the land
which I shall tell thee of. Sojourn in this land,
and I will be with thee, and I will bless thee; for
unto thee, and unto thy seed, I will give all
these countries, and I will perform the oath
which I sware unto Abraham thy father." Gen.
26 : 2, 3. It is worthy of remark that in this,
the only instance recorded of God speaking to
Isaac, he commences with renewing the promise
of the land, in fulfillment of his word and oath
unto Abraham. And in the only instance recorded of Isaac referring to God's promises to
his father, "the land" is the main subject of
mention. He sent away Jacob to take a wife of
his kindred in Padan-aram, saying: "And God
Almighty bless thee, and make thee fruitful, and
multiply thee, that thou mayest be a multitude of
people; and give thee the blessing of Abraham,
to thee, and to thy seed with thee that thou
mayest inherit the land wherein thou art a stranger, which God gave unto Abraham." Gen.
28 : 3, 4.

And Jacob went on his way, and he lodged in
Luz, and the Lord appeared also to him in a
dream, and said: "I am the Lord God of Abraham thy father, and the God of Isaac; the land
whereon thou liest, to thee will I give it and to
thy seed." Gen. 28 : 13. And again, after his
sojourn in that land, the Lord appeared unto

him as he came out of Padan-aram, and said unto him: "I am God Almighty: be fruitful and multiply; a nation and a company of nations shall be of thee, and kings shall come out of thy loins; and the land which I gave Abraham and Isaac, to thee will I give it, and to thy seed after thee will I give the land." Gen. 35 : 11, 12. And finally, Joseph charged his brethren to carry his bones out of Egypt, saying: "And God will surely visit you, and bring you out of this land unto the land which he sware to Abraham, to Isaac, and to Jacob." Gen. 50 : 24.

And thus it is clearly shown that the inheritance, the possession, the land, was the great object of promise in the Abrahamic covenant, without which the other promises could never be fulfilled.

By many it is supposed that all the promises of the possession of the land were fulfilled to the natural descendants of Abraham who dwelt in the land of Canaan. We have given to us in the Scriptures several lines of proof showing that the possession of the land of Canaan did not fulfill the promise; that that land, in the condition in which they received it, was not the true inheritance of Abraham's seed, but only typical of it.

1. The dwelling of the children of Israel in the land of Canaan was not a fulfillment of the promise that Abraham, Isaac, and Jacob should possess it. It was not said merely that their children should inherit it, but that *they and their seed* should receive it for an everlasting possession. Stephen said that Abraham had no inher-

itance in it, no not so much as to set his foot on. This is proved to be literally true, in that he had to buy of the inhabitants of the land a place to bury Sarah, his wife, in Hebron. And Paul said that Abraham, and Isaac, and Jacob, heirs with him of the same promise, died without receiving it, and confessed that they were strangers and pilgrims on the earth. This alone would be sufficient to prove that the promise remains to be fulfilled.

2. According to Paul's testimony in Gal. 3 : 16, Christ was the seed to whom the promise was made; and he, as Abraham, was a sojourner in the same land. He had "not where to lay his head." He was the world's Maker, destined to be the world's Redeemer, and yet spent a life of toil and suffering in the world without a resting-place or home upon the earth. He purchased the redemption of the earth by bearing in his person the curse of the earth, even as he will redeem man because he bore the curse of man. When the ground was cursed the Lord said it should bring forth thorns because of man's transgression; these it would never have produced if sin had not entered. And Jesus, when he was made an offering for sin; when he was placed in the hands of the powers of earth, was crowned with thorns. The old purple robe and the crown of thorns were a mockery of his right as king, but they became a part of the means of his final triumph—a means of vindicating the justice of God before men and angels in the Judgment. He was "the heir" whom the men of the vineyard

cast out and slew. But he will come again to claim his own, and they will be destroyed. Matt. 21 : 33–42.

3. There is an argument from analogy on this subject which is very conclusive, besides the direct declarations of the Scriptures, showing that *the whole earth* was contemplated in the original promise. This argument must be admitted by all who claim to be the seed of Abraham, and recognize as valid the covenant made with him. In this covenant we find three prominent points, namely, 1. The land of promise. 2. The seed to whom the promise was made. 3. The token of the covenant, which is circumcision. All that will be here claimed on points 2 and 3 will be readily accepted by all New Testament believers.

The seed. The reader of the Old Testament might easily conclude that "the seed" to whom the promises were made included only the literal descendants of Abraham. But the term was soon restricted, and was shown to refer, not to all who descended from Abraham, but to those descending from him through one of his sons, Isaac. And in the New Testament it is shown that the term refers primarily to Christ, the real child of promise, and secondarily to all who are Christ's by faith. Thus it is said:—

"He is not a Jew which is one outwardly; . . But he is a Jew which is one inwardly." Rom. 2 : 28, 29. And again: "For they are not all Israel, which are of Israel; neither because they are the seed of Abraham are they all children; but, In Isaac shall thy seed be called. That is,

They which are the children of the flesh, these are not the children of God; but the children of the promise are counted for the seed." Rom. 9 : 6-8.

Therefore the true heirs of the promise are not counted by natural descent, but are of all nationalities, as the apostle says:—

"There is neither Jew nor Greek, there is neither bond nor free, there is neither male nor female; for ye are all one in Christ Jesus. And if ye be Christ's, then are ye Abraham's seed, and heirs according to the promise." Gal. 3 : 28, 29.

"Wherefore remember, that ye being in time past Gentiles in the flesh, who are called uncircumcision by that which is called the circumcision in the flesh made by hands; that at that time ye were without Christ, being aliens from the commonwealth of Israel, and strangers from the covenants of promise, having no hope, and without God in the world; but now, in Christ Jesus, ye who sometime were far off are made nigh by the blood of Christ." Eph. 2 : 11-13.

The Gentiles were "aliens from the commonwealth of Israel, and strangers from the covenants of promise;" but the gospel of Christ is the means of their naturalization, so that now they belong to the true Israel of God if they are of faith, and are "fellow-heirs, and of the same body, and partakers of his promise in Christ by the gospel." Eph. 3 : 6.

The token. When the covenant was made with Abraham a sign, or token, was given to him. The Lord said to him: "Every man-child among

20

you shall be circumcised. And ye shall circumcise the flesh of your foreskin; and it shall be a token of the covenant betwixt me and you." Gen. 17 : 10, 11. This more than any other one thing was a mark of separation between the Jews and the Gentiles. And this, from its terms, was confined to the male portion of the children of Abraham, "Every man-child among you."

But in the New Testament everything on this subject is different, both in substance and manner. As we have seen that he is not a Jew, or child of Abraham, who is one outwardly, so "neither is that circumcision which is outward in the flesh. . . . Circumcision is that of the heart, in the spirit, and not in the letter; whose praise is not of men, but of God." Rom. 2 : 28, 29. "In whom also ye are circumcised with the circumcision made without hands, in putting off the body of the sins of the flesh by the circumcision of Christ." Col. 2 : 11.

Circumcision was called "a token of the covenant;" in the New Testament it is called a sign and a seal; Rom. 4 : 11. And the seal, or circumcision, of the New Testament is further explained as follows: "In whom also after that ye believed, ye were sealed with that Holy Spirit of promise, which is the earnest of our inheritance." Eph. 1 : 13, 14.

The *earnest* is the same as the *seal* or *token*. Again it is written:—

"Grieve not the Holy Spirit of God, whereby ye are sealed unto the day of redemption. Eph. 4 : 30. "Who hath also sealed us, and given the earnest of the Spirit in our hearts." 2 Cor. 1 : 22.

This is the circumcision of the heart, in the spirit; the true token or sign of our heirship. And as it was said to Abraham that the uncircumcised man-child should be cut off—he had no part in the covenant; so it is now said, "If any man have not the Spirit of Christ he is none of his." Rom. 8 : 9. He has not the seal or token of the covenant, and has no part in the covenant.

Now mark the analogy. All Christians believe that the seed or children of Abraham, and circumcision, have a place in the gospel; that they are brought over into this dispensation; only they are enlarged in their terms, and made to apply to those and that to which they did not *seem* to apply when first the covenant was made. Now an enlargement of them is the very opposite of nullifying them, or having them expire by limitation.

But if they to whom a certain promise is made, and the token or assurance of that promise, are brought into the New Testament, why not also *the promise itself?* And if the terms of the other are enlarged, it is only reasonable to expect that of this they would be also. And thus we find it written: "For the promise, that he should be the *heir of the world*, was not to Abraham, or to his seed, through the law, but through the righteousness of faith." Rom. 4 : 13. "Blessed are the meek, for they shall *inherit the earth*." Matt. 5 : 5.

We fully believe, as before remarked, that God's original purpose in the creation of the earth will be fulfilled; that the restoration of the earth from the curse, from thorns and thistles, and from everything that could annoy its inhabitants, was included in the promise that the seed of the woman should bruise the head of the serpent; or, in the words of the New Testament, that Christ should destroy the works of the devil. The "first dominion" given to man shall be returned to him, but the promise of restoration was made to and through Abraham and his seed, and we receive it as his heirs. The meek shall *inherit* the earth. To inherit is to possess by heirship; but our heirship is solely of Abraham our father.

In the book of Hebrews are several lines of argument proving the exalted nature, and office, and the Messiahship of Jesus of Nazareth. It is affirmed, and proved from the Scriptures, that he is superior to the angels, to Moses, to Joshua, and to Aaron. On the last point the writer dilates, giving a lengthy argument on the priesthood. That Moses, Joshua, and Aaron were types of Christ is beyond dispute. Of Moses it is written: "And Moses verily was faithful in all his house, as a servant, for a testimony of those things which were to be spoken after; but Christ as a son over his own house;" &c. This fixes the standing of Moses and the typical nature of his work. In like manner the writer argues that Joshua did not give to the house of Israel the rest or the inheritance which was promised, but that it remains yet to be given to the people of God.

That the Lord did give rest in the land of Canaan to the descendants of Abraham is no more proof that the promise was therein exhausted, than the fact that they were circumcised, and that they were descended from Abraham, fulfilled all that was designed in circumcision, and met in full all that was expressed by the term *seed.* But we have seen that this was not the case. And we have seen also that the promise was to Abraham as well as to his seed, and that it was not fulfilled to him in any sense; also that the promise was "that he should be the heir of the world," which has never been fulfilled to him or to any of his descendants. This is that "rest" which remains to the people of God, of which Paul speaks in Heb. 4 : 9.

It has been assumed, and is by many supposed, that, because *Sabbath* means *rest,* therefore whenever the word *rest* is found it is equivalent to the Sabbath. But this is not the case, as an examination of the Scriptures will plainly show.

When Lamech begat a son (Gen 5 : 28, 29) "he called his name Noah, saying, This shall comfort us concerning our work and toil of our hands." The margin says, "That is, *rest* or *comfort.*" The name was prophetic; it means *rest.* This word was used by Moses in his address to the two tribes and a half who chose their inheritance east of Jordan. He said: "I commanded you at that time, saying, The Lord your God hath given you this land to possess it; ye shall pass over armed

before your brethren the children of Israel, all
that are meet for the war. . . . Until the
Lord have given *rest* unto your brethren, as well
as unto you, and until they also possess the land
which the Lord your God hath given them beyond Jordan." Deut. 3 : 18–20. And again: "For
ye are not as yet come to the *rest* and to the *inheritance* which the Lord your God giveth you."
Chap. 12 : 9.

Joshua also uses the same word when speaking
on the same subject: "And to the Reubenites,
and to the Gadites, and to half the tribe of Ma-
nasseh, spake Joshua, saying, Remember the
word which Moses the servant of the Lord commanded you, saying, The Lord your God hath
given you *rest*, and hath given you *this land*.
. . . Ye shall pass before your brethren armed,
all the mighty men of valor, and help them; until
the Lord have given your brethren *rest*, as he
hath given you, and they also have *possessed the
land* which the Lord your God giveth them."
Josh. 1 : 12–15.

And again, after the land beyond Jordan was
subdued before them, it is written: "And the
Lord gave them *rest* round about, according to
all that he sware unto their fathers; and there
stood not a man of all their enemies before them."
Josh. 21 : 44. And to the two tribes and a half
Joshua said: "And now the Lord your God hath
given *rest* unto your brethren as he promised
them; therefore now return ye, and get ye unto
your tents, and unto the land of your possession,
which Moses the servant of God gave you on the
other side of Jordan." Chap. 22 : 4.

In these passages this word *rest* is used as the equivalent of *inheritance*, and as applied it refers to *the peaceable possession of the land.*

But the generation which came out of Egypt, with the exception of two men, rebelled against the Lord and were not permitted to see the goodly land. Of these the Lord spake, saying, "Forty years long was I grieved with this generation, and said, It is a people that do err in their heart, and they have not known my ways; unto whom I sware in my wrath that they should not enter into my rest." Ps. 95 : 10, 11. This refusal to permit them to enter into his rest is recorded in Num. 14 : 23, in these words: "Surely they shall not see the land which I sware unto their fathers, neither shall any of them that provoke me see it." And in verse 30: "Doubtless ye shall not come into the land concerning which I sware to make you dwell therein." By these texts we see again that "the rest" was the possession of the land promised to them.

This is the subject of the argument of the apostle in Heb. 3 and 4. "But with whom was he grieved forty years? Was it not with them that had sinned, whose carcasses fell in the wilderness? And to whom sware he that they should not enter into his rest, but to them that believed not? So we see they could not enter in because of unbelief." Heb. 3 : 17–19. He then proceeds to exhort his brethren (which exhortation is spoken unto us), saying: "Let us therefore fear, lest a promise being left us of entering into his rest, any of you should seem to come short of it." Chap. 4 : 1.

This exhortation contains the announcement that, as the rebellious Hebrews who fell in the wilderness did not enter into the rest because of unbelief, so we should fear lest we come short of it; and labor to "enter into that rest, lest any man fall after the same example of unbelief." Verse 11. This is equivalent to a declaration that the promise which was given to them remains to be fulfilled; that we may inherit the rest offered to them, or fail of receiving it—"come short of it"—if we follow their example of unbelief. And to sustain this idea is the intention of the argument in Heb. 4:1–9. But before examining this argument we must call attention to the uses of the Hebrew words to which we have referred.

The Hebrew verbs *sha-vath* and *noo-ah* may be used interchangeably as far as they simply convey the idea, "to rest." Of this it is sufficient proof to cite Ex. 20:11, where *noo-ah* is used: "And he rested the seventh day." But when used in a substantive form they, or their derivatives, differ in this respect: *Shab-bath* signifies *a time* or *a period of rest;* whereas *no-ah* (*menoohah*) passes to the idea of a resting-place; *a place of rest.* That *Shab-bath*, sabbath, relates to a period of rest every reader knows; that *noo-ah* carries the idea of a place of rest is sufficiently shown by the passages quoted. *Menoo-hah* (feminine termination *ah*, from the root *noo-ah*) is the word used in Ps. 95:11. And Paul's quotation from this Psalm in Heb. 3:7–11 proves that that rest, or resting-place, the possession, the inheritance, is the subject of his exhortation and his argument in chapter 4.

According to the New Testament the people of ancient times knew much more of the counsel of God, through the types and shadows given to them, than we are wont to give them credit for, and even more than some Christians are able to discover in those same types. Abraham had the gospel preached to him, Gal. 3 : 9; and he rejoiced to see, by faith, the day of Christ; John 8 : 56. The Jews in the desert of Arabia drank of the rock which followed them, and that rock was Christ; 1 Cor. 10 : 4. It was "the reproach of Christ" that Moses esteemed as greater riches than the treasures of Egypt; Heb. 11 : 24–26; and the gospel was preached to the rebellious ones whose carcasses fell in the wilderness. Heb. 4 : 2. We, in this age, are quite too apt to draw a line of distinction between the faith of the ancient worthies and that of the faithful of this dispensation, which does not exist. Their gospel, their faith, their hope, were identical with ours. Through the types they looked forward to the "blessed hope" which cheers our hearts. "The rest" which was promised to them is promised to us; and, as many of them fell under the displeasure of God, and were not permitted to see even the land which was typical of the true inheritance (and which, of course, worked their forfeiture of the true), so may we fail of receiving the true inheritance if we follow their example of unbelief.

But the question is raised: If the everlasting

inheritance is the subject of the argument, why does the writer introduce the seventh day, and also speak of another day? They who ask this question seem to think that the apostle is arguing concerning the weekly Sabbath, and its change to another day; but, surely, they never would gather such an idea if they carefully read or studied the connection. Besides the facts which have been already presented, showing that the inheritance is the subject of the discourse, we notice,

1. If the Sabbath is "the rest" spoken of, then the Lord must have sworn in his wrath that they should not keep the Sabbath! So far from this, he had some put to death who refused to regard the Sabbath. But he declared that they should not go into the land of Canaan.

2. They who fell in the wilderness did not come short of the Sabbath, but kept it on their journeyings. But they did not see "the rest" which was given to the survivors.

3. The rest which remains is the antitype of that which Joshua gave to them. But Joshua did not give them the Sabbath, he gave them "the rest and the inheritance," to possess which they left Egypt.

Looking at it in every light we see but this fact, that the inheritance only is the subject of the argument.

In answer to the question we first remark, that the inheritance of the saints, and the kingdom which shall be given to them, are very closely related. So far as territory is concerned, they are identical. As Abraham, with his seed, is to be the heir of the world, and possess the whole earth, so the Son of David is to receive the kingdoms of the world and reign unto the uttermost parts of the earth; the kingdom and dominion "under the whole heaven" shall be given to the saints. As this rest or inheritance was finished from the foundation of the world, so of the kingdom; it was prepared from the foundation of the world. Matt. 25 : 34. And by the text in question Paul proves that it was finished from the foundation of the world. At the end of the work of creation "God did rest the seventh day from all his works." This proves that "all his works" were finished at that time, for rest is subsequent to work. This was "the dominion" given to Adam, which he lost by sin. It is to be redeemed and restored by the last or second Adam; but he will do it as the seed of Abraham, under a covenant or promise made to Abraham. This is the use, the only use, which Paul makes of the seventh day. It stands related to the promised rest to attest that the promise was not a matter of uncertainty; it related to that which was already made. And now we are prepared to appreciate the remark which he makes on Ps. 95.

It is on the record that the children of Israel received a certain rest, or possession, under Joshua; also that some who came out of Egypt provoked the Lord, and came short of that rest. But the Holy Spirit by David, some four hundred years afterward, exhorted the children of Israel who were then in the land of Canaan, not to follow in the ways of the rebellious ones who failed to enter into the rest. And the conclusion is drawn by Paul that if *that land* were in truth the inheritance intended in the promise, then those who lived in the days of David did not need the exhortation, seeing they were already in possession of it. Thus he speaks:—

"Seeing therefore it remaineth that some should enter thereinto, and they to whom the good tidings were before preached failed to enter in because of disobedience, he again defineth a certain day, saying in David, after so long a time, To-day, as it hath been before said, To-day if ye shall hear his voice, harden not your hearts. For if Joshua had given them rest, he would not have spoken afterward of another day. There remaineth therefore a sabbath rest for the people of God." Heb. 4 : 6–9, Revised Version.

As Paul spoke by inspiration this must be conclusive; and this rest which remains must bear the same relation to that which Joshua gave to the house of Israel that Christ bears to Joshua—the latter is the antitype of the former. It is the substance of the original "promise made of God unto the fathers." And this proves that the house of Israel no more received the inheritance promised to Abraham and his seed, than that circumcision in the flesh, outward, is the real circumcision which God requires, or that an unconverted Israelite, one who rejects Christ, is of the seed of Abraham, an heir according to the promise.

The only apparent difficulty presented in Paul's argument on "the rest" in Heb. 4, is the change from the use of the Greek word *katepausis,* rest, to that of *sabbatismos,* literally "the keeping of a Sabbath," or a sabbath rest, in verse 9. But there is no real difficulty when we consider that *Sha-vath* and *noo-ah* are interchanged as verbs. *Katepausen* properly represents the latter, yet in verse 4, Paul follows the Septuagint and uses *katepausen* in a quotation from Gen 2 : 3, where *sha-vath* is used in the Hebrew. *Sabbatismos* has a signification, according to the lexicons and the most judicious commentators, beyond literal Sabbath-keeping. Thus Greenfield says: " spoken of an eternal rest with God. Heb. 4 : 9." Robinson the same: " in N. T. only of an eternal rest with God. Heb 4 : 9." Dr. Smith, in Bible Dictionary, notices the opinions which have been offered that it refers to the Sabbath, and says: "The objections, however, to this exposition are many and great, and most commentators regard the passage as having no reference to the weekly Sabbath."

The "Bible Commentary" says:—

" *There remaineth.*—Or, v. 6, 'there still remaineth,'—is still to be looked for hereafter, over and above that rest in the land of Canaan. This inference follows, since the Holy Ghost speaks in the Psalms to us. *A rest.*—Rather a Sabbath rest; lit. 'a keeping of sabbath;' when the people of God, the 'Israel of God,' Gal. 6 : 16, shall obtain rest from all that trouble them; 2 Thess.

1 :7; and when all enemies shall be put under the feet of Jesus, the Captain of the Lord's host. Then, at last, the faithful shall 'enter into the joy of their Lord.' (Matt. 25 : 21, 23)."

The Cyclopedia of M'Clintock and Strong has the following: "Sabbatism (*sabbatismos*, Heb. 4: 9, A. V. rest), a repose from labor like that enjoyed by God at creation; a type of the eternal Sabbath of Heaven. See Rest." And of "rest," it says: "Rest also signifies a fixed and secure habitation;" and refers to the texts quoted on that subject.

The great difficulty in referring Heb. 4 : 9 to a weekly Sabbath lies in this: it leaves the apostle's argument without any logical conclusion. Although the verse begins with the word "therefore" (in the Greek), if it refers to the weekly Sabbath, it has no logical connection with the argument preceding; certainly no relation to the declaration in verse 8, that if Joshua had given them rest—implying the rest of the promise—he would not afterward have spoken of another day —for receiving it. And this is the view taken by most authorities. Dr. Clarke says:—

" The apostle shows that, although Joshua did bring the children of Israel into the promised land, yet this could not be the intended 'rest; because, *long after* this time, the Holy Spirit, by David, speaks of this rest; the apostle therefore concludes—verse 9, 'There remaineth therefore a rest to the people of God.' It was not, 1. The rest of the Sabbath; it was not, 2. The rest in the promised land, for the psalmist wrote long after the days of Joshua; therefore there is another rest, a state of blessedness, for the people of God."

Dr. Barnes speaks at length on this subject, and marks clearly the relation of argument and conclusion. We quote briefly. On Heb. 3:11, he says:—

" The particular *rest* referred to here was that of the land of Canaan, but which was undoubtedly regarded as emblematic of the *rest* in Heaven. Into that rest God solemnly said they should never enter."

And on chap. 4:8, 9, he says:—

" The object is to prove that Joshua did *not* give the people of God such a rest as to make it improper to speak of *a rest* after that time. If Joshua had given them a complete and final rest; if by his conducting them to the promised land all had been done which had been contemplated by the promise, then it would not have been alluded to again, as it was in the time of David. Joshua did give them a *rest* in the promised land; but it was not all which was intended, and it did not exclude the promise of another and more important rest. . . .

" There remaineth, therefore, a rest. This is the conclusion to which the apostle comes. The meaning is this, that according to the Scriptures there is *now* a promise of rest made to the people of God. It did not pertain merely to those who were called to go to the promised land, nor to those who lived in the time of David, but it is *still* true that the promise of rest pertains to all the people of God of every generation. The *reasoning* by which the apostle comes to this conclusion is briefly this: 1. That there was a rest called 'the rest of God'—spoken of in the earliest period of the world,—implying that God meant that it should be enjoyed. 2. That the Israelites, to whom the promise was made, failed of obtaining that which was promised, by their unbelief. 3. That God intended that *some* should enter into his rest—since it would not be provided in vain. 4. That long after the Israelites had fallen in the wilderness, we find the same reference to *a rest* which David in his time exhorts those whom he addressed to endeavor to obtain. 5. That if all that had been meant by the word *rest*, and by the promise, had been accomplished when Joshua conducted the Israelites to the land of Canaan, we should not have heard another day spoken of when it was possible to forfeit that rest by unbelief. It followed, therefore, that there was something besides that; something that pertained to all the people of God to which the name *rest* might still be given, and which they were exhorted still to obtain. The word rest in this verse, *sabbatismos, sabbatism*, in the margin is rendered 'keeping of a Sabbath.' It is a different word from *sabbaton*—the Sabbath; and it occurs nowhere else in the New Testament, and is not found in the Septuagint. . . . It means here a resting, or an observance of sacred repose, and refers undoubtedly to Heaven, as *a place of eternal rest* with God. It cannot mean the rest in the land of Canaan, for the drift of the writer is to prove that that is *not* intended. It cannot mean the Sabbath, properly so called, for then the writer would have employed the usual word *sabbaton*, Sabbath. It cannot mean the Christian Sabbath, for the object is not to prove that there is such a day to be observed; and his reasoning about being excluded from it by unbelief and by hardening the heart would be irrelevant."

This is a very fair statement of the case, though the writer *appears* almost to lose sight of the *object* of the promise in referring it to Heaven. He is certainly correct when he says: "If Joshua had given them a complete and final rest; if by his conducting them to the promised land, all had been done which had been contemplated by the promise, then it would not have been alluded to again." It must be kept in mind that *the promise* which was not exhausted in their possession of Canaan, was "the promise made of God unto the fathers," especially unto Abraham and to his seed, and embraced "the land of promise," which according to the New Testament, was "the world," or "the earth,"—the whole earth, or as the angel said to Daniel, "under the whole heaven."

And here we rest the argument on this point, believing that it is abundantly proved that the children of Israel "according to the flesh," were not all "the seed of Abraham;" that their cir-

21

cumcision in the flesh was not all that was intended in that ordinance; and that a temporary
possession by Abraham's natural descendants of
the land of Palestine, was not all that was meant
in the promise that he and his seed should inherit
it for an everlasting possession. The promises to
Abraham will be fulfilled only when "the meek
shall inherit the earth, and shall delight themselves in the abundance of peace."

We will notice one more. objection; not so
much because of its strength or plausibility, as
that it has been urged by some eminent theological scholars, in whose opinions people may have
confidence. It has been said that the righteous,
the meek, do now possess the earth; that all the
blessings and enjoyments of this world really belong to the people of God. But this objection is
readily disposed of; indeed it seems strange that
any one with the New Testament in his hands
should urge that the meek now inherit the earth;
that the promises are now being fulfilled to them.
It is disproved by most explicit declarations of
the Scriptures.

(1) The poor of this world, the rich in faith,
are only " *heirs* of the kingdom which God hath
promised to them that love him;" the kingdom
prepared "from the foundation of the world."

(2) When the meek inherit the earth "they
shall delight themselves in the abundance of
peace." Ps. 37:11. This is not the case at present, as we all know by observation and experience; the following words of our Saviour settle it:

(3) "In the world ye shall have tribulation; but be of good cheer, I have overcome the world." John 16:33. The enjoyment or blessing of the Christian is not from or of the world, but from what Jesus has done for us to overcome the world. So far from the meek having "abundance of peace" in this world, they have persecutions and afflictions; their life is only a warfare, in which they are speedily overcome if they lay aside their armor.

(4) The wicked inherit more of this present world than the righteous do, the latter being "the poor of this world," while a woe is pronounced upon the rich. But the scripture says: "Cast out the bondwoman and her son, for the son of the bondwoman shall not be heir with the son of the freewoman." Gen. 21:10: Gal. 4:30. If the inheritance is of this present world, the son of the bondwoman has the largest share.

(5) Abraham dwelt in the land, but he did not inherit it. He with others, heirs with him of the same promise, dwelt in the land of promise as in a strange country. And so the apostle said his brethren were "strangers and pilgrims." 2 Peter 2:11. Abraham had to buy a place to bury his dead in the land which was promised to him for an everlasting possession; even so now, the children of Abraham have an abiding-place in the earth only by paying tribute to earthly powers. But of this we do not complain. The time for us to inherit the earth has not yet come.

(6) That the Spirit is an "earnest of our inher-

itance" is proof on this point. The earnest looks to the fulfillment of a promise in the future· When God promised the land to Abraham he gave him circumcision as a token, an assurance of his promise. So now we have the circumcision of the Spirit, "which is the earnest of our inheritance." How long do we need the earnest or token? Until we take possession of the inheritance. And how long is that in the future? "Until the redemption of the purchased possession." The meek will not inherit the earth before it is redeemed, for in its present state they can only possess it in common with the children of the bondwoman, and they cannot "delight themselves in the abundance of peace." Jesus purchased the earth with the right to redeem it from the curse. And he will surely claim his right, and his people shall receive their reward. The expectation of the poor shall not perish. "The kingdom and dominion, and the greatness of the kingdom *under the whole heaven*, shall be given to the people of the saints of the Most High." Dan. 7 :27.

CHAPTER XIII.

CONCLUSION.

THE Bible is eminently a practical book; its great object is to make the man of God perfect; to thoroughly furnish him unto all good works. 2 Tim. 3 : 15–17. To this purpose it presents duties, warnings, and promises, holding out inducements by every means to lead us into the path of life and peace. It gives both history and prophecy, spreading out before us the past, the present, and the future. Here we have the only reliable cosmogony—the only "science of sufficient reasons" of the origin of the heavens and the earth. Here only can we learn the future of man and his dwelling-place. Peter says: "By the word of God the heavens were of old, and the earth standing out of the water and in the water; whereby the world that then was, being overflowed with water, perished. But the heavens and the earth which are now, by the same word are kept in store, reserved unto fire against the day of Judgment and perdition of ungodly men " And in that day of the Lord "the heavens shall pass away with a great noise, and the elements shall melt with fervent heat, the earth also, and the works that are therein shall be burned up.' "Nevertheless we, according to his promise, look for a new heavens and a new earth, wherein dwelleth righteousness." 2 Peter 3 : 5–7, 10, 13.

The world was once overflowed with water; the foundations of the great deep were broken up; the earth was a wreck; its surface was so changed as perhaps not to be recognized by those who beheld it before; and its inhabitants, except eight souls who were tossed upon the boisterous deep, were gone—all gone. Its gay and busy millions suddenly disappeared.

The Lord promised that there should not be " any more a flood to destroy the earth." But he did not promise that the earth should not any more be destroyed. As it once "perished" by water, so it will once more perish, but by fire. "The heavens and the earth which are now," are presented in contrast with those before the flood. But the material is the same; the earth is only changed in its form or features. So it will be with the new heavens and earth; there will be a second change, wrought by the agency of fire, and the earth will come forth purified from all the works of a fallen race. Then will the "purchased possession" be redeemed from the curse, and the glorified saints shall possess "the. kingdom prepared from the foundation of the world," even "the first dominion." And then "God shall wipe away all tears from their eyes; and there shall be no more death, neither sorrow, nor crying, neither shall there be any more pain; for the former things are passed away." There is blessedness, there is joy, there is glory, far beyond our conception; as it is written, "Eye hath not seen, nor ear heard, neither have entered into the heart of man, the things which God hath prepared for them that love him."

> "No more fatigue, no more distress,
> No sin nor death can reach that place;
> No tears shall mingle with the songs
> That warble from immortal tongues."

Reader, is there not infinite value in the atonement? Is not the blood of Christ precious? Does not the eternal inheritance, the far more exceeding and eternal weight of glory, present attractions beyond all else of which your heart has conceived? Does not eternal life in the kingdom of God appear a boon most precious? Then join with all the saints in blessing God for the rich provision through his Son, and for the word, the Holy Book, wherein alone such matchless grace, and such endless joys are revealed. Without the revelation of God's will, how uncertain, how dark would all appear! Without this, who should teach us the knowledge of God? who should acquaint us with the principles of morality and truth, by which we may honor and please our Creator? who should lead the fallen, erring one to a remedy for sin, wherein justice and mercy may be harmonized? Only eternity can reveal, and only immortalized beings can realize, how great is our indebtedness to God for his word. Happy the man who can say,

> "Holy Bible, book divine,
> Precious treasure, thou art mine."

But to them who despise the riches of his grace, and scorn his counsel and will none of his reproof there is another revelation in the word of God. He has not only sent redemption to his people, but prepared for his enemies a doom commensurate with their crime.

Having shown that obedience to the law, and acceptance of the gospel, are necessary to salvation; that salvation on any other terms would be derogatory to the character and Government of God, it follows necessarily that those who reject these terms cannot be saved. The penalty of their sins hangs over them, soon to descend upon their guilty heads; for in strict justice God reserves the wicked to the day of Judgment to be punished. 2 Pet. 2 : 9. And as eternal life is the gift of God, so they who do not seek it through the Son, must of necessity receive the wages of their sin, which is death. "He that believeth not the Son shall not see life; but the wrath of God abideth on him."

There are two resurrections taught in the Bible; for what the impenitent lose involuntarily by the sin of Adam, will be restored to them without regard to their will and action. Besides the resurrection of life, already noticed, there is also "the resurrection of damnation." They who have part in the first resurrection are blessed and holy; on them the second death shall have no power. They are raised in power, in glory, in incorruption, while they that sow to the flesh, "shall of the flesh reap corruption." Gal. 6 : 8. They will be subject to the second death. Once they die on account of Adam's sin; from this state they are raised by Christ. But the second time they die on account of their own sin; and from this death there is no redemption. **No hope is** held out for those who fall under its power. **No** resurrection morning dawns upon the darkness and gloom of the second death.

In examining the type of the scape-goat, **we** found the devil confined in the abyss for one thousand years. At the end of that period, all the inhabitants of the grave are called forth; the wicked of all ages stand up in life, and the great enemy of God and man is once more among the victims of his deceptions. He has borne the heavy burden of many sins placed upon his head, but his punishment yet awaits him. The Judgment has been sitting, and its decisions remain to be executed. But with the certainty of destruction before him, his malignity is not abated. His hatred to the ever-glorious Son of God and to the saints, who, through the blood of their Master, have overcome his deceptions and his power, leads him to instigate the risen nations to raise their arms once more against their Maker. Vain effort! Those who *now* think they can oppose his power with success, find *then* how fatally they have been mistaken. "And fire came down from God out of Heaven and devoured them." Rev. 20 : 9. As once this earth was overflowed with water, then it will be overspread with fire. This is that "day of Judgment and perdition of ungodly men," to which this sin-cursed earth is "kept in store." This is that terrible day "that shall burn as an oven; and all the proud, yea, and all that do wickedly, shall be stubble; and the day that cometh shall burn them up, saith the

Lord of hosts, that it shall leave them neither root nor branch." High ascends "the smoke of their torment," who have often mocked at the judgments of God; for "the wicked shall perish and the enemies of the Lord shall be as the fat of lambs; they shall consume; into smoke shall they consume away." Ps. 37 : 20. And as it is written that the Lord "smote Egypt in their first-born, and overthrew Pharaoh and his host in the Red Sea; for his mercy endureth forever;" Ps. 136 : 10, 15; so in the terrors of that great, that burning day, we behold the power of Jesus' blood; for he suffered "that through death he might *destroy* him that had the power of death, that is the devil." Heb. 2 : 13. And with him all his works are destroyed. 1 John 3 : 8. This ends the world's great controversy.

When "everlasting destruction from the presence of the Lord and from the glory of his power," is visited upon the wicked; when the righteous are introduced " to an inheritance incorruptible and undefiled and that fadeth not away," the record of the great future is briefly given. No elaborate description of that eternity of joy is offered; for words cannot describe all its glories; nor could our minds, always having associated with meaner things, appreciate the description. But we are permitted by faith in the sacred revelation, to look beyond the scene of terror, which we have been considering. The fury of the crackling flames exhausts itself; where the seething fires burned deep and fierce they languish for want of prey. As the smoke rolls up from the earth, there is revealed to our view a scene both grand and lovely; its surpassing beauty words cannot express; but above it all a voice is heard, "Behold I make all things new!" And now awakes the universal chorus: "And every creature which is in Heaven, and on the earth, and under the earth, and such as are in the sea, and all that are in them, heard I saying, Blessing, and honor, and glory, and power, be unto Him that sitteth upon the throne, and unto the Lamb forever and ever." The universe again is free from sin. Redemption's work is done. Beyond lies the vast ocean of eternity, all radiant with glory.

Here the mind gladly rests in contemplation of the heavenly scene. And now, while yet the scoffer, who has never had a thought of the eternal and infinite justice of God, declares that the Atonement is unnecessary, what fitting words of wisdom shall I choose to persuade him of its truth, and check his irreverent railing? How weak the effort a mortal puts forth to frame an argument worthy of the theme. From that dying agony; from that precious flowing blood; from that interceding grace; from that bright resurrection morn; from the earth made new; from that far more exceeding and eternal weight of glory, I turn and look *at my own heart;* and looking there, O man, your scoffing is vain. That glory I long to possess; that blood, that grace, that love, I need to fit me for the presence of my God. And shall I, a worthless worm of earth, defiled by sin, behold that glory and enjoy it forever? Then truly God is love. Nothing but love divine can perfect a work so great. And to him alone, the God of grace, I look for "victory through our Lord Jesus Christ."

Reader, may you and I find it there.

APPENDIX.

APPENDIX A.

THOUGH a doctrine should be maintained or admitted on the strength or correctness of its principles, in the minds of some an objection is suffered to obscure a principle, however well it may be established. Many have been so thoroughly indoctrinated in the idea that the death of Christ is equivalent to the Atonement that it is really difficult for them to appreciate our argument on justification by faith, and to understand the relation of such justification to a future Judgment. And again, by assuming that the death of Christ and the Atonement are identical, they are involved in endless controversy in regard to the application of the benefits of the Atonement. It will not appear to be out of place to further notice these points.

We read that Christ died for all. Some who take the view that the death of Christ is the Atonement, readily conclude that the sins of all have been atoned for, and argue thence that no condemnation can remain to any. The argument is reasonable, but the premise is defective.

Others, assured from the Scriptures that all will not be saved, that some do now and will finally rest under condemnation, are shut up to the conclusion that the Atonement is not made for all. They also regard the death of Christ and the Atonement as the same thing, and therefore are necessarily precipitated to the opposite extreme, that Christ did not die for all, but only for a chosen part of mankind. Here again, the difficulties of ultra Calvinism lie in the assumption on which their argument is based. The distinction herein advocated and sustained by plain Scripture facts and declarations, removes the errors of " Universalists " and " Partialists," and, if recognized, would bring all together on the harmonious testimony of the word of God.

And we would urge upon the consideration of the reader that, assuming that the Atonement was made on Calvary, one of the above positions must necessarily be admitted. Either the death of Christ was for a limited number (as the Atonement is), or else the sins of all have been atoned for, and all must be saved. If the Atonement be already made, if the sanctuary be already cleansed, and sin blotted out by an act long passed, we are unable to see how the destiny of man is to be affected by the proclamation and belief of the truth. It will be said that our faith lays hold of that which has been done for us; and if the declaration referred merely to what the Scriptures say *has been done*, it would be correct. But if our sin was removed or blotted out long before we were born, it is hard to see how the fact could be more a fact, or made more certain by our belief of it; or if our sins were not so blotted out, our unbelief could not affect the omission. But "Christ died for all;" and yet the impenitent will be "punished with everlasting destruction." This is in harmony with what has been shown in commenting on Rom. 5 : 10, pages 193–195, namely, that the death of Christ does not of itself save any one, but it makes salvation possible to every one. It is a matter of wonder that Bible readers have ever for a moment recognized as true the idea that death makes an atonement, when the Atonement is *always* represented as the work of the priest, performed in the sanctuary, with the blood of the offering.

The position of an individual who is justified by faith may be illustrated thus: A owes B a sum which he is not able to pay, and C engages to take the responsibility of the debt on certain conditions; and in order to make it sure, C deposits with B an amount sufficient to cover the debt. Now it is stipulated that if A fulfills the conditions, B shall cancel the debt from the deposit made by C. And as long as A is faithfully fulfilling the conditions, so long is B satisfied in regard to the debt; and of course he will not trouble A for it, knowing it is secure. Thus A is accounted just, in the sight of B, though not really just in himself, because he fails to pay a just debt. He is considered as just, or justified through obedience to the conditions of C, who is his surety. But if A refuses or neglects to fulfill the conditions, the deposit of C no longer avails for him; he falls from the favor of B, which he had enjoyed through this arrangement, and the debt stands against him as fully as though C had never engaged to pay it on any condition.

That justification by faith, or the pardon we receive while on probation, is a *conditional pardon*, is proved by our Saviour's words in Matt. 18 : 23–35. Here is presented the case of a servant who owed his lord ten thousand talents; but having nothing to pay, and manifesting honesty of intention, " the lord of that servant was moved with compassion, and loosed him, *and forgave him the debt*." But this servant met his fellow-servant, who owed him the trifling sum of two hundred pence; and who plead for mercy in the same terms in which the first had so successfully plead before his lord. But this servant would not show mercy; he thrust his fellow-servant into prison till he should pay the debt. Hearing of this, his lord called him, and said unto him, " O thou wicked servant, *I forgave thee all that debt*, because thou desiredst me. Shouldest not thou also have had compassion on thy fellow-servant, even as I had pity on thee ? And his lord was wroth, and delivered him to the tormentors, *till he should pay all that was due unto him*." This we say is the Bible view of forgiveness in the gospel, or justification by faith, while we are waiting for the decisions of the Judgment. And on this plain case we are not left to merely draw a conclusion; the Saviour has made the application for us, and from this application there can be no appeal. He says: " *So likewise shall my Heavenly Father do unto you*, if ye from your hearts forgive not every one his brother their trespasses."

That this is a true representation of the position of the penitent, is evident from the declarations that "he that ondureth unto the end"—he that is "faithful unto death"—shall be saved; while he that is justified by faith may, by disobedience, lose that justification, and his righteousness will not be remembered. The blood of Jesus is the bounteous supply—the rich deposit where all may find a covering for their sins; but whether their sins are actually atoned for and removed by that blood, depends upon their acceptance of it and their faithfulness to the conditions of acceptance. Without faith and obedience this deposit will never avail for any one.

Yet we hear many say, with the utmost assurance: "My debt is all paid; I cannot be lost, since Christ has died for me." But this is not the language of *trust;* it is rather that of *presumption.* Faith claims the promise of God on the fulfillment of its condition. We cannot consent to the idea of *unconditional salvation.* Whether they are aware of it or not, this is the position of all who expect to be saved *because their debt is paid*, or because Christ died for them. Every human being can say the same.

But we must notice the real point of this doctrine, namely, that God chose a certain part of mankind, and predetermined that they should be saved, passing by or reprobating the remainder. In 2 Cor. 5 : 14 we are told that "Christ died for all;" in Heb. 2 : 9, "that he, by the grace of God should taste death for every man;" and in 1 John 2 : 2, that he is the propitiation "for the sins of the whole world." Did Christ shed his blood for these reprobate ones? Is he their mediator? And some of this faith will answer in the negative; they will say that he did not die for them, but only for the elect. But if he did not die for them, was anything done for them? And how can they be said to "*neglect* so great salvation" (Heb. 2 : 3), if no salvation was provided for them? or trample on divine grace, which was no grace to them?

On account of the inherent repulsiveness of the doctrine known as "Calvinism," we often find persons claiming to hold it in a modified form. But that is impossible; it cannot be modified. It is fixed and inflexibly rigid in every feature. It is a belief that God irrevocably decreed and determined all things; and the belief can no more be modified than a fixed decree of Deity can be modified. It may only be exchanged for something else; but in itself it admits of no degrees; for the moment, that a condition is incorporated into it, it *is* something else. Calvinism teaches unconditional personal election; and unconditional personal reprobation is its converse and necessary attendant.

The Scriptures clearly teach these things, namely: free grace, justification by faith, and the necessity of good works to salvation; and these are all in harmony.

It is not our purpose to examine at length the

various texts quoted on this subject; but rather to notice the principles on which the true doctrine rests, and introduce texts sufficient to corroborate the principles.

The great question to be decided is this: In what respect is the gospel plan unconditional, and in what respect is it conditional? If there is anywhere such a distinction, and if we can clearly trace the line, the subject must thereby be relieved of much difficulty. Examining this, we find that,

1. The introduction of the gospel, or setting forth of Christ as the way of salvation, was unconditional. But,

2. The application of the gospel to individual salvation, is conditional.

We do not see how any, who believe the Bible, can dissent from either of these declarations. It is not said to the world, nor to any class in the world, that if they would do some certain thing Christ should die for them. But it is said that if they will believe and do certain things, they shall be saved by his blood so freely shed for the sins of the world. "God so loved the world, that he gave his only begotten Son, that whosoever believeth in him should not perish, but have everlasting life." John 3 : 16. Freely and unconditionally he gave his Son to be a propitiation for the sins of the whole world, to die for all; but not so that they will be saved from perishing if they refuse to repent and believe. Salvation was freely purchased by the death of Christ, but will never be given to those who neglect it. Heb. 2 : 3. Eternal life through Christ was freely and unconditionally brought to man; Rom. 6 : 23; yet, if they would not perish they must "lay hold on eternal life;" 1 Tim. 6 : 19; which they can only secure "by patient continuance in well-doing;" Rom. 2 : 7; and so "work out their own salvation with fear and trembling." Phil. 2 : 12. But in uniting works to faith we detract nothing from the grace and glory of Christ, for we can do nothing in our own unassisted strength. John 15 : 5. With this distinction in view we find no difficulty in harmonizing all the Scriptures. But we will notice a few texts to further show the conditional nature of God's promises to man.

When the Lord sent Moses to the children of Israel, it was with this message: "Say unto them, The Lord God of your fathers, the God of Abraham, of Isaac, and of Jacob, appeared unto me, saying, I have surely visited you, and seen that which was done to you in Egypt; and I have said, I will bring you up out of the affliction of Egypt unto the land of the Canaanites, and the Hittites, and the Amorites, and the Perizzites, and the Hivites, and the Jebusites, unto a land flowing with milk and honey." Ex. 3 : 16, 17. Again he said to them: "And I will take you to me for a people, and I will be to you a God; and ye shall know that I am the Lord your God, which bringeth you out from under the burden of the Egyptians. And I will bring you in unto the land, concerning the which I did swear to give it to Abraham, to Isaac, and to Jacob; and I will give it to you for an heritage; I am the Lord." Ex. 6 : 7, 8. Yet, direct and positive as this promise was, the Lord did *not* bring them into that land, but destroyed them for their disobedience.

Again, it was said to Pharaoh: "Thus saith the Lord, Israel is my son, even my first-born. And I say unto thee, Let my son go, that he may serve me; and if thou refuse to let him go, behold, I will slay thy son, even thy first-born." Ex. 4: 22, 23. The first-born was the highly-prized and beloved. Yet on the institution of the Passover, they would have been destroyed with the first-born of Egypt, if they had not remained in their houses and sprinkled the blood on their door-posts; and were afterwards destroyed as noticed above. This teaches us that God's chosen—his first-born, will continue to enjoy his favor *only on condition of continued obedience.* The conditional nature of his gracious promises is shown by his word through Jeremiah, wherein he commanded Israel to obey him, saying: "*That I may perform the oath which I have sworn* unto your fathers." Jer. 11: 3–5. And again, where he has shown the fixed principle upon which he fulfills his promises and threatenings. "At what instant I shall speak concerning a nation, and concerning a kingdom, to pluck up, and to pull down, and to destroy; if that nation against whom I have pronounced, turn from their evil, I will repent of the evil that I thought to do unto them. And at what instant I shall speak concerning a nation, and concerning a kingdom, to build and to plant it; if it do evil in my sight, that it obey not my voice, then I will repent of the good wherewith I said I would benefit them." Jer. 18 : 7–10. And this is true not only of nations, but of individuals. Thus the Lord said to Eli: " *I said indeed* that thy house and the house of thy father should walk before me forever; but now the Lord saith, Be it far from me; for them that honor me I will honor, and they that despise me shall be lightly esteemed." 1 Sam. 2 : 30.

It is argued that he that has an interest in the Saviour cannot or will not lose it. See what our Lord himself says: "I am the vine, ye are the branches. . . . If a man abide not in me, he is cast forth as a branch, and is withered." John 15 : 5, 6; and in verse 2 : "Every branch *in me* that beareth not fruit he taketh away." This completely overthrows that doctrine which affirms that if any one be in Christ by faith he cannot be taken away. He may "depart from the faith." It is urged, and with truth, that none can pluck them out of his hand. But this supposes that they "bear fruit," or continue faithful. He that endures to the end shall be saved. As the Jews were rejected because of their unfaithfulness, so Paul says to the Gentile converts, who, by faith, were grafted into the good olive tree, they must continue faithful or they should be cut off also. According to the unconditional personal election scheme, there could be no danger of it, and if so, the warning of the apostle was deceptive. He says also that they in whom the Spirit of God dwells, which can refer only to accepted believers, are the temple of God; and if they defile the temple of God, that is, themselves or their own bodies, God shall destroy them. And Peter affirms that some shall arise in the church who shall *deny the Lord that bought them*, and bring upon themselves swift destruction. 2 Peter 2 : 1.

Again, it is said we are chosen in him before the foundation of the world. But all must admit that there is a time when we become Christ's, come into him, etc. "As many of you as have been baptized into Christ have put on Christ." We are also said to receive Christ by faith. So it is evident that we are not "in Christ" before we have faith—before we have put him on. Prior to that event, we were the "children of wrath, even as others." Eph. 2 : 3. That we are *personally* and *unconditionally* elected before the foundation of the world cannot, therefore, be the sense of that scripture. Jesus Christ was the one chosen— "the elect"—to be the Author of salvation to all who believe and obey; and all who receive him and put him on, or are baptized into him, become one with him, members of his body; and, of course, are partakers of his privileges and his election. That the election was a prior event is admitted; but that we have any part in it before we become members of Christ's body is denied. The choice is of Christ, and through him all that are "in him;" but, *personally*, does not reach them that are out of him, children of wrath, as we were all by nature. With this view, we see the reasonableness of Peter's exhortation to make our calling and election sure, 2 Pet. 1 : 10; but with the Calvinistic view, it cannot be made to appear reasonable. And so of all the exhortations and threatenings in the Bible; if man is not free to choose or refuse, to obtain through obedience or lose through disobedience, they cannot be what they purport to be.

The truth on this subject we chiefly rest on the difference between the death of Christ, and the Atonement, to the argument on which we refer the reader.

APPENDIX B.

CHRIST, MAHOMET, OR CONFUCIUS?

THEY who reject the Bible and the Atonement frequently refer to Mahomet and Confucius as being equally entitled with Christ, if not more than he, to honor and worship.

When persons compare the Koran with the Bible, and place Mahomet on an equality with Christ, we are constrained to think that they have never read the Koran (perhaps not the Bible), and have never inquired into the principles of the divine Government, nor sought to find a way to save fallen humanity, and vindicate divine justice. We have read the Koran with this thought in mind, desiring to find there these great principles and to give it credit for them if found; but did not find them. And from our reading of it, we should full sooner place the story of "Jack the Giant Killer" on a level with the American Encyclopedia, than place the Koran on a level with the Bible.

We shall all be agreed in regard to the infliction of punishment when it answers the end of justice; and that the divine Ruler has a perfect right to choose his own instruments to carry out his own purposes; that when nations become grossly immoral, he may use flood, fire, and tornado, the earthquake, or other nations, to effect their overthrow. When all the nations of earth had become corrupt, it became necessary to choose one family and plant them a separate people, and remove or destroy idolatry from their land, to acquaint them with the truth, and to preserve a genealogy that the world might be assured that the promises and prophecies were fulfilled in Messiah. As God overthrew the enraged Egyptians in mercy to his people, so the nations of Canaan, low sunken in idolatry and sensuality, were exterminated in mercy to the race, to unfold the doctrines and facts of the Messiah's future kingdom. We see the wisdom of God in the Levitical law, for the gradual development of the great plan of salvation, both to make it plain to human reason, and to impress it deeply on the human heart.*

The Bible reveals the faults of God's people, but does not justify them. It teaches love, kindness, good-will, humility, self-denial, purity, and all that is "lovely and of good report" in the human character; while it offers the only means to raise and restore the erring to the favor of a just Creator.

---

* See "Philosophy of the Plan of Salvation."

It offers only joys that are pure, free from vanity and corruption; free from all that is low and sensual. The Koran, on the contrary, leads to hatred, to violence, to bloodshed, without even an effort to make this a mere element or necessity of a plan to eventuate in redemption; it presents the hope of power here, and of lustful gratification hereafter; the hope of overthrowing their enemies here as the best means of enjoying a plurality of wives in paradise! Not one principle of justice to be gained— not one attribute of God honored and glorified. Truly, he must be ignorant or depraved (or both) who compares the Koran to the Bible; and that this is often done we take as evidence of the perverseness of humanity.

Bishop Sherlock made the following just comparison:—

"Go to your Natural Religion; lay before her Mahomet and his disciples arrayed in armor and in blood, riding in triumph over the spoils of thousands and tens of thousands who fell by his victorious sword. Show her the cities which he set in flames, the countries which he ravaged and destroyed, and the miserable distress of all the inhabitants of the earth. When she has viewed him in this scene, carry her into his retirements, show her the prophet's chamber, his concubines and wives, and let her see his adulteries, and hear him allege revelation, and his divine commission, to justify his lusts and his oppressions. When she is tired with this prospect, then show her the blessed Jesus, humble and meek, doing good to all the sons of men, patiently instructing the ignorant and the perverse. Let her see him in his most retired privacies; let her follow him to the mount, and hear his devotions and supplications to God. Carry her to his table, to view his poor fare, and hear his heavenly discourse. Let her see him injured, but not provoked. Let her attend him to the tribunal, and consider the patience with which he endured the scorns and reproaches of his enemies. Lead her to his cross, and let her view him in the agonies of death, and hear his last prayer for his persecutors: 'Father, forgive them, for they know not what they do.' When Natural Religion has viewed them both, ask which is the prophet of God. But her answer we have already had; when she saw part of this scene through the eyes of the centurion who attended him at the cross; by him she said, Truly, this is the Son of God."*

Confucius is doubtless entitled to more respect than Mahomet, for there appears to be no evidence that he was an imposter; for he was not a religious leader. And therefore they who put him forth as a rival to Christ are no more entitled to credit than the devotees or apologists of Mahomet. All that is known of Confucius is by Chinese tradition, which to those in anywise acquainted with

---

*The Cottage Bible says of Mahomet: "Most of the truths of divine revelation he has discarded, only he acknowledges the divine mission of Jesus, and *so far* may be considered a witness for Christianity." But even this is, I think, more than should be either claimed or granted, especially as some might thence infer that there is an agreement between the two; for though he may acknowledge the "*divine mission*" of Jesus, he does not acknowledge his *divinity*, for he says, Koran, Chap. iv., "God is but one God; far be it from him that he should have a son." Several other expressions show that he denied the divinity of Christ.

the Chinese character, will not seem entitled to any great credit. Holding that all beyond their own borders are barbarians, they shut themselves up in their self-conceit; and from the divine titles and honors paid to their rulers, we may readily and justly conclude that the memory of "the Teacher," as they term Confucius, has not suffered in their hands. They never speak of their rulers without using the most extravagant language; and if their emperor is sick, he can have nothing less than a "celestial disease"! Their literature is generally considered below mediocrity; their educational systems tax the memory rather than the judgment; how then shall we arrive at a certainty as to the *real* merits of Confucius?

As a specimen of their literature, take the following:—

"The great extreme is merely the immaterial principle. It is not an independent, separate existence; it is found in the male and female principles of nature, in the five elements, in all things; it is merely an immaterial principle, and because of its extending to the extreme limit, is therefore called the great extreme. . . . .

"The great extreme is simply the extreme point, beyond which one cannot go; that which is most elevated, most mysterious, most subtle, and most divine, beyond which there is no passing. . . . It is the immaterial principle of the two powers, the four forms, and the eight changes of nature; we cannot say that it does not exist, and yet no form or corporeity can be ascribed to it. From this point is produced the one male and the one female principle in nature, which are called the dual powers; the four forms and eight changes also proceed from this, all according to a certain natural order, irrespective of human strength in its arrangement. But from the time of Confucius no one has been able to get hold of this idea."— *Chinese Repository, Vol. 13.*

If this were a specimen of Confucius' philosophy (which it probably is not), we could not wonder that A. J. Davis should put him in the "Pantheon;" for the above resembles the *philosophy* of Davis enough to have been written by his twin brother!

The "Middle Kingdom," a history of the Chinese Empire, contains the following statement:—

"The remarks of Confucius upon religious subjects were very few; he never taught the duty of man to any higher power than the head of the State or family, though he supposed himself commissioned by Heaven to restore the doctrines and usages of the ancient kings. He admitted that he did not understand much about the gods; that they were beyond and above the comprehension of man, and that the obligations of man lay rather in doing his duty to his relatives and society, than worshiping spirits unknown."—*Vol. 2, p. 236.*

This is quite as good as we could expect from a heathen politician; but that professed reformers, who acknowledge moral relations and moral obligation, should quote him as an oracle, or place him on a level with Christ, and his teachings on a level with the morality of the Bible, is strange indeed. The gospel alone shows how God may be just and the justifier of him that believeth in Jesus; it alone shows the true relative importance of love to God and love to our fellow-men; it alone proclaims, " Glory to God in the highest, and on earth peace, good will toward men."

THE LOVE OF GOD.

"GOD IS LOVE." He is the same from everlasting to everlasting. With him is "no variableness, neither shadow of turning." Jas. 1:17. Many have made the serious mistake of supposing that God has changed with the changes of man's relations to his government. If they do not directly speak it in words, the thought often discovers itself in their reasonings, that God is different, either in purpose or disposition, in the fall of man, or in the changes of dispensations, from what he was in the remotest ages of his eternity. Many show that they look upon him as *only a cool deliberator* in the work of creation, having no deep, earnest, intense feelings of sympathy and love for the work of his hands; that he was but *a rigid lawgiver* in the Levitical dispensation, and that he manifested himself *as love* only in the present or gospel dispensation. In nothing that we can conceive could there be a greater misrepresentation of the divine character than in such a view as that. He has uttered a strong reproof to those who think he is such a one as themselves. Ps. 50:21. And in nothing is this error more manifest than in representing him as changeable in character and in purpose.

God *is* love, and he *always was* love. All his works have been and are done in love. It was

(351)

not a blind, unreasoning emotion that caused all the sons of God to shout for joy when the great Creator laid the foundations of the earth. A glorious system was presented to their enraptured view, and they well understood that it was to the pleasure and glory of the Creator that it was brought into existence. Rev. 4:11. He hath made his wonderful works to be remembered. Ps. 111:4. And the creatures of his power did not alone rejoice in that day. On the seventh day God rested from all his work, "and was refreshed." Ex. 31:17. This can only mean that he took delight in the work which he had made. And his pleasure in, and the importance of, his work are shown in this: that he always revealed himself, in contrast with the idols of the nations, as the God that made the heavens and the earth. Jer. 10:3–16; Acts 17:23, 24; Rev. 10:5, 6; 14:6, 7. Truly, "the heavens declare the glory of God" (Ps. 19:1), and therefore all men are without excuse before him, because his eternal power and Godhead are "understood by the things that are made." Rom. 1:20. To all these high purposes his work was pronounced "very good.'

Again, they all rejoiced because there was opened to their wondering sight an avenue for the immeasurable happiness of vast multitudes of the creatures of the Most High. Among that joyous, shouting throng there was no selfishness. They found their joy in that which brought joy to others. The creation of man presented to their minds *vast possibilities*, which would all redound to the glory of God and to the happiness of the race.

They looked forward to the time when the purpose of the Creator would be accomplished; when the earth should be subdued and filled with inhabitants, all happy as they were, who would share in the eternity and in the favor of God, and forever sing praises to his grace.

Of the happiness which was stored up for man in his creation, we, in our fallen state, with the effects of the curse on every hand and in ourselves, can have but a faint conception. Placed in a lovely garden, with the privilege of extending its loveliness over all the earth, in which was every tree that was good for food and pleasant to the sight, he need not labor hard to procure his food. or to minister to his sense of delight. Nature presented an inexhaustible fountain of intellectual pleasure. The botanist, who spends his time in the study of vegetation, can alone realize the enjoyment which may be found in holding converse with the flowers. He who trains the lower animals—who, by his association with them, learns somewhat of their intelligence, of their affection for and faithfulness to their friends and benefactors, can realize to a small degree the pleasure which their presence might have afforded to man if death and the curse had not fallen upon all races. The astronomer can best appreciate the words of inspiration, "that the heavens declare the glory of God." To him who enters into the secrets of nature, every twinkling star, every opening bud, every falling leaf, every stone in the mountain, every animal and insect, every combination of the elements, presents an open page,

23

interesting and instructing all leading the beholder to praise and adore the wisdom and goodness of the Creator.

Had Adam lived unto the present day, and all remained pure and peaceful, what treasures of knowledge he might now possess! What deep delight he could find in the dominion over which his loving Maker had placed him! And, compared to his immortal existence, these would be but his childhood day ; compared to what his ever expanding mind might grasp in eternity, he would yet be in the rudiments of his studies of the wonderful works of God. Who can measure the intellectual enjoyment which God prepared for man in the creation of the heavens and the earth? Who can measure the love of God manifested in creating man with such capacities, and placing him in the midst of such surroundings?

But intellectual enjoyment was not the highest, the dearest, which was prepared for man. Association with the lower races, the study of creation, pleasant as these would have been, could not have satisfied all his nature. The most pleasing employment, the most beautiful scenes, may all become wearisome without companionship. God, in his infinite wisdom and kindness, saw that it was not good for man to be alone. He made a "help meet" for him.* In our fallen condition, with our

---

*This term, "help meet," is a tame translation. It is, perhaps, difficult to give a literal translation which would be appreciated. The literal rendering is : "a help as before him," or in his presence. But Gesenius gives to this form of the word the following definition : "Things corresponding to or like each other, counterparts, hence, Gen. 2:18, *I will make for him a helper corresponding to him,* his counterpart." This is generally accepted ; if taken most literally, it might represent one "as in his presence," a part of himself, to behold whom, or of whose companionship, he would never weary.

sensibilities blunted by continual contact with sin; with all our powers impaired, and especially our moral natures weakened, we can have but a faint conception of the love which animated the breasts of Adam and Eve; of the happiness for him, and for his race, which was stored in the marriage institution. Heaven smiled upon them, and angels rejoiced with them in their fullness of joy.

But there was *one* who was jealous of their joy; jealous of the glory which the new-made earth brought to its Creator. And he stirred up others to share in his jealousy, and to join him in his work of evil. He determined, if possible, to mar the work so that it might become a scene of misery to its inhabitants, and bring reproach upon its Maker. He would tempt the woman—the weaker of the noble pair—to distrust the loving-kindness of God, and to regard her Creator as an abitrary ruler. He would stir up feelings of selfishness and self-will in her heart, and cause her to transmit these baneful qualities to her posterity. He would work the ruin, the destruction of man, and turn the rejoicings of the angels into weeping over the desolations which he would work in the earth. And, alas, too well he succeeded. Choosing one of the brightest and wisest of the creatures of earth as his instrument, he approached the woman (who, presuming on her strength to stand alone, had left the side of her husband, as many of her daughters have since done), and, with insinuating manner, thus he suggestively addressed her:—

"Hath God even denied you the privilege of

eating of all the trees of the garden? And especially of this, the most desirable of all the trees to make one wise? God knows that if you eat thereof your eyes will be opened, and you will be godlike. It is for this reason he would deprive you of its benefits. He is jealous of your happiness; jealous for his own exaltation, lest you should rise to be more nearly like himself. For this he deprives you of the greatest benefit the garden possesses. And as for the threatening of death—you shall not die; you cannot die. Your body at best is only of the dust. Look beyond this to the development of your higher nature. You have an immortal part, over which death can have no control. Do not suffer your high immortal nature to be thus dwarfed, but assert your liberty—your right to the joys of that knowledge which this tree alone can impart."

"And when the woman saw that the tree was good for food, and that it was pleasant to the eyes, and a tree to be desired to make one wise, she took of the fruit thereof, and did eat, and gave also unto her husband with her; and he did eat." *

In the transgression Adam was not deceived. 1 Tim. 2 : 14. He full well understood the consequences of his action. But to be separated from her who was a part of his being, and dearer to him than his life,—to lose her by death, and remain to walk the earth alone,—this was more than he could bear. Had he never known her, life might have been pleasant without her. But to be deprived

---

* The words here ascribed to the tempter are not altogether "a fancy sketch," as the reader might consider them. Gen. 3 : 6, here quoted, shows that the woman was deceived to that extent. In this manner, by the strength of the deception, she "saw" that the tree was good, and greatly to be desired; she saw what did not actually exist. For the same manner of speaking, see 2 Thess. 2 : 4, " showing himself that he is God." That is, he so deceives his followers that he appears to possess the powers and attributes of God.

of her after having known her and being associated with her, life was not endurable. Through what a struggle he must have passed to come to this conclusion! He had enjoyed the presence and conversation of his Maker; he had associated with the angels; he had seen the glory of God—a glory of which we have no conception; his mind grasped the loveliness of the garden and the beauty of the earth as it would be, when subdued by the hands of himself and his children; eternal beauties, eternal blessings, and the eternal favor of God, stood revealed before him; and he sacrificed all to perish with his beloved wife. He fell because he, too, distrusted God. He could not believe that God could provide any blessing which could atone for the loss of this.

But when he sinned, the scene changed—all was changed. All his noble powers fell in his fall. His love for his wife degenerated. Before his fall he chose to sacrifice life, unspeakable joys, the favor of God, everything, for love of her. But now, he who was not deceived, who sinned by choice, was willing to throw the blame upon his wife, and indirectly upon his Maker, who, in the depth of love, had provided for him a counterpart. " *The woman* whom *thou gavest* to be with me, she gave me of the tree, and I did eat." And thus it has been from that day to this. The purity and unselfishness of man's first love has been lost. Man has continued to excuse himself, and to throw the blame of his actions upon another. He abuses the best gifts of Heaven, and blames the Giver because they do not well answer their intended purpose when thus perverted. But every evasion of responsibility, every excuse which is offered, is proof of a fallen, selfish, perverse nature. Poor fallen man! He chose his own destiny; and the sentence went forth that he must die, and return unto the ground from which he was taken.

But God's mercy did not fail; he still loved his fallen creatures. It was necessary that man, intelligent and well-instructed, should form his own character, and be held responsible for his actions. The work of the Creator was marred, but his counsel cannot be overthrown. Justice demands that man must die, but love pleads that a way may be opened for his recovery. The purpose of God in creating the earth must be vindicated. "He created it not in vain; he formed it to be inhabited." Isa. 45 : 18.* Satan triumphed over man, but the triumph of evil is not forever. God's love for man is deeper than that of a mother for her infant child. Isa. 49 : 15. It was *the same love* which prompted the creation of man, which prompted the institution of means for his redemption. The gospel brings to man that which was embraced in God's original purpose. And his honor and glory are concerned in the success of this plan; in the salvation of man, and in the restitution of his dominion. The universe shall not be robbed of this jewel in the crown of its Creator's glory.

---

*These words of the Lord do not leave us to conjecture whether the countless orbs in the heavens, immensely larger than the earth, are inhabited. If not inhabited this earth would be made in vain. We may not admit that all the other worlds were made in vain; they must be inhabited. If sin is found only in this world, as we are led to believe by the Son of God coming here to suffer and die, what an aggregate of happiness has God conferred upon the universe which he has framed! What an infinite number of intelligences are the recipients of his love.

As by man himself came the curse, so by man must come the recovery. "Since by man came death," it was ordained that by man shall also come the resurrection of the dead. 1 Cor. 15 : 21. As the woman was led into temptation by the serpent, it was determined that the seed of the woman should bruise the serpent's head. *Another Adam* (see 1 Cor. 15 : 45) must appear to take away the reproach of the first; to do that which the first failed to do, and to undo what he did amiss. And from the time of the giving of the promise, the Father multiplied instruction to lead the fallen race into the knowledge of the great plan which he had devised to destroy the enemy and his works. 1 John 3 : 8; Heb. 2 : 14.

And when the nations were multiplied, and all had chosen their own way,—"they did not like to retain God in their knowledge,"—his love still followed them. He separated Abraham and his seed from the nations, to make them the special depositaries of his truth, missionaries to the world, the people among whom his knowledge might be perpetuated, and among whom the Lord's Christ should be revealed. And thenceforth the promise was kept ever before them by signs and symbols, by types and figures, of the coming of the hope of the world, the Anointed One. The altar, the prophet, the priest, and the king, all announced, and all likewise represented, the promised Messiah. With much anxiety this "chosen people" looked forward to the time when *the Deliverer* should appear. All their service took character from this hope: "*Messiah shall* come;" the "Lord's Anointed" shall be revealed. This was the watchword of Israel through the ages.

But with the passing of centuries they grew weary of waiting. Many times they turned to their own way, and God left them to the power of their foes. Many calamities befell them. And when the "nation of fierce countenance" (Deut. 28:50) overflowed the land, they, as the nations around them, made an alliance with the conquering power, in hope of finding that peace and security for which they had not faith and patience to wait in the fulfillment of God's all-wise plan. God had purposed that Israel should "not be reckoned among the nations." Num. 23:9. And so it was that the tie unto which they had consented became irksome. That to which they looked for relief became a burden. In their sorrow they longed exceedingly for deliverance, and came at length to make freedom from the Roman yoke the chief end of Messiah's coming—the object of their hopes and the burden of their prayers. As their hope degenerated to a worldly object, they became worldly in their religion. They longed for the restoration of the kingdom, but it must be by methods of their own choosing, or in a way to gratify their ambitious desires. The Roman yoke was heavy upon them; but the bondage of sin, the corruptions of a fallen nature and the carnal heart, they did not feel.

But God did not leave himself without witnesses. He gave abundant evidence of the time, and the nature of the work to be accomplished by the coming of his Son. Born in obscurity, not as the kings of the earth, not in the manner to meet the minds of the ambitious and the worldly, Jesus has yet a heavenly host to herald his advent, and to sing, "Glory to God in the highest," over his despised birth-place. Holy, waiting ones were inspired to announce that the infant Jesus was the hope of Israel, and a great prophet. John the Baptist was specially commissioned to formally present him to the people, and to declare that in his day the axe was laid at the root of the tree, and that the fruit of righteousness was required in order to find acceptance with the Lord and his Anointed.

In due time Messiah appeared. But instead of seeking the display and pomp of power, he was meek and lowly, and announced that the kingdom of Heaven was for the poor in spirit; that exalted positions in the church, a desire to be counted scrupulously pious, already have their reward in the praise of men, which they are seeking, and that they could not believe in him while they received honor one of another, and sought not that honor which comes from God.

To us in this day it looks marvelous that, with the prophecies plainly pointing to his coming; with inspired ones then living who declared he was the salvation of God, the hope of Israel; with the testimony of John (in whose light they for a time rejoiced) that Jesus was the Lamb of God that taketh away the sin of the world; with the witness of the Spirit, which rested visibly upon him at his baptism; with the testimony of the

Father speaking from Heaven, saying, This is my beloved Son; with the evidence of his own miracles, which seem to put all doubt out of question,—we say it looks marvelous that Israel, the church of God, his own chosen people, should shut *their* eyes against all these evidences, and even demand his shameful death. It shows the great danger of perverting or neglecting the words of the prophets, and of lowering our religion so that it shall embrace exalted position in this world.

And it may be questioned why God reveals his plans and purposes thus gradually and by types and symbols; why he suffers evil influences, and trials, and unfavorable surroundings to blind the minds of the people, and to impede the progress of those who would fain escape from the snares of the enemy. It is not only just, but necessary, that God should be honored right where he was dishonored. Man fell by giving way to temptation; he must rise by overcoming temptation. He fell by suffering himself to be tempted to distrust God; he must rise, if he rises at all, by a work of faith. The first step in the fall was the harboring of a desire to rise above the position which a loving Father had assigned to him; the first step in their recovery is by self-renunciation, by humility, by cross-bearing. The descendants of Abraham lost sight of the faith of Abraham, by means of which "he was called the friend of God." and walked in the way of their first representative, Adam, and rebelled against the word of their Creator. A Saviour from sin—a Messiah in lowliness of mind—they could not accept. "He came unto his own, and his own received him not."

We cannot say that God is moved by more love at one time than at another, but we can say it is so manifested as to be appreciated by us more at one time, or in one event, than in another. Of all that the God of love and grace has done for man, nothing so manifests his love for us—nothing so appeals to our hearts—as *the gift of his Son* to die for our redemption. "God so loved the world, that he gave his only begotten Son, that whosoever believeth in him should not perish, but have everlasting life." "Not that we loved God, but that he loved us, and sent his Son to be the propitiation for our sins." "But God commendeth his love toward us, in that, while we were yet sinners, Christ died for us." God by his own Son made the worlds. Heb. 1: 1, 2. And the Son of God, without whom was not anything made that was made, died for his own creatures who were in open rebellion against him; who were his avowed enemies. If we cannot conceive the joy, the happiness, that was stored up for man in his creation, in the surroundings and privileges conferred upon him, and in the institutions which the Lord ordained for his benefit, much less can we conceive the love which devised and conferred these things; and less, far less, can we conceive the love by which the Maker of all laid down his life—not for his friends and followers, but—for his bitter foes! The love of the Father, the incarnation of his Son, "the mystery of godliness," can never be understood by finite minds. Through all the ages to come we shall learn more of "the love of Christ, which passeth knowledge," and day by day will all eternity increase the joy with which we shall praise the glory of his grace.

By wicked hands he was crucified and slain. In the bitterness of their disappointment even his disciples, despised of men and fearing for their own lives, forgot the words of the prophets, and the instruction they had received from their beloved Teacher. Their hope was gone. He whom they had trusted should redeem Israel, lay in the grave.

"But God raised him from the dead." Acts 13: 30. With a revival of their joy in his presence, their hope was revived in the immediate restoration of the kingdom of Israel. Acts 1: 6. But they were told that they must wait; that they must be his witnesses to all nations to gather out a people to the glory of his name. And he was parted from them, and returned to his Father in Heaven. Then was renewed by heavenly messengers the promise which he had made to them, that, after he has prepared mansions for them in his Father's house, *he will come again* and receive them unto himself. From that time his *second advent* was, to his longing people, "the blessed hope." Tit. 2: 13. It was their hope of salvation. Heb. 9: 28. They looked forward to it as the time when they shall appear with him in glory. Col. 3: 4. When they shall be like him, and see him as he is. 1 John 2: 4. When they shall receive a crown of life. 1 Pet. 5: 4. When they shall put on immortality and triumph over death and the grave. 1 Cor. 15: 51-55. When they shall be restored to the sweet companionship of their loved ones who had fallen asleep. 1 Thess. 4 : 13–18. And to "love his appearing" was made an assurance of receiving a "crown of righteousness." 2 Tim. 4 : 8. All hope, all joy, all glory, clustered around the promise of his "*second advent.*"

It was only on the day of atonement—once every year—that the high priest went into the most holy place to blot out the sins of the people. On this day, the chief of their solemnities, all Israel was commanded to afflict their souls under penalty of being cut off. Special orders were given to insure the successful performance of the work of the priest. How anxiously did the people wait around the sanctuary, praying that their sins might be removed; that the sanctuary might be cleansed from the defilement of their iniquities. They understood that it was *the judgment,* the great assize for the determination of their cases, which were then pending before the throne of God.* In that day the glory of God appeared over the mercy-seat. It was upon the mercy-seat that the blood was sprinkled which blotted out their sins.

What a solemn moment for Israel! How anxiously they marked each step as the priest approached the second vail which separated between the holy—the place of ordinary or continual service—and the most holy, the place of service for this day only. Now the vail is removed, and he passes into that place of most awful sacredness!

*We once inquired of a Jewish Rabbi in what light he regarded the day of atonement. He said to the Jews it was the day of Judgment.

The cloud of incense rises before him to shield his eyes from the fullness of that glory upon which a mortal cannot look and live. All breathless the people wait. The stillness and solemnity of death rest upon the congregation. The blood has been sprinkled upon the mercy-seat; the offering is accepted; the high priest returns to the holy to perform the last rites there. He moves from the golden altar toward the outer door. With shouts of rapturous triumph they cry, He is coming! he is coming! The singers raise their voices; all hearts anticipate the joyful moment when their high priest shall appear to pronounce upon them the divine benediction, to assure them of their acquittal, and that the blessing of Heaven was theirs.

This service in the most holy place, this finishing work of the priest, and his coming out to bless the people, typified the second advent of the Messiah, our great High Priest, and not his first. His first advent was in humility, as a pattern of suffering and of patience; his second will be in glory, and for the redemption of his people. As Israel watched and prayed, and afflicted their souls, so must the "little flock" watch for the return of their Lord. As Israel rejoiced when they marked the closing of his work, and the nearness of his coming to bless them, so should the saints look up and rejoice when they see their redemption drawing nigh. Luke 21: 28. Thus the word of God marks the parallel. But as *the first house of Israel* overlooked the humiliation of the Messiah, and desired that he should come only as a

king, so *the second Israel* now rejects the prophecy
of his second coming, and can see but one advent
—that of humiliation and suffering. *Each rejects
the truth given for its own time.*

To the early Christian Church, who prayed
earnestly that the beloved Saviour would come
again, and "come quickly," it was a strange revelation that his professed followers should cease to
"love his appearing." But it is even so; the
great apostasy has done its work; the love of
many has waxed cold. From saying, "My Lord
delayeth his coming,"—from putting it off indefi-
nitely, they have come to question, "Where is the
promise of his coming?"—their eyes are closed
to the evidence of the blessed hope.

But the mercies of God are unfailing. His
word of truth is as steadfast as his eternal throne.
Though all men should deny him, he cannot deny
himself. He is long-suffering, not wishing that
any should perish, but that all should come to
repentance. 2 Pet. 3: 9, R. V. He has never
done any great work for or among his people
"but he revealeth his secret unto his servants the
prophets." Amos. 3:7. He has never sent sore
judgments upon the earth without sending a
warning, and giving the inhabitants a chance to
escape. It was so in the time of the flood, so in
the case of Egypt, so with Nineveh, so with the
nation of Israel, whom he would gladly have
saved from ruin, and so it will be in the last days.
He has commanded that an alarm shall be sounded
before the great day of the Lord shall come.
Joel 2: 1. Messiah gave signs which should pre-

cede his second coming, whereby we may know when it is near, even at the doors. Matt. 24. He has revealed to his people that although the wicked will not understand, and that day shall come as a thief upon the world and a world-loving church, even as the flood came unawares to those who did not accept the warning, yet the wise shall understand; his watching ones shall not be in darkness that that day should come upon them as a thief. Dan. 12 : 4; 1 Thess. 5 : 1–4.

Yes, he will come, and the weary shall find rest. 2 Thess. 1: 6, 7. He will glorify his ransomed ones. He will redeem the earth from the curse. He will vindicate the counsel of the Most High, and all creatures shall rejoice together in the works of his hands. All things shall be made new; sorrow and sighing shall be no more. And as countless ages roll over the redeemed millions who people the earth; as they forever magnify the cleansing power of Jesus' blood, which has "restored all things;" as they rejoice before the "tabernacle of God" with joy unspeakable and full of glory, they fully understand that the eternal purpose of God is now accomplished. Here, and here only, do they realize THE LOVE OF GOD IN CREATION !

We'd love to have you download our catalog of titles we publish at:

www.TEACHServices.com

or write or email us your thoughts, reactions, or criticism about this or any other book we publish at:

TEACH Services, Inc.
254 Donovan Road
Brushton, NY 12916

info@TEACHServices.com

or you may call us at:

518/358-3494

Produced in partnership with
LNFBooks.com